7. **Copy system and public files to the server:**
   - Choose System Options ➤ Copy System and Public Files.

8. **Load LAN drivers:**
   - Type LOAD *driver.*
   - Specify the frame type if necessary.
   - Bind protocol to LAN driver.

9. **Create STARTUP.NCF and AUTOEXEC.NCF files:**
   - Add any additional necessary commands.

10. **Add name space support to the volumes (optional):**
    - Type ADD NAME SPACE *namespace* TO VOLUME *volume.*

Expert Advice from the Network Experts

At Novell Press, we know that your network is vital to your business, and good, solid advice about your network is priceless. That's why Novell, in partnership with SYBEX Inc., prides itself on publishing the best networking books in the business.

Each book combines Novell's technical expertise with SYBEX's editorial and trade publishing experience, resulting in networking books of unparalleled accuracy, reliability, and readability. All Novell Press books are written by acknowledged experts in their field who have a special insight into the challenges and advantages of today's most popular networking products. Many Novell Press authors are past and current members of networking product development teams. For this reason, Novell Press fills the unique needs of networking professionals as no other publisher can.

Our books will help you work with the many versions of NetWare, use UnixWare, integrate UnixWare and NetWare, solve and avoid network problems, and much more. You can even study to become a Certified NetWare Administrator (CNA) or a Certified NetWare Engineer (CNE) with the help of Novell Press.

When you need advice about your network, you need an expert. Look for the network experts from Novell Press.

For a complete catalog of Novell Press and SYBEX books contact:

SYBEX Inc.
2021 Challenger Drive, Alameda, CA 94501
Tel: (510) 523-8233/(800) 227-2346 Telex: 336311
Fax: (510) 523-2373

SYBEX is committed to using natural resources wisely to preserve and improve our environment. As a leader in the computer book publishing industry, we are aware that over 40% of America's solid waste is paper. This is why we have been printing the text of books like this one on recycled paper since 1982.

This year our use of recycled paper will result in the saving of more than 15,300 trees. We will lower air pollution effluents by 54,000 pounds, save 6,300,000 gallons of water, and reduce landfill by 2,700 cubic yards.

In choosing a SYBEX book you are not only making a choice for the best in skills and information, you are also choosing to enhance the quality of life for all of us.

TALK TO NOVELL PRESS AND SYBEX ONLINE.

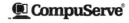

NOVELL'S® NETWARE® 3.12

Administrator's
HANDBOOK

KELLEY J. P. LINDBERG

NOVELL
PRESS

Novell Press, San Jose

Publisher: Rosalie Kearsley
Editor-in-Chief: Dr. R.S. Langer
Executive Editor, Novell Press: David Kolodney
Acquisitions Manager: Kristine Plachy
Developmental Editor: Guy Hart-Davis
Editor: Dusty Bernard
Project Editor: Kristen Vanberg-Wolff
Assistant Editors: Malcolm Faulds and Michelle Khazai
Technical Editor: Howard Olson
Novell Technical Advisor: Howard Olson
Technical Art: Cuong Le
Proofreader/Production Assistant: Emily Smith
Indexer: Kelley J. P. Lindberg
Cover Designer: Archer Design
Logo Design: Jennifer Gill
Cover Photographer: Zeilon

Library of Congress Card Number: 94-69701
ISBN: 0-7821-1635-3

Manufactured in the United States of America
10 9 8 7 6 5 4 3 2 1

For my great friend and brother, Ray Pollard, who has now joined me in the computer industry—just where did Mom and Dad go wrong with us, anyway?

Acknowledgments

Writing the acknowledgments is always my light at the end of the tunnel. The research is over, the editing is all but done, the late nights at the keyboard are about to fade into memory. Best of all, I get to find a few moments to sincerely thank the people who helped me with this project.

First, I have to thank Novell. In January of 1986 I answered a help-wanted ad in the newspaper for Novell, a little company I'd never heard of. I stepped through the door into what had once been a carpet ware-house and discovered a transformed world of lunatics and heroes. These were people who would work all night because they couldn't wait to see their code work, who knew the take-out menu of every restaurant in town, and who could achieve Herculean accomplishments at the prom-ise of a T-shirt. I never dreamed that in a few short years these people would revolutionize the way companies work and would create an entire industry out of a simple, but great, concept.

The breathtaking entrepreneurial atmosphere has calmed down quite a bit after all these years, and the warehouse has been replaced with a complex of buildings, but the offices in them are still filled with people who care passionately about what they do. It's an honor to work with these folks every day, and I thank Novell for letting me be part of this NetWare world.

Of course, there are a few key people I'd like to thank as well, who helped me make this book a reality.

The people at Sybex were, as always, great to work with. Kris Vanberg-Wolff kept the process running smoothly and Dusty Bernard's editing was always right on the mark. And many thanks go to David Kolodney, the series editor, for his unwavering confidence and sincere enthusiasm and for patiently waiting until I suffered a moment of weakness before springing this book idea upon me.

I'd also like to thank Rose Kearsley, at Novell Press, for her ongoing support and help.

A ton of gratitude goes to Howard Olson, who fearlessly volunteered to do the technical review of this book. I think his exact words were, "You want me to do *what?*" His broad technical knowledge of NetWare is equaled only by his unfailing sense of humor, and I have taken considerable advantage of both over the last couple of years, on this and other projects. Thanks, Howard.

Finally, I want to thank my husband, Andy, for not even flinching when I told him I was going to write another book. His support and encouragement never fail me. Without him, life would be one long, dreary Monday.

CONTENTS AT A *Glance*

TABLE OF *Contents*

TABLE OF CONTENTS

Introduction

If you're the administrator of a NetWare 3.12 network, chances are good you've got your hands full—full of users with questions about applications they're running; full of hardware and software upgrades and new acquisitions; and full of changing organizational structures within the company that may affect your network users, their files, and their trustee rights. And especially full of manuals, trade magazines, and technical notes. Sorting through all that information to find the one parameter you need to set to improve something can be a frustrating experience.

This book is designed to be a handy on-site tool you can refer to as you set up, reconfigure, use, or troubleshoot the various components of your NetWare 3.12 network. As you flip through the pages, you'll see they are filled with tables, lists, quick paths, step-by-step instructions, and other types of information that will help keep all those essential procedures, values, and parameters at your fingertips.

Is This Book for You?

Whether you're a network administrator, workgroup manager, or systems engineer, if you need quick access to information about running a NetWare 3.12 network, this handbook will be an important piece of your network toolbox.

Additionally, since NetWare 3.12 is an enhancement of NetWare 3.11, most (if not all) of the information in this handbook applies equally well to NetWare 3.11 networks.

What You Need to Know before Using This Book

This handbook is aimed at providing you with quick lookup information about your NetWare 3.12 network. It provides those pieces of information that are essential but very easy to forget, such as utility syntax and file server parameters.

Before using this book, make sure you understand how NetWare works. You should know the basic principles of setting up and using file servers and workstations. This book assumes you have access to the Novell documentation or other manuals for detailed instructions and explanations of any concepts that are unfamiliar to you. (For a list of additional books and other resources, see Appendix B.)

In addition, you should be familiar with the operating systems running on your workstations. If you have PCs on your network, use the manufacturer's documentation to learn how to install and run DOS, OS/2, or Microsoft Windows on a computer. If you have Macintoshes, you should know how to set them up and how to create, copy, and delete Macintosh files, too.

What This Book Contains

The chapters and appendices in this book cover all the major aspects of your NetWare 3.12 local area network:

- ▶ Chapter 1 explains the typical tasks of a network administrator and includes tips on documenting your network and effective troubleshooting techniques.

- ▶ Chapter 2 contains helpful information about installing and monitoring a NetWare file server. It includes an installation quick path and procedures, as well as descriptions of SET parameters and server boot files. It also explains how to use Remote Console and how to find key server statistics data that will help you optimize your server's performance.

▶ Chapter 3 provides a quick path for installing network workstations and describes the workstation boot files you'll need.

▶ Chapter 4 describes the essential elements of NetWare security, such as trustee rights and file and directory attributes.

▶ Chapter 5 covers the information you need to automate your users' working environments using login scripts and menu programs.

▶ Chapter 6 describes network printing and contains an installation quick path.

▶ Chapter 7 explains how to install and use Novell ElectroText and DynaText online documentation.

▶ Chapter 8 covers NetWare for Macintosh 3.12, including installation quick paths for both servers and workstations and a description of the NetWare for Macintosh utilities.

▶ Chapter 9 explains NetWare Loadable Modules (NLMs) and lists all the available NLMs in NetWare 3.12.

▶ Chapter 10 lists all the NetWare 3.12 console utilities.

▶ Chapter 11 lists all the workstation utilities included in NetWare 3.12.

▶ Appendix A is a set of worksheets you can use to keep track of various types of information about your network.

▶ Appendix B is a list of additional resources and phone numbers you may find helpful.

▶ Appendix C is a glossary that provides definitions of common networking terms.

NetWare 3.12's Hardware Requirements

To run the NetWare 3.12 network operating system, your file server must meet the following minimum requirements:

- ► It must be a DOS-based or OS/2-based personal computer using an 80386 or higher processor. (This book discusses only the DOS-based version of NetWare 3.12.)

- ► It must have enough RAM (random-access memory). As a minimum, you should probably have 8MB (megabytes) of RAM, but you may need additional RAM, depending on the file server's hardware configuration and the applications you will be running on your file server.

- ► It should have a hard disk for storing network applications and files. You can add external hard disks to the file server for extra storage. If you want to use the disk-mirroring feature, which stores identical copies of all your network files on two separate hard disks in case one fails, you'll need two or more hard disks. (Disks of identical make and size are best.) For more protection, you can put each of the disks on a separate disk controller. (This is called disk duplexing.)

- ► It must have a network board installed that supports the network topology your workstations are using, such as Ethernet, Arcnet, or Token-Ring.

A PC workstation on a NetWare network must meet the following minimum requirements:

- ► It must be an IBM-compatible personal computer, running DOS, OS/2, or NT. (DOS workstations may also run MS Windows.)

▶ It must have a minimum of 512K of memory, although you will almost certainly need more, depending on the type of applications that will run on the workstation.

▶ It must contain a network board that matches the network board installed in the file server (such as Ethernet, Token-Ring, or Arcnet).

Macintosh workstations on a NetWare for Macintosh network must be running the following software:

▶ System version 6.0 or above

▶ Finder version 6.1 or above

▶ AppleShare workstation software version 2.0 or above

CHAPTER 1

Laying the Foundation: Maintaining and Troubleshooting Your Network

You have two primary goals as the supervisor of a NetWare 3.12 network: to get the network up and running smoothly and to keep it that way. How you go about doing this, of course, depends greatly on the kind of network you're running, the business your users are in, and the type of person you are.

Regardless of your specific situation, however, your tasks as network supervisor can be distilled to a few common categories:

- ▶ **Routine maintenance:** Upgrading software and hardware, adding and deleting users, monitoring network security, and so on

- ▶ **Documenting your network:** Registering software and hardware for warranties, maintaining a current inventory of all hardware, documenting network information about each workstation, justifying new purchases of software and hardware to management, and so on

- ▶ **Troubleshooting your network:** Answering questions from users and solving problems

Of these duties, the most difficult to anticipate is the last one: troubleshooting. The only way to minimize the amount of time you'll spend troubleshooting your network is to try to stay on top of the other aspects of your network supervisor duties. The more organized you are about routine maintenance and record keeping, the better off you and your users will be.

Routine Maintenance

Network maintenance may be different for every network, depending on the networking hardware and machines, the applications that are running, and the particular network features that are being used. However, there are some common routine tasks that generally add to the stability and longevity of a network:

- ▸ **Maintaining hardware:** Adding new workstations and printers, replacing broken cables, installing additional memory in computers, tracking down and replacing faulty network boards and other hardware, and so on

- ▸ **Maintaining the software:** Purging old files from the network, upgrading existing applications, installing new applications, and so on

- ▸ **Adding and deleting network users:** Updating the network as people are hired, leave, or move around in the company's organization

- ▸ **Ensuring the network is secure:** Protecting the network from unauthorized users, preventing users from accessing sensitive files, insulating the network from viruses, and so on

- ▸ **Backing up files on a regular basis:** Ensuring that you always have a recent copy of network files if something happens to the originals

- ▸ **Deleting and purging unnecessary files:** Freeing up disk space

- ▸ **Monitoring your file server's statistics:** Checking to see whether it is running out of memory, cache buffers, and so on

- ▸ **Monitoring the error log files:** Checking the error log files for the file server, the volumes, and the Transaction Tracking System

Of these, the only task you should do on a daily basis is backing up files. Most backup systems allow you to perform incremental backups, meaning you back up only those files that have changed since the last time they were backed up. This allows you to do complete backups on a weekly or biweekly basis, using incremental backups to make up the difference.

Some of the other tasks should probably be scheduled tasks, which you do on a regular basis. These tasks include monitoring the error log files, purging old files, and monitoring the file server's statistics.

You perform other tasks as needed, such as restoring files or updating software applications.

Documenting the Network

When something goes wrong with your network, your first line of defense is knowledge about your network. How is the network cabled? Which pieces of hardware are most likely to have problems? Which users should have access to which applications and files? Which interrupts and addresses are being used on workstations?

To answer questions like these, it is essential that you maintain accurate, up-to-date records about your network. It's a distasteful task to most people, but you'll be thankful you've done it the next time you need to add new hardware to the network, resolve an interrupt conflict, balance your equipment budget, get a workstation repaired under warranty, justify a new purchase to management, or train your backup network supervisor (or your replacement when you move on to bigger and better things).

How you keep track of your network information is your decision. You can store records in folders, in a three-ring binder labeled *Network Maintenance,* in a database, or in any other system that fits your style.

The types of records you need to keep include

- ► Existing inventory and new purchases of hardware and software

- ► Hardware configuration of network machines (such as workstations, file servers, and printers) and their components (network boards, disk controllers, disk subsystems, and so on)

► Maintenance records, including when equipment was repaired, how much it cost, who did the repair, and so on

► Your network layout

► Login scripts, menus, boot and batch files, and so on

► Your backup schedule and the location of backup tapes or disks

The following sections describe these types of records. Appendix A contains worksheets you can copy and use to track this information.

RECORDING EXISTING INVENTORY AND NEW PURCHASES

First, inventory all your existing hardware and software. Then, with each new hardware and software purchase you make, record that new item's information in the inventory. Record the name of the product, the version number, the serial number, the vendor you bought it from, the price, the purchase date, the length of the warranty, and so on.

An inventory can be very useful for many reasons, most of which are financial. By keeping your inventory records up to date, you can supply management with information about current capital assets, track your expenditures against your budget, and plan for the coming year's budget. By tracking purchases you can tell at a glance whether a workstation is under warranty, which vendor you used, and which products you have that may need to be upgraded soon.

Also, make sure you fill out and return all registration cards and forms. Some companies will not honor a warranty unless you have registered your purchase with them. In addition, many companies offer incentives for registering, such as free technical support, free or reduced cost updates or bug fixes, notification of upgrade programs, newsletters, special offers, and sometimes even free gifts.

RECORDING HARDWARE CONFIGURATIONS

A configuration conflict between two pieces of hardware is one of the more common problems on a network. For example, if two workstations have the same address or if two cards in the same workstation are configured to use the same interrupt setting, a conflict will occur.

It can be time consuming to track down the conflicting pieces of hardware when problems occur. Therefore, recording the configuration settings of each piece of hardware can help you plan addresses and interrupts that won't interfere with each other in the first place, as well as help you identify the potential culprit when a problem does occur.

You also may need to supply this configuration information in various software programs. For example, if you use settings that are different from the default configuration on a network board, you may need to specify those settings in the workstation's NET.CFG file before the workstation will be able to access the network.

RECORDING MAINTENANCE HISTORIES

Keep a history of all repairs made to your network hardware, both for warranty and budgeting reasons. You may want to file all paperwork associated with repairs along with the worksheet that documents your original purchase of the item.

RECORDING YOUR NETWORK LAYOUT

You may find it useful to have a drawing of your network on file, showing how all the workstations, file servers, printers, and peripheral equipment are connected. Such a drawing can be helpful when you try to explain to a new employee or to upper management how your network operates.

To draw the network, sketch out the general layout. (It doesn't necessarily have to be to scale, depending on how you plan to use this drawing.) Label each workstation with its make and model (such as PS/2 Model 50), its location (Accounting department), and its user. Show the cable that connects each piece of hardware to the network, and show which type of cable it is. Also show any hubs, wiring closets, or other types of important cabling information.

RECORDING YOUR LOGIN SCRIPTS, MENUS, AND BOOT FILES

Creating login scripts, menus, and boot files for your users takes some careful planning and probably some trial and error to get them working correctly. After going to that much effort, the last thing you need is to have to re-create them if they become lost or corrupted.

Therefore, keeping both a printed and a diskette copy of those files can be a time saver. Login scripts, boot files, and the source files for most menu-creation programs (including NetWare's trimmed-down version of the Saber menu program included in NetWare 3.12) are all ASCII text files. You can print them from any word processing or text editor application that allows you to work with ASCII text files.

Table 1.1 shows the probable locations for these types of files.

RECORDING BACKUP INFORMATION

It is important to keep a written record of your backup schedule. Most network supervisors have a set schedule so that they do different types of backups at certain times. For example, you may do a full backup, including a backup of the NetWare bindery, once a month. Then you may do a weekly backup of all files on the network (excluding the bindery and application directories, for example) and daily backups of just those files that have been changed since the last backup.

Whatever your schedule is, be sure to document it clearly so that if you're gone, someone else can restore necessary files. Record not only your schedule, but also the type of backup system you use, the labeling system you use to identify your tapes or disks, the location of the tapes or disks, and any other information you think someone may need in order to restore files if you're not there.

▶ **T A B L E   1.1**   *Location of Login Scripts, Menus, and Boot Files*

FILE	LOCATION
System login script	Text file named NET$LOG.DAT, in SYS:PUBLIC
User login script	Text file named LOGIN, in the user's ID directory under SYS:MAIL (ID directories are named with each user's ID number, which can be found using SYSCON.)
Menu source files	If menus are for general usage, the source files are probably in SYS:PUBLIC. If menus are for specific users, the files may be in those users' directories. Menu source files for the Saber menu program are named with .SRC extensions
Boot files	Users' boot and batch files, such as AUTOEXEC.BAT, STARTNET.BAT, CONFIG.SYS, NET.CFG, and LAN drivers, are located on the users' boot disks. Users may have additional batch files located in their home or working directories that should be archived, as well

General Troubleshooting Guidelines

Performing routine maintenance and keeping accurate records will help ensure that your network runs smoothly and efficiently. However, even the best of preventive maintenance can't eliminate all possible network problems. When a problem with your network occurs, where do you start looking for the solution?

On a NetWare 3.12 network the possible combinations of networking hardware, networking software, computers, printers, and applications are endless. Therefore, it is impossible to predict every type of problem you might encounter and equally impossible to predict the solutions. But it may be helpful to know where to begin looking for the sources of problems and what to do after you locate them.

When it comes to troubleshooting your network (or almost anything that consists of more than one component), the first step is to isolate the problem. Isolating a network problem means trying to identify which component is causing the problem. Only then can you fix it. The following sections provide some guidelines to follow when troubleshooting a network problem.

Narrow the Search   Were there any error messages? Did the problem occur on only one workstation, on several workstations, or at the file server? Can you pinpoint the problem area? For example, is it a printing problem, a communication problem, an application problem, or a problem in another area of the network? For communication problems, reduce the number of workstations and cables on the network. Then add the cables and workstations back to the network until you pinpoint the offending hardware.

Check the Equipment   If the problem is with a piece of equipment, such as a workstation, printer, or peripheral, try hooking up the machine in stand-alone mode. If it functions correctly by itself, you'll know that the problem has something to do with the connection to the network. If the machine has the same problem when running in stand-alone mode as it did on the network, you can eliminate the network components and concentrate on the configuration of the machine itself.

Check the Documentation   Try looking in the NetWare documentation for ideas. The *NetWare 3.12 System Administration* manual has troubleshooting sections that point out several common problems and solutions. In addition, the *System Messages* manual explains error messages that may appear.

Check Other Resources   Appendix B contains a list of other resources you might find helpful.

Try Each Solution Independently   After you have narrowed down the search to a particularly suspicious area, begin trying solutions, *but try them one at a time.* Start with the easiest, cheapest solution and work up from there. Changing one element at a time may take longer, but it can save you money. It can also help you solve the problem much more quickly if it happens again.

Look for Patches   Check NetWire (Novell's online service, on CompuServe) or check with your reseller for any patches that may solve the problem you're having.

Call a Support Line As a Last Resort   If all else fails, call your reseller or Novell Technical Support for help. Because calling for technical support can often cost you money, make sure you have used every other avenue (especially the documentation) first. Nothing is more frustrating than spending a chunk of money on a support call and then finding that the answer was on page 45 of the installation manual.

Document the Solution   When you find the solution, document it. That way, you or the next person who supervises the network may be able to avoid duplicating efforts if the problem recurs later.

By using the one-component-at-a-time technique, you may be able to save both your money and your sanity. For example, suppose you have a workstation that can't seem to communicate with the file server. Frustrated, you change the network board, replace the network cable, and update the workstation's shell files. When you reboot the workstation, it works. Great—but which one of the elements you changed was the one that caused the problem? If the problem was a corrupted shell file, you just wasted money on a new network board and cable.

Each chapter in this book contains specific tips for troubleshooting some of the more common problems you may encounter with network components.

CHAPTER 2

Installing and Monitoring the NetWare Server

The first step in setting up a network is to install the NetWare file server. This chapter explains how to install your file server and how to manage it once it's up and running.

Installation Quick Path

You can purchase NetWare 3.12 on either floppy diskettes or CD-ROM. Installing NetWare 3.12 from CD-ROM is much faster than installing from floppies. In fact, for the amount of time (at your salary rate) it takes you to install or upgrade two or three file servers from floppy diskettes, you could probably cover the cost of a CD-ROM drive.

Figure 2.1 shows the major steps in installing a NetWare 3.12 file server, regardless of whether you use CD-ROM or floppy diskettes. The following sections explain how to install the NetWare 3.12 operating system on a server, how to load the disk drivers, and how to run INSTALL.NLM to complete the installation by creating volumes, loading LAN drivers, and modifying the server boot files.

PREPARING THE SERVER

You must prepare the computer before you begin the installation program. To do this, complete the following steps:

1 · Install the network board in the file server and record the board settings.

2 · Install any external hard disks and their corresponding controller boards in the file server, and record all pertinent information, such as disk type, disk size, and board settings. If you intend to mirror or duplex the disks, the disks should be similar in type and size; extra space on the larger disk will be wasted because the smaller disk limits the amount of information that

FIGURE 2.1 *File server installation quick path*

I. **Prepare the file server:**

- Install hard disks and network boards.
- Make backups of existing files.
- Create DOS partition (5MB minimum) and leave room for NetWare partition.
- Install CD-ROM drive (optional).

2. **Install the NetWare 3.12 operating system:**

- Run INSTALL.EXE.
- Give the server a name and an IPX internal network number.
- Specify country code, code page, and keyboard mapping.
- Specify whether SERVER.EXE is added to AUTOEXEC.BAT.

3. **Load the disk driver:**

- Type LOAD *driver.*

4. **Load INSTALL.NLM:**

- Type LOAD INSTALL.

5. **Create disk partitions:**

- Create NetWare partitions.
- Mirror or duplex disk partitions (optional).

6. **Create and mount volumes:**

- Create volume SYS.
- Create additional volumes (optional).
- Mount volumes.

7. **Copy system and public files to the server:**

   • Choose System Options ➤ Copy System and Public Files.

8. **Load LAN drivers:**

   • Type LOAD *driver.*

   • Specify the frame type if necessary.

   • Bind protocol to LAN driver.

9. **Create STARTUP.NCF and AUTOEXEC.NCF files:**

   • Add any additional necessary commands.

10. **Add name space support to the volumes (optional):**

   • Type ADD NAME SPACE *namespace* TO VOLUME *volume.*

can be stored. (In disk mirroring, both disks share the same controller board. In disk duplexing, the disks each have a separate controller board.)

3 · If you're installing from floppy diskettes, make duplicates of all the diskettes for safekeeping.

4 · If the computer you're going to turn into a file server has important files on its hard disk, make backup copies of those files because they will be deleted during the installation process. If the computer was a file server running an earlier version of Net-Ware and you are upgrading it to NetWare 3.12, make two backup copies, just in case something goes wrong with the first copy.

5 · Boot DOS on the file server and create a DOS partition if one does not already exist. Use DOS's FDISK command to create a DOS partition of at least 5MB, and then use the FORMAT command to format the partition. The DOS partition will let the server boot from the hard disk (rather than from a floppy). After creating a DOS partition, leave the rest of the disk available for a NetWare partition, which will be created during installation.

6 · (CD-ROM only) Connect the CD-ROM drive to the file server. Follow the manufacturer's instructions to connect the drive, and modify the computer's AUTOEXEC.BAT and CONFIG.SYS files to load the necessary CD-ROM drivers. When the drive is connected, insert the NetWare 3.12 CD-ROM and reboot the computer so that it will now recognize the drive.

INSTALLING THE NETWARE 3.12 OPERATING SYSTEM

After the server is prepared, use the INSTALL.EXE utility to install the operating system (a file called SERVER.EXE) on it:

1 · If you're using floppy diskettes, insert the Install diskette in drive A of the file server and change to drive A. If you're using a CD-ROM, change to the drive that is mapped to the CD-ROM drive, and then move to the NETWARE.312\ENGLISH directory on the CD-ROM (by typing CD NETWARE.312\ENGLISH).

2 · Start the installation program by typing

```
INSTALL
```

3 · Choose Select an Installation Option ➤ Install New Net-Ware v3.12.

4 · When asked if you want to create or retain DOS disk partitions, select Retain Current Disk Partitions.

5 · When prompted, give the file server a name. The name can be up to 47 characters long and cannot contain any periods or spaces.

6 · When prompted for an IPX internal network number, either accept the default number that is randomly generated or specify your own number. The number must differ from IPX internal network numbers for any other file servers on this network, it must differ from the physical network number, it must be between 1 and 8 digits long, and it must be in hexadecimal format (numbers 0 through 9 and letters A through F).

7 · Copy the server's boot files (SERVER.EXE, INSTALL.NLM, disk drivers, and name space modules) to the server's hard disk by pressing the Enter key. Unless you specify a different destination directory (by pressing the F4 key and typing a new directory name), the files will be copied to a directory called SERVER.312, which is automatically created on the hard disk. If you are installing from diskettes, insert the necessary diskettes as you are prompted for them.

8 · You are prompted for a country code, code page, and keyboard mapping. Computer hardware and DOS versions can vary from country to country. Therefore, computers use DOS code pages, which determine which numerals, letters, and symbols are supported by the version of DOS running on the computer. If you are using a keyboard and a DOS code page created for use with United States English, you do not need to change the default values presented by the installation program. If you are using a different DOS code page and a keyboard designed for use in countries other than the United States, such as a German keyboard with German-specific characters, you can specify the country code and code page the computer should use. To determine which values you must enter, refer to either your DOS documentation or your reseller. (To see a list of alternate choices for each option, highlight the field and press the Enter key.)

9 · Choose the DOS Filename Format option for your files. This format enforces DOS file name conventions. In previous versions of NetWare you were allowed to use nonconventional file names. (If you are upgrading a server that used nonconventional file names, you will have to run VREPAIR.NLM after the upgrade before you can mount any volumes. VREPAIR changes the invalid DOS file names to valid ones.)

10 · You are asked whether you want to specify any startup SET commands. If you do not require any special startup commands, select No and press Enter to continue. If your disk driver requires memory below 16MB (typically 16-bit boards or any bus mastering board), select Yes and type the following command in the STARTUP.NCF file:

```
SET RESERVED BUFFERS BELOW 16 MEG=40
```

(Add 20 buffers for each additional SCSI device.) Then press F10 to save the commands. This line will be added to the STARTUP.NCF file so that the drivers will have available memory below 16MB. If the driver itself must load below the 16MB boundary, see the section "Loading a Disk Driver Below 16MB" later in this chapter for more information.

II • Specify whether or not you want SERVER.EXE added to the server's AUTOEXEC.BAT file. If you want SERVER (the NetWare operating system) to load automatically every time you reboot the server, select Yes. If you want to manually load the NetWare operating system from DOS (by typing SERVER) every time the server is rebooted, select No. Many people select No so that they can have more control over the computer in case the SERVER.EXE file somehow becomes corrupted.

At this point the installation program automatically loads SERVER.EXE. The NetWare 3.12 operating system is now running on the server. Next you must load the disk driver.

LOADING THE DISK DRIVER

Once the server is running and the colon prompt (:) is displayed, you must load the disk driver. Table 2.1 lists the disk drivers that are available.

▸**T A B L E 2.1**   *Disk Drivers*

DISK ARCHITECTURE	CONTROLLER TYPE	DISK DRIVER
(EISA) Extended Industry Standard Architecture	AT Vendor's proprietary controller	ISADISK Vendor's driver
ISA (Industry Standard Architecture)	ARLL, AT, MFM, RLL ESDI IDE Novell SCSI	ISADISK ISADISK /B IDE DCB
Microchannel	ESDI MFM IBM SCSI	PS2ESDI PS2MFM PS2OPT

To load a disk driver, complete the following steps. If you are using a disk driver that must be loaded below the 16MB memory boundary, use the steps in the next section, "Loading Disk Drivers Below 16MB," instead.

1 • Choose your driver from the third column in Table 2.1, and then type the following command at the server's console:

    LOAD driver parameters

substituting the name of your driver, such as PS2OPT, for the word *driver* and including any necessary parameters, such as a memory address, interrupt number, or slot number.

2 • Depending on the type of board you are using, if you did not include any parameters in the LOAD command, you may have to answer prompts for necessary parameters.

3 • If you have more than one disk controller board, load the next driver.

4 • If you are using the DCB disk driver with an external disk subsystem, run the DISKSET utility.

After you load the disk driver, you can finish configuring NetWare 3.12 on your server, as explained in the section "Creating Disk Partitions" later in this chapter.

Loading Disk Drivers Below 16MB

If your disk drive must be loaded below the 16MB memory boundary, complete the following steps:

1 • If an AUTOEXEC.NCF file already exists, copy it to the server's startup directory (C:\SERVER.312). Both STARTUP.NCF and AUTOEXEC.NCF must be located in the same directory as SERVER.EXE. (If AUTOEXEC.NCF exists in SYS:SYSTEM, delete or rename it.)

2 · Make sure the following commands are in STARTUP.NCF:

```
SET AUTO REGISTER MEMORY ABOVE 16 MEG=OFF
SET RESERVED BUFFERS BELOW 16 MEG=40
```

(In the second command, add 20 buffers for each additional SCSI device.)

3 · Create or edit the AUTOEXEC.NCF file so that the commands are loaded in the following order:

```
FILE SERVER NAME name
IPX INTERNAL NET number
LOAD diskdriver [parameters]
LOAD (any other modules)
REGISTER MEMORY 1000000 xxxxxx
MOUNT volume
LOAD (any other modules)
SET (any SET parameters)
```

The REGISTER MEMORY 1000000 command registers memory above 16MB. *xxxxxx* is total memory above 16MB. (1000000 is 16MB in hex.) If your machine had 32MB, the syntax would be "REGISTER MEMORY 1000000 1000000".

When you reboot the server, the disk driver will be loaded before memory above the 16MB limit is available.

CREATING DISK PARTITIONS

After you've loaded SERVER.EXE and the disk drivers, you must create NetWare disk partitions where network files will be stored. To do this you use the INSTALL.NLM utility, as explained in the following steps:

1 · At the server's console prompt (:), load INSTALL.NLM by typing

```
LOAD INSTALL
```

2 · Select Disk Options ➤ Partition Tables.

3 · If you have more than one disk, select the disk you want to partition from the list shown.

4 · (Optional) You need only one DOS partition for the NetWare server; the rest of the disk's space should be used as a NetWare partition. Therefore, if you have additional DOS partitions, you should delete them so the space can be used for the NetWare partition. (To delete a partition, select Delete Partition from the menu.)

5 · Choose Create NetWare Partition from the menu to create a new partition.

6 · Accept the default size of the partition and its Hot Fix redirection area, or specify a different size if you wish. For disk mirroring or duplexing, modify the size of the partition by adjusting the number of Hot Fix redirection blocks for the disk with the most disk blocks, until the available blocks on both disks match. For disk mirroring or duplexing, the disk blocks available on both disks must match.

7 · Press the Esc key to create the partition.

8 · After the partition has been created, press the Esc key to return to the Available Disk Options menu. If you have more than one disk, select the next disk you want to partition from the Available Disk Drivers menu and repeat the process. If you are finished partitioning disks, press the Esc key again to return to the Installation Options menu.

9 · (Optional) To mirror or duplex disks, select Mirroring. Then, from the list of partitions displayed, select the primary partition by pressing Enter. Then press the Ins key, and select the secondary partition that you want to mirror the primary partition. Then press the Esc key twice to return to the Installation Options menu.

CREATING AND MOUNTING VOLUMES

Next, you will create at least one volume on the server's hard disk. Every server must have one volume named SYS. This volume contains all the files and utilities required to run the server. You should reserve SYS for NetWare's own files and create at least one additional volume for your other files. If you are using NetWare for Macintosh, you may want to create a separate volume just for your Macintosh files.

Each NetWare partition has one logical disk segment. Each volume created on a single NetWare partition will create its own logical segment. If you remove a volume from a drive, you can add its logical segment to another existing volume.

If a volume is made up of two or more logical segments, the speed of disk reads and writes may degrade during heavy load times. If disk read and write performance is critical and you have volumes with multiple segments, you may want to re-create the volume so it has only one segment. To do this, back up the disk and remove the volume and the NetWare partition. Then re-create the partition and the volume and restore the data. The volume will then have only one segment.

To create and mount volumes, follow these steps:

1 · Select Installation Options ➤ Volume Options, and then press the Ins key to create a new volume. For the first volume (SYS), the installation procedure by default allocates the entire disk to volume SYS.

2 · Since you probably want to create more than one volume, lower the size of volume SYS in the Initial Segment Size field. You can use any space left over for additional volumes.

3 · Press the Esc key to create the volume SYS.

4 · When volume SYS appears in the Volumes list, select it by highlighting it and pressing the Enter key. Then select the Status field and select Mount Volume. Press Esc to return to the Volumes screen.

5 · To create additional volumes, press the Ins key at the Volumes screen. If you have more than one disk drive, press Ins at the Volumes menu and select a drive on which you have created NetWare partitions. Create additional volumes until all free space is used.

6 · When you're finished, press Esc again to return to the Installation Options menu.

Next, you will copy the NetWare files onto the server.

COPYING SYSTEM AND PUBLIC FILES ONTO THE SERVER

Now that the volumes are mounted, you can copy the NetWare files from the installation diskettes or CD-ROM onto the server. These files, which include program files and utilities, will be copied into the SYS volume, in the directories SYSTEM, PUBLIC, and LOGIN. The following steps show how:

1 · Select Installation Options ➤ System Options ➤ Copy System and Public Files.

2 · (Diskette only) If you're installing from diskettes, insert the Install diskette and press Enter.

3 · (CD-ROM only) If you're installing from CD-ROM, press the F6 key and type the directory path to the CD-ROM (D:\NETWARE.312\ENGLISH).

The copying process will take several minutes, especially if you're installing from diskettes. (You will be prompted for diskettes to insert.) After the files are copied, you can load the LAN drivers.

LOADING LAN DRIVERS

You must load a LAN driver for each network board installed in your file server and then bind a protocol to the driver. To do this, complete the following steps:

1 · To load a driver, type the following command at the server's console:

```
LOAD driver FRAME=type
```

The FRAME=*type* portion of the command is optional. You need to specify a frame type only if you are using a frame type that is not the default. The default frame type for Novell Ethernet drivers is Ethernet_802.2.

2 · Bind a protocol to the LAN driver. For example, to bind the IPX protocol to an NE2 LAN driver, type

```
BIND IPX TO NE2
```

3 · When prompted, type in the network board's network address, which is unique to the network to which the board is attached. Each network segment requires a unique network address, which must be between 1 and 8 digits long and must be in hexadecimal format (numbers 0 through 9 and letters A through F). All network boards in other servers that are attached to this network segment must share the same network address.

CREATING STARTUP.NCF AND AUTOEXEC.NCF FILES

Next, you will create two boot files for the server: STARTUP.NCF and AUTOEXEC.NCF.

▶ STARTUP.NCF: Executes automatically after SERVER.EXE (when located in the same directory as SERVER.EXE) and loads disk drivers to support the server's hard disks. It includes other commands required to boot the server. In addition, it can load name space modules to support differing file formats (such as Macintosh or OS/2). It can also contain SET parameters, which configure cache buffer and packet sizes, and so on

▸ **AUTOEXEC.NCF**: Executes automatically after STARTUP.NCF and continues the process of preparing the server to run the network by specifying the server's name, specifying the internal network number, mounting volumes, loading LAN drivers, automatically loading additional NLMs (such as MONITOR), specifying SET parameters, and so on

To create these files, complete the following steps:

1 · If INSTALL.NLM is loaded, press Alt+Esc until the INSTALL screen is the active screen. If INSTALL.NLM is not loaded, type

```
LOAD INSTALL
```

2 · Choose Available System Options ➤ Create STARTUP.NCF File, and enter the driver letter for the boot file's location (drive C). The file appears on the screen, displaying a few commands reflecting information you entered earlier during the installation process.

3 · Add any useful commands to the file, such as commands to load additional name spaces or SET parameters.

4 · Press Esc and answer Yes to save the file.

5 · Choose Available System Options ➤ Create AUTOEXEC.NCF File. The file contents appear on the screen, displaying a few commands reflecting information you entered earlier during the installation process.

6 · Add any useful commands to the file, such as commands to load additional NLMs, console commands, or SET parameters.

If other volumes besides SYS exist on the server, enter the following command to mount all volumes automatically when the server is booted:

```
MOUNT ALL
```

7 · Press Esc and answer Yes to save the file.

When you have finished editing the startup files, either you can press Alt+Esc to move to a different console screen or you can unload IN-STALL.NLM by pressing the Esc key until you are asked whether you want to exit the utility.

ADDING NAME SPACE SUPPORT TO THE VOLUMES

If you want to store non–DOS file formats, such as Macintosh or NFS, on the file server, you must load a name space module and add name space support to the volume. If you have not already loaded the name space, type the following command at the console prompt:

```
LOAD namespace
```

For example, to load the Macintosh name space, type

```
LOAD MAC
```

Include this command in the STARTUP.NCF file so it will be available for any volumes needing that name space support module.

Next, to add the name space to a volume, type the following command:

```
ADD NAME SPACE namespace TO VOLUME volume
```

For example, to add Macintosh name space support to a volume named Apple, type

```
ADD NAME SPACE MAC TO VOLUME APPLE
```

You need to type this command only once, at the console prompt. It does not need to be included in the STARTUP.NCF or AUTOEXEC.NCF file. Once a name space has been added to a volume, you must use the VREPAIR utility to remove it.

Using Remote Console

Once the file server is up and running, you can use a variety of commands and programs (called NetWare Loadable Modules, or NLMs) to add functionality or enhance the server's performance.

These commands and programs must be executed from the server's console. However, sometimes the server is in a room separate from your office and regular workstation, so it is not always convenient to access the server's keyboard.

For this reason NetWare 3.12 includes Remote Console, a feature that lets you turn your workstation into the file server's console. Using Remote Console you can execute server utilities and type commands to load NLMs without leaving your workstation (if you have the correct password). In fact, Remote Console lets you access any server on the network from your workstation.

For a server to be accessible from a Remote Console, the server must have special NLMs loaded on it. Then you can execute RCONSOLE (or ACONSOLE, for asynchronous connections) from the workstation and enter the correct password to start the remote session with the file server. (You can use either the SUPERVISOR's password or a password entered when REMOTE.NLM is loaded on the server.)

Table 2.2 shows which files to load on the server and the workstation to start Remote Console on a workstation that is connected directly to the server's network. Table 2.3 shows how to start Remote Console across an asynchronous connection (via a modem). In both cases the two required NLMs must be loaded on the file server before you execute the workstation utility, or the remote session cannot be started.

▸ T A B L E 2.2   *Remote Console Files Required for a Direct Workstation Connection*

FILE	WHERE LOADED	DESCRIPTION
REMOTE.NLM	Server	Allows the server to communicate with the workstation, sending and receiving keystrokes, screen displays, and so on. Also lets you specify the Remote Console password
RSPX.NLM	Server	Communications driver that allows the workstation and server to communicate across an SPX connection
RCONSOLE.EXE	Workstation	Utility that makes the workstation become the server's console

After you've started a Remote Console session, you can work with the console as follows:

▸ To access RCONSOLE or ACONSOLE's Available Options menu, press the asterisk (*) key on the number pad of your keyboard.

▸ To move between active file server screens, such as between MONITOR and the console prompt, press the minus (−) and plus (+) keys. Note that these keys do not work in the Available Options menu.

▸ **T A B L E** 2.3   *Remote Console Files Required for an Asynchronous Workstation Connection*

FILE	WHERE LOADED	DESCRIPTION
REMOTE.NLM	Server	Allows the server to communicate with the workstation, sending and receiving keystrokes, screen displays, and so on. Also lets you specify the Remote Console password
RS232.NLM	Server	A communications driver that allows the workstation and server to communicate across an asynchronous connection (usually via a modem and phone lines)
ACONSOLE.EXE	Workstation	Utility that makes the workstation become the server's console. This utility works just like RCONSOLE but includes additional prompts to specify the modem baud rate, phone number, and so on

▸ To run a server utility or load an NLM, go to the console prompt and type the appropriate command (such as LOAD MONITOR).

▸ To exit Remote Console, press the asterisk on the keypad and select Available Options ➤ End Remote Session with Server, or press Shift+Esc.

Monitoring File Server Statistics

It's a good idea to monitor various file server statistics periodically to see how your server is performing. You can see how the server's memory is being used, how many cache buffers it is using, and so on. These statistics can help you determine whether you need to add enhancements to your file server, such as more memory or more disk space.

There are three error log files you should check. In addition, there are several utilities you can use to monitor the information about your server. These log files and monitoring utilities are explained in the following sections.

MONITORING THE ERROR LOG FILES

Whenever an error occurs with the file server or the volume, NetWare records the error in error log files. Periodically, you may want to check these files to see which types of errors have occurred. There are three error log files:

- SYS$LOG.ERR, for file server errors

- VOL$LOG.ERR, for volume errors

- TTS$LOG.ERR, for NetWare's Transaction Tracking System (TTS protects files, especially database files such as the NetWare bindery, from being corrupted.)

Use a text editor to read and print the error log files. The file server and TTS error logs are both in the SYS volume. The volume error log is in whichever volume the log belongs to.

You can also read the file server error log from within the SYSCON utility. (The volume error log and the TTS error log can be opened only with a text editor.)

To see the log files from the server's console, load EDIT.NLM and specify the directory path and name of the file you want to see. For example, type

```
LOAD EDIT SYS:VOL$LOG.ERR
```

After you review the error log files, you can delete them. New ones will be created if new errors occur.

USING UTILITIES TO TRACK SERVER STATISTICS

You can use the utilities listed in Table 2.4 to track various aspects of the server's performance and storage statistics.

▸ **T A B L E 2.4** *Utilities Used to Track Server Statistics*

UTILITY	INFORMATION TO MONITOR
MONITOR.NLM (loaded on the server)	Utilization of the server's CPU Packet receive buffers allocated Service process allocated Memory statistics (especially the total number of cache buffers versus the original number of cache buffers) Disks' mirroring status (whether or not they are mirrored) Number of Hot Fix redirection blocks used Number of packet errors for each LAN driver
VOLINFO.EXE (executed at a workstation)	Disk space and directory entries in use (and available) on each volume
UPS STATUS (executed at the server)	Status of UPS's battery Status of current network power

In addition to these utilities, you can use the SET command at the server to view and set a large number of server parameters, controlling everything from the number of cache buffers to the number of subdirectory levels allowed.

SET PARAMETERS

Using the SET command at the file server console, you can view and modify the NetWare 3.12 operating system's current configuration. There are many parameters you can change with SET. The parameters are divided into nine categories:

- ► Communications

- ► Memory

- ► File caching

- ► Directory caching

- ► File system

- ► Locks

- ► Transaction tracking

- ► Disk

- ► Miscellaneous

To see the current value of SET parameters, type SET and then select the category. The values for all parameters in that category will be displayed.

To change a SET parameter, type the complete SET command and parameter with a value.

You can set SET parameters at the console prompt, which leaves the parameter in effect until the server is rebooted, or in the STARTUP.NCF or AUTOEXEC.NCF file.

Tables 2.5 through 2.13 list the SET parameters in each category, show their limits and default values, and indicate whether the parameter can be set at the console prompt, in STARTUP.NCF, or in AUTOEXEC.NCF.

▶ **T A B L E 2.5** *Communications SET Parameters*

SET PARAMETER	VALUES	WHERE EXECUTED
Console Display Watchdog Logouts= ___ If ON, displays a console message when a workstation's connection is cleared by the server "watchdog"	ON, OFF. Default=OFF	AUTOEXEC.NCF or console
New Packet Receive Buffer Wait Time= ___ Sets the time the operating system waits after allocating the minimum number of buffers before granting the next packet receive buffer. This allows the server to optimize buffer allocation over a period of time	0.1 to 20 seconds. Default=0.1 seconds	AUTOEXEC.NCF or console
Maximum Physical Receive Packet Size= ___ Sets the maximum size of packets allowable on the network	618 to 4202. Default=1514	STARTUP.NCF only
Maximum Packet Receive Buffers= ___ Sets the maximum number of packet receive buffers allocated when the server boots	50 to 2000. Default=400	STARTUP.NCF, AUTOEXEC.NCF, or console
Minimum Packet Receive Buffers= ___ Sets the minimum number of packet receive buffers that can be allocated	10 to 1000. Default=10	STARTUP.NCF only
Number of Watchdog Packets= ___ Sets the number of packets the server sends to an unresponsive workstation before clearing the workstation's connection	5 to 100. Default=100	AUTOEXEC.NCF or console

▶ T A B L E   2.5   *Communications SET Parameters (continued)*

SET PARAMETER	VALUES	WHERE EXECUTED
Delay between Watchdog Packets=___ Sets the time the server waits before sending each watchdog packet	9.9 seconds to 10 minutes 26.2 seconds. Default=59.3 seconds	AUTOEXEC.NCF or console
Delay before First Watchdog Packet=___ Sets the time the server waits before sending the first watchdog packet to an unresponsive workstation	15.7 seconds to 20 minutes 52.3 seconds. Default=4 minutes 56.6 seconds	AUTOEXEC.NCF or console
NCP Packet Signature Option=___ Sets the server's NCP Packet Signature security level	0 to 3. Default=1	STARTUP.NCF, AUTOEXEC.NCF, or console
Enable Packet Burst Statistics Screen=___ Displays the NCP Packet Burst statistics screen	ON, OFF. Default=OFF	AUTOEXEC.NCF or console
Reply to Get Nearest Server=___ Determines whether this server responds to workstations that request a connection to the nearest server	ON, OFF. Default=ON	STARTUP.NCF, AUTOEXEC.NCF, or console

▶ T A B L E 2.5 Communications SET Parameters (continued)

SET PARAMETER	VALUES	WHERE EXECUTED
Enable IPX Checksums= ___ Sets the IPX checksum level. 0=No checksums. 1=Checksums performed if enabled on the client. 2=Checksums required	0, 1, 2. Default=1	AUTOEXEC.NCF or console
Allow LIP= ___ Enables Large Internet Packet support	ON, OFF. Default=ON	AUTOEXEC.NCF or console

▶ T A B L E 2.6 Memory SET Parameters

SET PARAMETER	VALUES	WHERE EXECUTED
Cache Buffer Size= ___ Sets the size of cache buffers. Cannot be larger than the volume's block size	4096, 8192, or 16384 bytes. Default=4096	STARTUP.NCF only
Maximum Alloc Short Term Memory= ___ Specifies how much dynamic memory the server can allocate to the Alloc Short Term Memory pool, which is used for storing various types of network information	50000 to 33554432. Default=8388608	STARTUP.NCF, AUTOEXEC.NCF, or console
Auto Register Memory above 16 Megabytes= ___ Automatically adds memory above 16MB that can be detected on EISA bus computers	ON, OFF. Default=ON	STARTUP.NCF only

▶ T A B L E 2.7 *File-Caching SET Parameters*

SET PARAMETER	VALUES	WHERE EXECUTED
Maximum Concurrent Disk Cache Writes= ___ Sets the maximum number of write requests that can be stored before the disk head begins a sweep across the disk	10 to 1000. Default=50	AUTOEXEC.NCF or console
Dirty Disk Cache Delay Time= ___ Sets how long the server will keep a write request in memory before writing it to the disk	0.1 to 10 seconds. Default=3.3 seconds	AUTOEXEC.NCF or console
Minimum File Cache Report Threshold= ___ Causes a warning message to be sent when the number of available file cache buffers drops to this threshold. With this command you set the threshold to be a certain number of buffers above the minimum buffers allowed	0 to 1000. Default=20	AUTOEXEC.NCF or console
Minimum File Cache Buffers= ___ Sets the minimum number of cache buffers that must be reserved for file caching	20 to 1000. Default=20	AUTOEXEC.NCF or console
Read Ahead Enabled= ___ Allows background reads to be done during sequential file access so that blocks are placed into the cache ahead of time	ON, OFF. Default=ON	AUTOEXEC.NCF or console

► T A B L E 2.7 *File-Caching SET Parameters (continued)*

SET PARAMETER	VALUES	WHERE EXECUTED
Read Ahead LRU Sitting Time Threshold=___ Sets the time the server will wait before doing a read ahead	0 seconds to 1 hour. Default=10 seconds	AUTOEXEC.NCF or console
Reserved Buffers below 16 Meg=___ Sets a number of cache buffers in lower memory for device drivers that cannot access memory above 16MB	8 to 300. Default=16	STARTUP.NCF only

► T A B L E 2.8 *Directory-Caching SET Parameters*

SET PARAMETER	VALUES	WHERE EXECUTED
Dirty Directory Cache Delay Time=___ Specifies how long a directory table write request is kept in memory before it is written to disk	0 to 10 seconds. Default=0.5 seconds	AUTOEXEC.NCF or console
Maximum Concurrent Directory Cache Writes=___ Sets the maximum number of write requests that can be stored before the disk head begins a sweep across the disk	5 to 50. Default=10	AUTOEXEC.NCF or console
Directory Cache Allocation Wait Time=___ Specifies how long the server waits after allocating one directory cache buffer before it can allocate another buffer	0.5 seconds to 2 minutes. Default=2.2 seconds	AUTOEXEC.NCF or console

▶ T A B L E 2.8   *Directory-Caching SET Parameters (continued)*

SET PARAMETER	VALUES	WHERE EXECUTED
Directory Cache Buffer NonReferenced Delay= ___ Sets how long a directory entry is held in cache before it is overwritten	1 second to 5 minutes. Default=5.5 seconds	AUTOEXEC.NCF or console
Maximum Directory Cache Buffers= ___ Sets the maximum number of directory cache buffers that the server can allocate	20 to 4000. Default=500	AUTOEXEC.NCF or console
Minimum Directory Cache Buffers= ___ Sets the minimum number of directory cache buffers to be allocated by the server before using the Directory Cache Allocation Wait Time to determine whether another directory cache buffer should be allocated. Allocating buffers too quickly will cause the server to eat up memory resources during peak loads. Waiting too long may cause a delay in file searches. This wait time creates a leveling factor between peak and low access times	10 to 2000. Default=20	AUTOEXEC.NCF or console

▶ **T A B L E 2.9** File System SET Parameters

SET PARAMETER	VALUES	WHERE EXECUTED
Maximum Extended Attributes per File or Path= ___ Limits the number of extended attributes that a file or directory can have (Applies to all volumes.)	4 to 512. Default=8	AUTOEXEC.NCF or console
Immediate Purge of Deleted Files= ___ Specifies whether files are purged immediately when they are deleted or stored in a salvageable state	ON, OFF. Default=OFF	AUTOEXEC.NCF or console
Maximum Subdirectory Tree Depth= ___ Sets the maximum level of subdirectories the server can support	10 to 100. Default=25	STARTUP.NCF only
Volume Low Warn All Users= ___ Notifies all users when the free space on a volume reaches a minimum level	ON, OFF. Default=ON	AUTOEXEC.NCF or console
Volume Low Warning Reset Threshold= ___ Specifies the number of disk blocks above the Volume Low Warning Threshold that must be freed up to reset the "low volume" warning. This parameter controls how often you receive the low-volume warning if your free space is fluctuating around the threshold	0 to 100000. Default=256	AUTOEXEC.NCF or console
Volume Low Warning Threshold= ___ Sets the minimum amount of free space (in blocks) that a volume can have before it issues a warning	0 to 100000. Default=256	AUTOEXEC.NCF or console

▶ T A B L E 2.9   *File System SET Parameters (continued)*

SET PARAMETER	VALUES	WHERE EXECUTED
Turbo FAT Re-Use Wait Time= _____ Sets how long a turbo FAT (File Allocation Table) buffer stays in memory after an indexed file is closed	0.3 seconds to 1 hour 5 minutes 54.6 seconds. Default=5 minutes 29.6 seconds	AUTOEXEC.NCF or console
Minimum File Delete Wait Time= _____ Specifies how long a file must be stored before it can be purged	0 seconds to 7 days. Default=1 minute 5.9 seconds	AUTOEXEC.NCF or console
File Delete Wait Time= _____ Sets the maximum amount of time a file must be stored in a salvageable state. After this time has elapsed, the file can be purged if the space is needed	0 seconds to 7 days. Default=5 minutes 29.6 seconds	AUTOEXEC.NCF or console
NCP File Commit= _____ Specifies whether an application can issue a File Commit NCP and flush the file immediately from cache to disk	ON, OFF. Default=ON	AUTOEXEC.NCF or console
Maximum Percent of Volume Used by Directory= _____ Limits the amount of disk space that can be used as directory space	5 to 50. Default=13	AUTOEXEC.NCF or console
Maximum Percent of Volume Space Allowed for Extended Attributes= _____ Limits the amount of disk space that can be used to store extended attributes	5 to 50. Default=10	AUTOEXEC.NCF or console

► **T A B L E 2.10** *Locks SET Parameters*

SET PARAMETER	VALUES	WHERE EXECUTED
Maximum Record Locks per Connection=___ Sets the number of record locks a workstation can use simultaneously	10 to 10000. Default=500	AUTOEXEC.NCF or console
Maximum File Locks per Connection=___ Sets the number of opened and locked files a workstation can use simultaneously	10 to 1000. Default=250	AUTOEXEC.NCF or console
Maximum Record Locks=___ Sets how many record locks the server can support across all connections	100 to 200000. Default=20000	AUTOEXEC.NCF or console
Maximum File Locks=___ Sets how many opened and locked files the server can support across all connections	100 to 100000. Default=10000	AUTOEXEC.NCF or console

▶ T A B L E 2.11   *Transaction-Tracking SET Parameters*

SET PARAMETER	VALUES	WHERE EXECUTED
Auto TTS Backout Flag=___ Specifies whether incomplete transactions can be backed out automatically when a downed server is rebooted	ON, OFF. Default=OFF	STARTUP.NCF only
TTS Abort Dump Flag=___ Specifies whether the TTS$LOG.ERR file is created to record backout data in the event of a failure	ON, OFF. Default=OFF	AUTOEXEC.NC F or console
Maximum Transactions=___ Specifies how many transactions can occur simultaneously, across all connections	100 to 10000. Default=10000	AUTOEXEC.NC F or console
TTS Unwritten Cache Wait Time=___ Sets the time that a block of transactional data can be held in memory	11 seconds to 10 minutes 59.1 seconds. Default =1 minute 5.9 seconds	AUTOEXEC.NC F or console
TTS Backout File Truncation Wait Time=___ Sets the minimum amount of time that allocated blocks remain available for the TTS backout file	1 minute 5.9 seconds to 1 day 2 hours 21 minutes 51.3 seconds. Default = 59 minutes 19.2 seconds	AUTOEXEC.NC F or console

▶ T A B L E   2.12   *Disk SET Parameters*

SET PARAMETER	VALUES	WHERE EXECUTED
Enable Disk Read after Write Verify=____ Sets how data written to disk is compared with the data in memory to verify its accuracy. If set On, this parameter tells the driver to perform the highest level of read after write verification that it can. If set Off, this parameter turns off any form of read after write verification that the driver may do. It is still possible that the disk controller has a built-in function that performs read-after-write verification. This function may be configurable through a utility or jumper setting on the controller board	ON, OFF. Default=ON	STARTUP.NCF, AUTOEXEC.NCF, or console
Concurrent Remirror Requests=____ Sets the number of simultaneous remirror requests per logical disk partition	2 to 30. Default=2	STARTUP.NCF only

▶ T A B L E   2.13   *Miscellaneous SET Parameters*

SET PARAMETER	VALUES	WHERE EXECUTED
Maximum Outstanding NCP Searches=____ Sets the maximum number of NCP directory searches that can be performed simultaneously	10 to 1000. Default=51	AUTOEXEC.NCF or console
Allow Unencrypted Passwords=____ Specifies whether or not unencrypted passwords will be accepted by the server	ON, OFF. Default=OFF	AUTOEXEC.NCF or console

▶ T A B L E   2.13   *Miscellaneous SET Parameters (continued)*

SET PARAMETER	VALUES	WHERE EXECUTED
New Service Process Wait Time=___ Sets how long the server waits to allocate another service process after receiving an NCP request. If a service process is freed up during this time, a new one will not be allocated	0.3 to 20 seconds. Default=2.2 seconds	AUTOEXEC.NCF or console
Pseudo Preemption Time=___ Prevents an NLM from using too much CPU time	1000 to 10000. Default=2000	AUTOEXEC.NCF or console
Display Spurious Interrupt Alerts=___ Specifies whether error messages are displayed when the server hardware creates an interrupt that has been reserved for another device	ON, OFF. Default=ON	STARTUP.NCF, AUTOEXEC.NCF, or console
Display Lost Interrupt Alerts=___ Specifies whether error messages are displayed when a driver or board makes an interrupt call but drops the request before it's filled	ON, OFF. Default=ON	STARTUP.NCF, AUTOEXEC.NCF, or console
Display Disk Device Alerts=___ Specifies whether messages are displayed when hard disks are added, activated, deactivated, mounted, or dismounted	ON, OFF. Default=OFF	STARTUP.NCF, AUTOEXEC.NCF, or console
Display Relinquish Control Alerts=___ Specifies whether messages are displayed when an NLM uses the server's processor for more than 0.4 seconds without giving up control to other processes	ON, OFF. Default=OFF	STARTUP.NCF, AUTOEXEC.NCF, or console

► T A B L E   2.13   Miscellaneous SET Parameters (continued)

SET PARAMETER	VALUES	WHERE EXECUTED
Display Old API Names=_____ Specifies whether messages are displayed when old NetWare 3.0 API calls are used by an NLM	ON, OFF. Default=OFF	STARTUP.NCF, AUTOEXEC.NCF, or console
Maximum Service Processes=_____ Sets the maximum number of service processes the server can create	5 to 40. Default=20	AUTOEXEC.NCF or console
Display Incomplete IPX Packet Alerts=_____ Specifies whether alert messages are displayed when IPX receives incomplete packets	ON, OFF. Default=ON	STARTUP.NCF, AUTOEXEC.NCF, or console
Replace Console Prompt with Server Name=_____ Specifies whether the server name should be displayed on the server's screen instead of the normal console prompt (:)	ON, OFF. Default=ON	STARTUP.NCF, AUTOEXEC.NCF, or console
Allow Change to Client Rights=_____ Specifies whether a server can assume a client's rights to complete a task	ON, OFF. Default=ON	STARTUP.NCF, AUTOEXEC.NCF, or console

Troubleshooting Common File Server Problems

With any server installation, problems may occur. If you're having problems with your file server, check the following areas:

▸ Are the network boards configured correctly? Are their board settings conflicting with any other boards or LPT and COM ports enabled on the server's hardware?

▸ Does the LAN driver's configuration (including frame type) loaded on the server match the network board's configuration? Did you use the BIND server utility to bind the correct protocol (such as IPX) to the LAN board?

▸ Is the cable that connects the server to the rest of the network functioning?

▸ If you just installed or upgraded your server, did you follow the instructions in the documentation exactly? Check for missed steps, shortcuts you took that may have bypassed an important file, and so on.

▸ Are you using the correct version of LAN drivers, disk drivers, utilities, and other files on this server? You can't use a NetWare version 3.11 VREPAIR utility on a NetWare 3.12 network, for example.

▸ Does the server need more memory?

▸ Is the server's volume out of disk space or directory entries?

▸ Do you need to reconfigure certain aspects of the server to make it run differently? You can use the SET and MONITOR utilities to check the server's parameters and change some if necessary.

- Is the network board or disk controller board faulty? Try replacing the boards one at a time to see whether the problem goes away.

- Check, and replace if necessary, any T connectors, cable terminators, or hubs, or reset the hubs.

- Memory problems can produce numerous side effects. Double-check the memory configuration. If more than 16MB exist, manually register the memory by setting Auto Register Memory off and use the REGISTER MEMORY command. Remove the memory above 16MB if possible and try to restart the server. It may be necessary to replace the memory. It's a good idea to use memory from one manufacturer and to avoid mixing the different speeds of chips in the same machine.

REPAIRING CORRUPTED DATA

Unfortunately, data sometimes gets corrupted; disks develop faulty spots that corrupt the files that were stored there, a power failure damages a volume, and so on. Or you may encounter problems with your bindery. For example, someone may not be able to change his or her password, or you may not be able to delete a user.

If the problem is a corrupted file, you can probably delete the file and restore an earlier version of that file from a backup copy.

If the problem is with a volume on the server's hard disk or with the bindery, you may be able to use NetWare utilities to make repairs:

- VREPAIR.NLM is a NetWare Loadable Module (NLM) that repairs partition, volume, and file structure problems that may have been caused by a server abend, memory corruption, or a power outage. VREPAIR cannot fix problems with faulty hard disks. VREPAIR is copied to SYS:SYSTEM and the server's boot partition during the installation process. This way, you can load VREPAIR from the server's boot partition if you can't get to the SYS:SYSTEM directory.

▸ BINDFIX is a command-line utility that repairs bindery problems. In addition, BINDFIX can clean up your bindery by deleting the mail directories and the trustee rights of users you have already deleted. It is a good idea to have all users log out before running BINDFIX. When BINDFIX is finished running, a message will indicate whether it successfully repaired the bindery.

▸ BINDREST is a command-line utility that restores an older version of the bindery if BINDFIX was not successful. If you still have problems after you have run BINDFIX, you can try to restore your bindery from a backup copy. However, any changes that were made to the bindery since it was last backed up will be lost. For example, users may need to go back to using previous passwords if they changed their passwords since the last backup copy was made.

Refer to the NetWare documentation for specific instructions for using these utilities.

CHAPTER 3

Installing Network Workstations

The installation of a workstation involves two stages: installing the network hardware (the board and cables) and copying the necessary files to a disk where the workstation can get to them. The following sections discuss the procedures for installing DOS, Windows, and OS/2 workstations. Chapter 8 contains information about setting up Macintosh workstations.

If You Are Using the CD-ROM Version

If you have the CD-ROM version of NetWare 3.12, the documentation that explains how to install workstations is located in the online documentation. You will have to run the online documentation from a stand-alone computer to read how to install workstations. (You can either install the online documentation onto the computer's hard disk or attach a CD-ROM drive to the workstation and run the online documentation from the CD-ROM.)

You can install workstation software directly from the CD-ROM if the CD-ROM drive is attached to the workstation. However, since you may not have a CD-ROM drive attached to every workstation on your network, it will probably be easier to make diskettes with the workstation software on them. To create the workstation diskettes, you can use the MAKEDISK batch file, as explained in the following steps.

1 · Install the CD-ROM drive on a stand-alone computer.

2 · Use the DOS FORMAT command to format and name three high-density diskettes. Use the following names for the diskettes:

DISKETTE	DISKETTE 1	DISKETTE 2	DISKETTE 3
Label for DOS and Windows	WSDOS_1	WSWIN_1	WSDRV_2
Label for OS/2	WSOS2_1	WSOS2_2	WSDRV_1

3 • Change your current drive to the CLIENT\DOSWIN directory for DOS or Microsoft Windows workstations (CLIENT\OS2 for OS/2 workstations).

4 • Insert the first of the newly formatted diskettes into drive A or B. Then, from the DOSWIN or OS2 directory, type the following command, which will create the diskettes for you. (If you used drive B, substitute "B:" for "A:"):

```
MAKEDISK A:
```

5 • When prompted, insert each of the newly formatted diskettes in order.

Now you have a complete set of diskettes, from which you can install all of your workstations.

Installing DOS and Windows Workstations

NetWare 3.12 includes two different types of workstation software that can be used on DOS workstations.

The original type of DOS workstation software, used in previous versions of NetWare, is the NETX shell software. The newer type of workstation software is called the NetWare DOS Requester, which includes files called VLMs (Virtual Loadable Modules).

The following sections include quick paths for installing both NETX and the NetWare DOS Requester.

INSTALLING THE NETWARE DOS REQUESTER

The NetWare DOS Requester consists of several VLMs that control various aspects of the workstation's communications with the network.

A VLM manager, called VLM.EXE, is the executable that loads and manages the various VLMs as necessary.

To install the NetWare DOS Requester on a workstation, complete the steps shown in Figure 3.1. If you want to install NetWare workstation software that will support Microsoft Windows, Windows must already be installed on this workstation.

Each workstation you will install must have its own network board and its own legal copy of DOS. Each Microsoft Windows workstation should have its own legal copy of Windows.

During the installation, boot files (which include configuration and batch files) are created on the workstation's hard disk, in the NWCLIENT directory. Boot files are discussed in more detail later in this chapter.

INSTALLING NETX

To install a workstation using NETX, complete the steps shown in Figure 3.2.

Each workstation you will install must have its own network board and its own legal copy of DOS. If you want to use Microsoft Windows, use the NetWare DOS Requester instead of NETX.

Instructions for creating a boot disk are in the next section.

Creating a Boot Disk

Each workstation must have a boot disk, which can be either a floppy diskette or the workstation's hard disk. The boot disk contains the files necessary for booting the workstation with DOS, configuring the workstation's environment, loading the NetWare shell files, and logging the user into the network.

FIGURE 3.1 *Workstation installation quick path, NetWare DOS Requester*

1. Configure and install a network board, and connect the board to the network cabling.

2. Boot DOS on the workstation. (Do not run Windows.)

3. From the WSDOS_1 diskette, type INSTALL.

4. Specify the directory to use (default is C:\NWCLIENT).

5. Specify whether or not to modify the CONFIG.SYS and AUTOEXEC.BAT files.

6. (Optional) Specify whether to install support for Microsoft Windows.

7. Select the LAN driver for the workstation network board:

- Press Enter.

- To select a driver supplied with NetWare 3.12, insert the WSDRV_2 diskette in drive A and press Enter.

- To select a different driver, press Esc, insert the manufacturer's diskette, and press Enter.

8. When all selections are correct, press Enter.

9. When the installation is finished, press Enter to exit the program.

10. When prompted to "Insert disk with batch file, Press any key to continue...," insert the WSDOS_1 diskette. It's looking for the INSTALL.BAT file.

11. If this workstation previously had NETX installed on it, edit the AUTOEXEC.BAT file to remove commands that loaded the IPX or IPXODI driver, the LSL driver, and the NETX file. These commands are now included in the STARTNET.BAT file instead.

FIGURE 3.2 *Workstation installation quick path, NETX*

1. Configure and install a network board, and connect the board to the network cabling.

2. Decide which version of the shell file each workstation will use:

   • NETX: For ordinary workstation memory

   • EMSNETX: For expanded memory

   • XMSNETX: For extended memory

3. Boot **DOS** on the workstation.

4. From the **WSDOS_1** diskette, type **INSTALL**.

5. Specify the directory to use (default is **C:\NWCLIENT**).

6. Specify whether or not to modify the **CONFIG.SYS** and **AUTOEXEC.BAT** files.

7. Select the **LAN** driver for the workstation's network board:

   • Press Enter.

   • To select a driver supplied with NetWare 3.12, insert the WSDRV_2 diskette in drive A and press Enter.

   • To select a different driver, press Esc, insert the manufacturer's diskette, and press Enter.

8. When all selections are correct, press Enter.

9. When the installation is finished, press Enter to exit the program.

10. When prompted to "Insert disk with batch file, Press any key to continue...," insert the **WSDOS_1** diskette. It's looking for the **INSTALL.BAT** file.

FIGURE 3.2 *Workstation installation quick path, NETX (continued)*

11. If this workstation previously had **NETX** installed on it, edit the **AUTOEXEC.BAT** file to remove commands that loaded the **IPX** or **IPXODI** driver, the **LAN** driver, the **LSL** driver, and the **NETX** file. These commands will now be included in the **STARTNET.BAT** file instead.

12. Copy **NETX, EMSNETX,** or **XMSNETX** from **SYS:LOGIN** (usually drive F) to the boot disk (such as drive C).

13. Edit the **CONFIG.SYS** file and change the line **LASTDRIVE=Z** to **LASTDRIVE=E**.

14. Edit the **STARTNET.BAT** file to remove the **VLM** command and insert the **NETX** (or **EMSNETX** or **XMSNETX**) command.

Even if the workstation is diskless, you must still create a boot diskette. Using diskless workstations is discussed in the section "Installing Diskless Workstations" later in this chapter. The following sections explain how to create a boot disk.

If you intend for your workstation to run DOS utilities from the network, the DOS system files must be on the workstation's boot disk in order for it to boot. The DOS system files on the boot disk must be the same version as the DOS that the workstation will access from a network directory.

DECIDING WHICH FILES TO INCLUDE ON THE BOOT DISK

The next step in creating a boot disk is to determine which configuration and batch files to include. With the NetWare DOS Requester, most boot files are automatically copied to the boot disk. With NETX, you must create the boot disk manually by copying some files from NetWare diskettes and creating others with a text editor.

The files you need on the boot disk depend on whether the workstation is using the NetWare DOS Requester or NETX.

BOOT FILES FOR NETWARE DOS REQUESTER WORKSTATIONS

The installation program for the NetWare DOS Requester creates most necessary configuration and batch files required for booting the workstation. Some of these batch files are placed at the root of the boot disk (generally drive C), while other files are placed in a directory on the boot disk named NWCLIENT. The following list explains the batch files:

- **DOS system files**: Placed on the boot disk when you format the disk with the system file option (FORMAT /S). Their purpose is to boot DOS on the workstation.

- **CONFIG.SYS**: (Optional) Created when you install DR DOS 6.0 or MS DOS 5.0, or you can create (or edit) it with a text editor. It is located at the root of the boot disk. It configures the DOS environment on the workstation. This file is modified by the NetWare DOS Requester installation program.

- **AUTOEXEC.BAT**: Created when you install DR DOS 6.0 or MS DOS 5.0, or you can create (or edit) it with a text editor. It is a batch file, located at the root, that can automatically load the NetWare files and log the user in to the network. It can also include other commands. This file is modified by the NetWare DOS Requester installation program to add a line that calls the STARTNET.BAT file.

▸ **STARTNET.BAT:** Located in the NWCLIENT directory and executed by the AUTOEXEC.BAT file. This batch file loads the LSL, LAN driver, and IPXODI files and then executes the VLM.EXE command, which loads all the necessary VLM files. (Most of these commands are already in the AUTOEXEC.BAT file in previous versions of NetWare. If this workstation was previously using NETX, you will need to edit the AUTOEXEC.BAT file and remove any lines that loaded the LSL, LAN driver, IPXODI, IPX, or NETX files.)

▸ **NET.CFG:** Created by the NetWare DOS Requester installation program; can be edited with a text editor. It configures the Requester and the LAN driver to work for the workstation's given configuration. It's located in the NWCLIENT directory.

▸ **VLMs:** Several VLM files (Virtual Loadable Modules) that are placed in the NWCLIENT directory. VLMs control different aspects of the workstation's communication on the network. VLMs are explained more fully in the next section.

▸ **Unicode files:** Automatically copied into the NWCLIENT\NLS subdirectory. These files are necessary for the VLMs to work with the versions of DOS and Windows used in different countries and in different languages. Unicode files are explained in the section "Unicode Files" later in this chapter.

▸ **LSL.COM:** The Link Support Layer file, located in the NWCLIENT directory. It allows the workstation to communicate with different protocols.

▸ **LAN driver:** The driver file, such as NE2000.COM, is located in the NWCLIENT directory. It allows the network board to communicate with the network.

- ▸ Protocol driver: The protocol driver file, such as IPXODI.COM, is located in the NWCLIENT directory. It allows the LAN driver to communicate with various protocols.

- ▸ NETBIOS.EXE: (Optional) Located in the NWCLIENT directory. Use it only if you have applications that require NetBIOS.

- ▸ ROUTE.COM: (Optional) Located in the NWCLIENT directory. Use it only if your workstations are on a Token-Ring network that is using source routing.

- ▸ LANSUP.COM: (Optional) Located in the NWCLIENT directory. Use it only if your workstations are using the IBM LAN Support program. You load LANSUP.COM from the CONFIG.SYS file.

Additonal NetWare files (including TBMI2.COM, used for task switching) are copied to the WINDOWS and WINDOWS\SYSTEM directories on the hard disk if you specify that you are using Windows on the workstation.

Virtual Loadable Modules (VLMs)

When the NetWare 3.12 DOS Requester is installed on a workstation, the NET.CFG file is created. A portion of the NET.CFG file includes commands that specify which VLM files are loaded when the VLM.EXE command is executed from the STARTNET.BAT file.

In NET.CFG, under the heading "USE DEFAULTS = OFF," each of the VLM files that will execute is listed. By default, the VLM commands shown here are included in the NET.CFG file:

```
USE DEFAULTS=OFF
        VLM=CONN.VLM
        VLM=IPXNCP.VLM
        VLM=TRAN.VLM
        VLM=SECURITY.VLM
    ;   VLM=NDS.VLM
        VLM=BIND.VLM
```

```
VLM=NWP.VLM
VLM=FIO.VLM
VLM=GENERAL.VLM
VLM=REDIR.VLM
VLM=PRINT.VLM
VLM=NETX.VLM
```

Every VLM file that is listed is executed, and they are executed in the order in which they appear in the NET.CFG file. The order in which the files execute is important, so be sure not to change their order.

If you look at the NET.CFG file after installing a workstation using the installation program that comes with NetWare 3.12, you will notice that one line, "VLM=NDS.VLM," has a semicolon (;) in front of it. The semicolon "comments out" (or turns off) the command.

The NDS.VLM command is turned off because that VLM file is used only when the workstation needs to use NetWare Directory Services to log in to a NetWare 4 file server. To log in to a NetWare 3.12 server, BIND.VLM is required instead. Although a workstation will work fine if both NDS.VLM and BIND.VLM are loaded in the NET.CFG file, the workstation will take a little longer to log in to a NetWare 3.12 file server. Therefore, to make logging in faster and to optimize memory usage, the installation program automatically adds the semicolon to the NDS.VLM command. Then the workstation skips NDS.VLM and goes straight to BIND.VLM.

If you ever upgrade your network to NetWare 4, or if you add a NetWare 4 server to your NetWare 3.12 network and you want this workstation to be able to log in to NetWare 4 using NetWare Directory Services, edit the NET.CFG file and delete the semicolon. Then unload and reload the VLMs by typing the following commands from the NWCLIENT directory:

```
VLM /U
VLM
```

By unloading and then reloading the VLMs, you activate NDS.VLM, and the workstation can then use use both NDS.VLM and BIND.VLM to log in to both versions of NetWare servers. (Unloading the VLMs logs the workstation out of all servers it was logged in to.)

The following list explains the VLM files that are included in NET.CFG by default:

- **CONN.VLM:** Tracks the connection information for the workstation. Allows up to 50 connections to servers, although the default is 8

- **IPXNCP.VLM:** Builds and delivers IPX packets to the IPX protocol

- **TRAN.VLM:** Handles protocols and manages IPXNCP.VLM

- **SECURITY.VLM:** (Optional) Helps provide security at the transport layer

- **NDS.VLM:** (Optional) Allows the workstation to communicate with a NetWare 4 server running NetWare Directory Services (NDS)

- **BIND.VLM:** Allows the workstation to communicate with a NetWare server using the bindery instead of NDS

- **NWP.VLM:** NetWare protocol module, which allows other modules to log in and out and to connect to services

- **FIO.VLM:** Controls file input/output tasks for accessing network files. This module includes file caching, Large Internet Packet (LIP) support, and packet burst support

- **GENERAL.VLM:** Provides services to other VLMs, such as handling of search drives, server and queue information, and so on

- **REDIR.VLM:** The DOS redirector—redirects requests to the network, when appropriate

▸ PRINT.VLM: (Optional) Provides printer redirection using the FIO.VLM module

▸ NETX.VLM: (Optional) Provides backward compatibility for applications that require APIs in NETX

Two additional VLMS are not loaded by default, but they are available:

▸ AUTO.VLM: (Optional) Automatically reconnects the workstation to a server after that connection has been broken; stores and reestablishes drive mappings, printer connections, and so on

▸ RSA.VLM: (Optional) Used for authenticating the connection in a NetWare 4 network

Unicode Files

Unicode files are automatically copied into the NWCLIENT\NLS subdirectory by the NetWare DOS Requester installation program. The VLMs require these files, but the exact files that are required depend on the country code and code page (character set) configuration set in the workstation's CONFIG.SYS and AUTOEXEC.BAT files. Different versions of DOS and Windows are used in each country for different languages. The Unicode files make sure the VLMs display the correct characters for that country and language. The United States English default values are country code 001 and code page 437. (If you need to modify the country code or code page on the workstation, consult your DOS manual.)

All the Unicode files are copied onto the workstation, but you can delete the files you do not need if you need to save disk space. (All Unicode files together use about 248K, but the English files only, for example, use about .15K.)

Each Unicode file has a file name extension that indicates the country and language it supports. (Usually, the country code is the country's international long-distance telephone code preceded by a zero (0).) You need to keep only the files with the extension that matches your country and language. For example, if your DOS is using United States English, you need to keep only the files with the .001 extension.

Table 3.1 lists the Unicode file name extensions and the country and language each supports.

▶ **T A B L E   3.1**   *Unicode Files Required by Each Country and Language*

UNICODE FILE NAME EXTENSION	COUNTRIES	LANGUAGES
.001	United States, Canada	English
.002	Canada	French
.003	Latin America	Spanish, Portuguese
.031	Netherlands	Dutch
.032	Belgium	Dutch, French, German
.033	France	French
.034	Spain	Spanish
.039	Italy	Italian
.041	Switzerland	French, German
.044	United Kingdom	English
.045	Denmark	Danish
.046	Sweden	Swedish
.047	Norway	Norwegian
.049	Germany	German
.061	Australia	English
.081	Japan	Japanese
.351	Portugal	Portuguese
.358	Finland	Finnish

BOOT FILES FOR WORKSTATIONS USING NETX

To create a boot disk for a workstation that will use NETX, you must copy some files from NetWare diskettes and create others with a text editor. The files you may need to create yourself are CONFIG.SYS, NET.CFG, and AUTOEXEC.BAT.

The files you will need on the boot disk are described in the following list:

- ► **DOS system files:** Located on your DOS diskette and copied to the boot disk when you format the boot disk using the system files option (FORMAT /S). Their purpose is to boot DOS on the workstation.

- ► **CONFIG.SYS:** (Optional) Created when you install DR DOS 6.0 or MS DOS 5.0, or you can create (or edit) it with a text editor. It configures the DOS environment on the workstation.

- ► **AUTOEXEC.BAT:** Created when you install DR DOS 6.0 or MS DOS 5.0, or you can create (or edit) it with a text editor. It is a batch file that automatically loads the NetWare files and logs the user in to the network. It can also include other commands.

- ► **NET.CFG:** You also create this file with a text editor. It configures certain options in NetWare files.

- ► **LSL.COM:** The Link Support Layer file, which is located on the NetWare workstation software diskette. It allows the workstation to communicate with different protocols.

- ► **LAN driver:** The driver file, such as NE2000.COM, is located on the NetWare workstation software diskette. It allows the network board to communicate with the network.

- ► **Protocol driver:** The protocol driver file, such as IPXODI.COM, is located on the NetWare workstation software diskette. It allows the LAN driver to communicate with various protocols.

▸ **NETX, EMSNETX, or XMSNETX:** The NetWare shell file is copied to the SYS:LOGIN directory during the server installation. Use the file for the type of memory the workstation has available: NETX for conventional memory, EMSNETX for expanded memory, or XMSNETX for extended memory.

▸ **NETBIOS.EXE:** (Optional) Located on the NetWare workstation software diskette. Use it only if you have applications that require NetBIOS.

▸ **INT2F.COM:** (Optional) Located on the NetWare workstation software diskette. Use it only if you have applications that require NetBIOS.

▸ **ROUTE.COM:** (Optional) Located on the NetWare workstation software diskette. Use it only if your workstations are on a Token-Ring network that is using source routing.

▸ **LANSUP.COM:** (Optional) Located on the NetWare workstation software diskette. Use it only if your workstations are using the IBM LAN Support program. You load LANSUP.COM from the CONFIG.SYS file.

Installing OS/2 Workstations

To install an OS/2 workstation on a NetWare 3.12 network, complete the steps in Figure 3.3.

Installing Diskless Workstations

A diskless workstation cannot boot from a local disk because it doesn't have one. Therefore, it must be able to find all the necessary DOS and NetWare files on the file server and boot from there. This method of

F I G U R E 3.3 *OS/2 workstation installation quick path*

1. Install OS/2.

2. Insert the WSOS2_I diskette into drive A.

3. From the desktop, select the Drive A icon.

4. From the Drive A TreeView, select the Drive A icon.

5. Select Installation ➤ Requester on workstation..., and follow the instructions.

6. (Optional) Configure the workstation by selecting Configuration ➤ This Workstation.

booting diskless workstations from the network instead of from a local disk is called remote booting, or remote reset.

If you decide to use diskless workstations, you must have one workstation with a floppy disk drive available, at least until you get all your applications copied onto the network and the rest of the workstations installed. (This workstation will be used to create an image file for the diskless workstations to use during the boot process.) You can then remove the workstation with the floppy drive.

To install diskless workstations, you will actually have to create a boot diskette for the diskless workstations, following the instructions given in the section "Creating a Boot Disk" earlier in this chapter. If you have several workstations with identical hardware configurations, you can create a single boot diskette for them all to use. This seems like an odd step since the diskless workstation can't use a diskette. However, you will use the DOSGEN utility to copy this boot diskette into a network directory, so it is important to make the boot diskette.

Figure 3.4 shows the quick path for installing a diskless workstation. See the NetWare documentation for more details.

F I G U R E   3.4   *Diskless workstation installation quick path*

1. Configure and install a network board, and connect the board to the network cabling.

2. Install a Remote Reset PROM chip in the workstation.

3. Load RPL.NLM on the server and bind the RPL protocol to the LAN driver.

4. If all your diskless workstations have identical hardware configurations, make a single boot diskette. If your workstations have different configurations, make a separate boot diskette for each configuration.

5. Run DOSGEN, which creates a boot disk image file, called NET$DOS.SYS, in SYS:LOGIN.

6. If your diskless workstations have varying hardware configurations, create a BOOTCONF.SYS file in the SYS:LOGIN directory. This file tells the workstation which remote boot files to use.

7. Give users rights to access the remote boot files.

8. Load DOS into directories under SYS:PUBLIC so the workstation can run DOS:

  • Create a DOS directory for each type of DOS you have.

  • Name directories with the machine name and DOS version: SYS:PUBLIC\machine\MSDOS\version

NET.CFG Parameters

The NET.CFG file contains commands that configure various aspects of the NetWare software on the workstation. If your workstation will use NETX, you must create NET.CFG with a text editor and place the file in the same directory as the NETX file. If you are using the NetWare DOS Requester, NET.CFG is created by the installation program, and you can edit it with a text editor. It's located in the NWCLIENT directory on the boot disk.

In NET.CFG you can specify options and values in the following categories:

- **Link driver**: Configures the LAN driver in the workstation

- **Link support**: Configures parameters for the Link Support Layer (LSL.COM), such as the size of packet receive buffers, the size of memory pool buffers, and so on

- **Protocol**: Configures the IPXODI protocol

- **NETBIOS**: (Not used by NETX) Configures NetBIOS

- **NetWare DOS Requester**: (Not used by NETX) Configures the NetWare DOS Requester and VLM files

- **TBMI2**: (Not used by NETX) Configures the workstation's task-switching environment

How you format the commands in NET.CFG depends on which category the command falls into. NETBIOS parameter commands are typed flush with the left margin of the file. Commands in the other categories are indented beneath a heading.

For example, to specify the Ethernet frame type and other pertinent information for the LAN driver 3C523, the configuration commands are indented beneath the heading "Link Driver 3C523" as shown here:

```
Link Driver 3C523
    SLOT 5
    FRAME Ethernet_802.2
    INT 3
    PORT 300
    MEM C0000
    protocol ipx e0 ethernet_802.2
```

Tables 3.2 through 3.7 list the available NET.CFG parameters, by category.

▸ **T A B L E   3.2**   *NET.CFG File: Link Driver Options*

LINK DRIVER *driver*	*driver* = LAN driver name
alternate	Specifies an alternate board
dma [*#1 or #2*] *channelnumber*	Configures the hardware's DMA channels
frame type	Sets the frame type the board will use
int [*#1 or #2*] *IRQnumber*	Sets the interrupt the board will use
link stations number	Specifies the number of link stations for the LANSUP driver, used with the IBM LAN Support Program
max frame size number	Specifies the maximum frame size, in bytes, the LAN driver can transmit
mem [*#1 or #2*] *address [length]*	Sets the memory range the network board can use. *Address* = the hex starting address of the memory used by the board. *Length* = the number of hex paragraphs (16 bytes) of the memory address range
node address *address*	Sets the hex address number for the board, which overrides the hard-coded address

▶ **T A B L E** 3.2 *NET.CFG File: Link Driver Options (continued)*

port [#1 *or* #2] address [*number*]	Sets the hex address for the starting port and the number of ports in the range
protocol *name ID type*	Adds additional protocols to the LAN driver. *Name* = the new protocol's name. *ID* = the protocol's hex ID number. *Type* = the protocol's frame type
saps *number*	Sets the number of Service Access Points needed by the LANSUP driver, used with the IBM LAN Support Program. Default: 1
slot *number*	Specifies the board's slot number so the driver doesn't have to scan the slots to find the board

▶ **T A B L E** 3.3 *NET.CFG File: Link Support Options*

LINK SUPPORT

buffers *number* [*size*]	Sets the number and size of receive buffers that LSL.COM can handle. Default number = 0. Default size = 1130
max boards *number*	Sets the maximum number of logical boards the LSL.COM can maintain. Default: 4. Range: 1 to 16
max stacks *number*	Sets the maximum number of logical protocol stack IDs that LSL.COM can support. Default: 4. Range: 1 to 16
mempool *number*[k]	Configures the size of the memory pool buffers for some protocols (not used with IPXODI). [k] means multiply by 1024

Protocol *name*	*name* = protocol name, such as IPXODI
bind *number*	Binds the protocol to a network board. *number* = board name or logical board number
config option *number*	Used with NETX to temporarily change the board's configuration options, overriding options set in the IPX file
int64 [on or off]	If an application requires interrupt 64h, change this parameter to Off. Default: On
int7A [on or off]	If an application requires interrupt 7Ah, change this parameter to Off. Default: On
ipatch *offset, value*	Allows an address in IPXODI.COM to be patched with the specified byte offset value
ipx packet size limit *number*	Sets the maximum size of packets to reduce wasted memory. Default: 4160 or the size specified by the LAN driver, if smaller. Range: 576 to 6500 bytes
ipx retry count *number*	Specifies the number of times a workstation resends a packet that failed. Default: 20
ipx sockets *number*	Sets the maximum number of sockets that IPX can have open. Default: 20
minimum spx retries *number*	Sets the minimum number of unacknowledged transmit requests that occur before assuming the connection has failed. Default: 20. Range: 0 to 255

► **T A B L E 3.4** *NET.CFG File: Protocol Options (continued)*

spx abort timeout *number*	Sets the time that SPX waits for a response before terminating a connection. Default: 540 ticks (approximately 30 seconds)
spx connections *number*	Sets the maximum number of simultaneous SPX connections a workstation can have. Default: 15
spx listen timeout *number*	Sets the time that SPX waits for a packet before requesting another packet to make sure the connection is still valid. Default: 108 ticks (approximately 6 seconds)
spx verify timeout *number*	Sets the interval between packets that SPX sends to verify a connection is working. Default: 54 ticks (approximately 3 seconds)

► **T A B L E 3.5** *NET.DFG File: NetBIOS Options*

Netbios abort timeout *number*	Sets the time NetBIOS waits before ending a session. default: 540 ticks (30 seconds)
Netbios broadcast count *number*	When multiplied by "NetBIOS Broadcast Delay" number, sets the time required to broadcast a name resolution packet across the network. Default (with NetBIOS Internet = On): 4. Default (with NetBIOS Internet = Off): 2. Range: 2 to 65,535

▸ **T A B L E** 3.5 *NET.DFG File: NetBIOS Options (continued)*

Netbios broadcast delay *number*	When multiplied by "NetBIOS Broadcast Count" number, sets the time required to broadcast a name resolution packet across the network. Default (with NetBIOS Internet = On): 36. Default (with NetBIOS Internet = Off): 18. Range: 18 to 65,535
Netbios commands *number*	Specifies the number of NetBIOS commands available. Default: 12. Range: 4 to 250
Netbios internet *number*	If you are using NetBIOS applications on a single network, set to Off to speed up packets. If using multiple networks through bridges, leave On. Default: On
Netbios listen timeout *number*	Sets the time NetBIOS waits before requesting another packet to make sure the connection is still valid. Default: 108 ticks (6 seconds). Range: 1 to 65,535
Netbios receive buffers *number*	Sets the number of IPX receive buffers that NetBIOS uses. Default: 6. Range: 4 to 20
Netbios retry count *number*	Specifies how many times NetBIOS resends a packet to establish a NetBIOS session with a remote partner. Default (with NetBIOS Internet = On): 20. Default (with NetBIOS Internet = Off): 10. Range: 4 to 20

► **T A B L E   3.5**   *NET.DFG File: NetBIOS Options (continued)*

Netbios retry delay *number*	Specifies how long NetBIOS waits between sending packets to establish a session. Default: 10 ticks (0.5 seconds). Range: 10 to 65,535
Netbios send buffers *number*	Sets the number of IPX send buffers that NetBIOS uses. Default: 6. Range: 4 to 250
Netbios session *number*	Specifies the maximum number of simultaneous virtual circuits. Default: 32. Range: 4 to 250
Netbios verify timeout *number*	Sets the interval between packets to keep a connection open. Default: 54 ticks (3 seconds). Range: 4 to 65,535
Npatch *offset, value*	Patches any location in the NETBIOS.EXE data segment with the specified value

(Note: NetBIOS commands do not need to be indented.)

► **T A B L E   3.6**   *NetWare DOS Requester Options*

Netware dos requester	
auto large table = [on or off]	When turned On, creates a connection table of 178 bytes for bindery reconnects. When set to Off, creates a small table of 34 bytes. Default: Off
auto reconnect = [on or off]	When turned On, AUTO.VLM reconnects the workstation after a connection has been broken. Default: On (Bind Reconnect = On must also be set.)

`auto retry = number`	Sets the time AUTO.VLM waits before retrying. Default: 0. Range: 0 (no retries) to 3640
`average name length = number`	Sets the average length of server names, which is used to create a table to store those names. Default: 48 characters. Range: 2 to 48
`bind reconnect = [on or off]`	Rebuilds bindery connections after a connection has been broken (Auto Reconnect = On must also be set.)
`cache buffers = number`	Specifies the number of cache buffers used for local caching. Default: 5. Range: 0 to 64
`cache buffers size = number`	Sets the size of cache buffers used by FIO.VLM. Default: 512 bytes. Range: 64 to 4096
`cache writes = [on or off]`	Specifies whether writes are cached. Default: On
`checksum = number`	Sets level at which NCP packets are validated. Default: 1. Range: 0=disabled; 1=enabled but not preferred; 2=enabled and preferred; 3=required
`connections = number`	Sets the maximum number of connections. Default: 8. Range: 2 to 8
`dos name = name`	Specifies the name of DOS on the workstation. Default: MSDOS
`first network drive = drive`	Specifies which drive letter will be the first network drive. Default: First available. Range: A to Z

▸ T A B L E 3.6   *NetWare DOS Requester Options (continued)*

`handle net errors = [on or off]`	Sets how network errors are handled. Default: On. On=interrupt 24 handles errors. Off=NET_RECV_ERROR is returned
`large internet packets = [on or off]`	Allows maximum packet size to be used. Default: On
`load conn table low = [on or off]`	Used only for initial release of NetWare 4.0 utilities. Default: Off
`load low conn = [on or off]`	If set to Off, makes CONN.VLM load in upper memory. Default: On
`load low ipxncp = [on or off]`	If set to Off, makes IPXNCP.VLM load in upper memory. Default: On
`local printers = number`	Tells the workstation how many local printers are attached. Default: 3. Range: 0 to 9. Set to 0 to prevent Shift+PrtScrn from hanging the workstation if CAPTURE isn't in effect
`long machine type = name`	Specifies the type of computer being used. Default: IBM_PC
`max tasks = number`	Sets the maximum number of simultaneously active tasks. Default: 31. Range: 20 to 128
`message level = number`	Sets which messages are displayed during load. Default: 1. Range: 0=copyright and critical errors; 1=warning messages; 2=load information for VLMs; 3=configuration information; 4=diagnostic information

▶ **T A B L E 3.6** *NetWare DOS Requester Options (continued)*

`message timeout = number`	Sets how long before broadcast messages are cleared from the screen. Default: 0 ticks. Range: 0 to 10,000 (6 hours)
`network printers = number`	Specifies how many LPT ports can be captured. Default: 3. Range: 0 to 9 (If set to 0, PRINT.VLM will not load.)
`pb buffers = number`	Turns Packet Burst on and off. Default: 3. Range: 0 (off) to 3
`pburst read window size = number`	Specifies how many bytes of data can be sent in a read request to the server before the workstation receives a reply. Default: 16 bytes. Range: 2 to 128
`pburst write window size = number`	Specifies how many bytes of data can be sent in a write request to the server before the workstation receives a reply. Default: 10 bytes. Range: 2 to 128
`preferred server = name`	Specifies which server to attach to first. Default: No preferred server
`print buffer size = number`	Sets the size for the print buffer. Default: 64 bytes. Range: 0 to 256
`print header = number`	Specifies the size of the buffer to hold initialization information for each print job. Default: 64 bytes. Range: 0 to 64

`print tail = number`	Specifies the size of the buffer to hold reset information after a print job. Default: 16 bytes. Range: 0 to 16
`read only compatibility = [on or off]`	Specifies whether a Read Only file can be opened with a read/write access call. Default: Off
`search mode = number`	Sets the search mode for finding files in directories. Default: 1. Range: 0 to 7
`set station time = [on or off]`	Synchronizes the workstation's time to the server's time. Default: On
`show dots = [on or off]`	Set to On to display dots (. and ..) for parent directories in Windows 3.x. Default: Off
`short machine type = name`	Sets the computer name for use with overlay files. Default: IBM
`signature level = number`	Sets the level of NCP Packet Signature security. Default: 1. Range: 0=no signing; 1=signs if server requests; 2=signs if server can sign; 3=required
`true commit = [on or off]`	Specifies whether the commit NCP is sent on DOS commit requests. Default: Off
`use defaults = [on or off]`	If turned Off, lets you override default loading of VLMs and specify exact files to load. Default: On
`vlm = path vlm`	Loads a VLM file

▸**T A B L E 3.7** *NET.CFG File: TBMI2 Options*

TBMI2

data ecb count *number*	Sets the number of data ECBs (event control blocks) allocated by DOS programs needing virtualization. Default: 60. Range: 10 to 89
ecb count *number*	Sets the number of nondata ECBs allocated by DOS programs needing virtualization. Default: 20. Range: 10 to 255
int64 [on or off]	If an application requires interrupt 64h, change this parameter to Off. Default: On
int7A [on or off]	If an application requires interrupt 7Ah, change this parameter to Off. Default: On
use max packets	Lets TBMI2 use the maximum IPX packet size
using windows 3.0	Lets TBMI2 use TASKID, which identifies tasks in each DOS Box as separate tasks

Examples of Boot Files

For examples of typical boot files used by a workstation running the NetWare DOS Requester, see Figures 3.5 through 3.8.

Figure 3.5 shows an example AUTOEXEC.BAT file, Figure 3.6 shows a CONFIG.SYS file, Figure 3.7 shows a STARTNET.BAT file, and Figure 3.8 shows a NET.CFG file.

```
PATH C:\NWCLIENT\;C:\WINDOWS;C:\DOS;C:\NOTEUT;C:\;C:\WP51

loadhigh C:\DOS\SHARE.EXE/1:500/f:5100

LOADHIGH C:\WINDOWS\SMARTDRV.EXE

PROMPT $P$G

SET TEMP=C:\DOS

LOADHIGH C:\DOS\mouse.COM/Y

set nwlanguage=english

set emailuser=lsnow

set wp=/u-lks

echo on

@CALL C:\NWCLIENT\STARTNET

f:

login lsnow
```

Troubleshooting Common Problems

If you're having trouble with a workstation, check the following areas:

▶ Is the problem with a single workstation or several? If the problem is with several workstations, it may be caused by the network cabling or related hardware. A network analyzer, such as NetWare LANalyzer, can be a useful tool for diagnosing cabling problems.

F I G U R E 3.6 *Example CONFIG.SYS file*

```
DEVICE=C:\DOS\SETVER.EXE
DEVICE=C:\DOS\HIMEM.SYS
DEVICE=C:\DOS\EMM386.EXE NOEMS
DOS=HIGH,UMB
SHELL=c:\command.com /p c:\ /e:4096
DEVICE:C:\DOS\POWER.EXE
FILES=50
LASTDRIVE=Z
```

F I G U R E 3.7 *Example STARTNET.BAT file*

```
SET NWLANGUAGE=ENGLISH
loadhigh C:\NWCLIENT\LSL.COM
:DRIVER1
loadhigh C:\NWCLIENT\3C523.COM
loadhigh C:\NWCLIENT\IPXODI.COM
loadhigh C:\NWCLIENT\VLM.EXE
```

FIGURE 3.8 *Example NET.CFG file*

```
Link Driver 3C523

    SLOT 5

    FRAME Ethernet_802.2

    FRAME Ethernet_II

    INT3

    PORT 300

    MEM C0000

    protocol ipx e0 ethernet_802.2

    protocol ip 800 ethernet_II


USE DEFAULTS=OFF

    VLM=CONN.VLM

    VLM=IPXNCP.VLM

    VLM=TRAN.VLM

    VLM=SECURITY.VLM

;   VLM=NDS.VLM

    VLM=BIND.VLM

    VLM=NWP.VLM

    VLM=FIO.VLM

    VLM=GENERAL.VLM

    VLM=REDIR.VLM

    VLM=PRINT.VLM

    VLM=NETX.VLM
```

FIGURE 3.8
Example NET.CFG file (continued)

```
NetWare DOS Requester

    FIRST NETWORK DRIVE=F

    NETWARE PROTOCOL=BIND

    PREFERRED SERVER=PHOTO

    NETWORK PRINTERS=3

    LOCAL PRINTERS=0

    PRINT HEADER=100

    PRINT TAIL=100

    SHOW DOTS=ON

    AUTO RECONNECT=ON

    BIND RECONNECT=ON

    AUTO RETRY=1

    VLM=AUTO.VLM

    VLM=RSA.VLM


Link Support

    Buffers 8 1500

    MemPool 4096

    Max Stacks 8
```

- Is the cable that connects the workstation to the rest of the network functioning?

- Are all the cables correctly connected or terminated? Check for any loose connections and tighten them.

- Are the network boards and any other boards (video, and so on) seated firmly in their slots?

- Do any of the cable segments exceed the length limits for your type of networking hardware?

- If the network is Ethernet, is the workstation using the same Ethernet frame type as the server? If the workstation is using a different Ethernet frame type, it won't be able to find the server.

- Is the network board configured correctly? Are the board settings conflicting with any other boards or printers attached to the workstation? Check the boards' documentation for instructions on avoiding conflicts with other boards. You may need to run a memory manager program to resolve memory conflicts.

- Does the LAN driver loaded on the workstation's boot disk match the network board?

- If you just installed or upgraded the workstation, did you follow the instructions in the documentation exactly? Check for missed steps, shortcuts that may have bypassed an important file, and so on.

- Are you using the right NetWare boot files on this workstation? The boot disk should have the correct versions of LSL, IPXODI, NETX or VLMs, and the LAN driver.

- Is the workstation running on a Token-Ring network that is using source routing? If so, make sure the ROUTE.COM file is on the workstation's boot disk (and is loaded).

- Is the workstation using the IBM LAN Support program? If so, make sure the LANSUP.COM file is on the boot disk and is loaded from the CONFIG.SYS file.

- Does the workstation need more DOS environment space? If so, you can increase the DOS environment size by using the SHELL command in the workstation's CONFIG.SYS file.

- Is the workstation finding the right DOS COMMAND.COM file? Use the COMSPEC command in the user's login script or the SHELL command in the workstation's CONFIG.SYS file to point to the COMMAND.COM file.

- Does the workstation seem to be running too slowly on the network? You may need to increase the number of cache buffers the workstation uses to manage incoming and outgoing network data. You can change the number of cache buffers by using the CACHE BUFFERS command in the NET.CFG file.

- Are the NCP Packet Signature levels correct on both the workstation and the server? If the server is requesting packet signatures, is the workstation's LOGIN utility, DOS Requester, or shell file an older version that doesn't support packet signatures? (For more information about NCP Packet Signature, see Chapter 4.)

- If the image on the monitor's screen is rolling or bouncing, make sure the video cable isn't loose. Also make sure no other monitors are situated near the monitor; monitors in close proximity can cause interference with each other.

- If workstations are running Windows from the network instead of from a local hard disk, the DOS Requester Install program may not work. This should be fixed in the next release of the DOS Requester.

► If, when entering Windows, you receive an error saying that the Unicode files could not be found, it may be because you are running a shell program from a directory other than C:\WINDOWS, which is where the Unicode files are copied during installation. Try copying the necessary Unicode files from the WINDOWS\NLS directory into the WINDOWS directory or another directory that is in the workstation's DOS path.

► The Auto Reconnect feature currently does not reconnect the workstation when multiple server connections are lost. This feature may be added in the future.

► If the DOS Requester is installed after Windows for Workgroups is installed, Windows for Workgroups may not run properly. Install the DOS Requester first, and then install Windows for Workgroups.

► If you set the search mode (using SMODE) to 5, the DOS Requester may not work properly with the CAPTURE utility.

CHAPTER 4

NetWare Security

NetWare 3.12 provides several security tools for protecting your network and its data. Using these tools, you can

- Prevent unauthorized users from logging in to your network and accessing your files

- Control whether users can access files and what they can do with the files they open

- Protect applications from being copied, deleted, changed, or pirated

- Prevent users from accidentally deleting or overwriting important files

- Prevent intruders from forging NCP packets and illegally gaining access to network resources

The security tools NetWare provides are

- **Login security:** Passwords and account restrictions specify if and when users can log in and how much disk space they can access.

- **Trustee rights:** Trustee rights control what users can do with a particular file or directory (such as reading, changing, renaming, deleting, and so on). An Inherited Rights Mask controls whether or not a user can inherit trustee rights from a parent directory and exercise those rights in the subdirectory.

- **Directory and file attributes:** Attributes are assigned to files and directories, controlling what users can do with the file or directory. Attributes affect all users and override trustee rights.

- **NCP Packet Signature:** Packet Signatures ensure that forged packets cannot access network files and other resources.

The following sections explain each of these security tools.

Login Security

Passwords and account restrictions are both elements of login security in a NetWare network. Passwords should be required to prevent unauthorized users from easily logging in using another person's user name. Account restrictions control such things as the time of day users can log in, how much disk space they can access, and how often they must change their passwords.

TIPS FOR CHOOSING PASSWORDS

To keep passwords from being easily guessed, encourage your users to observe some key tips for choosing passwords:

▶ Passwords must be at least 5 characters long, by default, although the network supervisor can change the minimum length.

▶ DOS users can have passwords up to 127 characters long, but Macintosh users can have passwords only up to 8 characters long.

▶ There is no difference between upper- and lowercase letters.

▶ Avoid passwords that can be easily guessed, such as birthdays, names of family members, favorite sports or hobbies, and so on.

▶ Avoid words that can be found in a dictionary. In other words, combine words or letters and numbers into a single word, such as IDRATHERBESAILING or 2HOT4ICE.

ACCOUNT RESTRICTIONS

You can use account restrictions to restrict users' work with the network in various ways. For example, you can limit the hours during which users can log in to the network, the workstations they can use, the amount of disk space they can fill up, or the length of time they can use the same password. Some of these restrictions will prevent a user from violating set limits. Other restrictions may actually disable the user's account if the user exceeds one of these restrictions, locking the user out of the network.

You can assign account restrictions on a system-wide basis or to individual users. When you specify system-wide restrictions, those restrictions apply to every user who is created from that point on. Any users who already exist will not be affected by the new restrictions. Therefore, you should apply system-wide restrictions before you create any users. When you assign account restrictions to individual users, the individual assignments override any system-wide restrictions you may have also set.

If you are supervisor equivalent, you can set account restrictions by using NetWare's SYSCON menu. To set system-wide account restrictions, select SYSCON's Supervisor Options menu; to set a user's restrictions, select the User Information menu.

Each of the options you can select are described below. To change Yes/No options, type either Y or N and press the Enter key. To enter values for an option, highlight the field where the information belongs, type in the value, and then press the Enter key.

Time Restrictions   The Time Restrictions option lets you restrict the days and times that users can log in. Each asterisk in the Time Restrictions chart means that users are allowed to log in at that time on that day. To restrict users from logging in at certain times, delete the asterisks in those time slots by positioning the cursor over those asterisks and pressing the Del key. To allow users to log in, press the Ins key or type an asterisk. When you are finished, press the Esc key and then choose Yes to save the changes.

Account Has Expiration Date   The Account Has Expiration Date option is useful only if you know most of your network users will be leaving at the same time. For example, if you are managing a network that is used primarily by students, and at the end of the semester the current users will leave and a new batch of students will become users instead, you could set this option to Yes. Otherwise, make sure this option is set to No.

Date Account Expires   If you choose to make user accounts expire, fill in an expiration date.

Limit Concurrent Connections   Set the Limit Concurrent Connections option to Yes only if you need to restrict the number of workstations users can log in from simultaneously.

Maximum Connections   If you choose to limit concurrent connections, enter the maximum number of connections.

Create Home Directory for User   Specify Yes for the Create Home Directory for User option so that every time you add a new user, a home directory for that user is created automatically.

Require Password   In most cases you should specify Yes for the Require Password option so that passwords are required. If you require passwords you will probably also want to specify values for the remaining password restrictions, which will help ensure that the passwords cannot be used by intruders.

Minimum Password Length   Usually, requiring passwords to be at least 5 characters long is a safe practice.

Force Periodic Password Changes   Select Yes to require users to change their passwords periodically.

Days Between Forced Changes If you choose to have users change their passwords periodically, enter the number of days the users can go between changes.

Limit Grace Logins When a user's password expires, the user is notified when trying to log in. A message appears explaining that the password has expired and asking whether the user would like to change the password. A grace login allows the user to finish logging in using the old password without changing it. Grace logins are useful if the user doesn't want to create a new password this time. If you want users to have an unlimited number of grace logins (effectively allowing users to never change their passwords), enter No. If you want users to have a limited number of grace logins, enter Yes.

Grace Logins Allowed If you choose to limit the number of grace logins, enter the maximum number you want to allow.

Require Unique Passwords To prevent users from using the same passwords over and over, set the Require Unique Passwords option to Yes. NetWare then checks to make sure the new password a user just created is different from the last eight passwords that user had.

Account Balance, Allow Unlimited Credit, and Low Balance Limit The Account Balance, Allow Unlimited Credit, and Low Balance Limit options appear only if you install NetWare's accounting feature on your file server (by choosing the Accounting option from SYSCON's Available Topics menu). The accounting feature tracks the amount of time, disk space, and other network resources each person uses on the network. Accounting is useful if your network provides services to outside clients and you need to track their usage statistics so that you can charge them for using those resources.

Trustee Rights

Trustee rights give users or groups permission to perform various tasks with a file or directory. For example, trustee rights control whether a user can see the files in a directory, read the files, delete them, change them, rename them, or change other users' rights to those files.

You can assign a user any combination of trustee rights to a directory or file. This allows you greater flexibility in controlling exactly how a user can work with a directory or file.

Once you have given a user trustee rights to a directory, the user can inherit those trustee rights in all of that directory's subdirectories (in fact, in the entire directory structure below that directory). You need to keep this in mind as you create subdirectories. When you first create a subdirectory, any user who has rights to the parent directory will get identical rights to the new subdirectory.

You can change users' rights to a subdirectory in two ways:

▶ Give the users new rights to the subdirectory, which will override the rights the users would have otherwise inherited from the parent directory.

▶ Block some or all of the users' rights by assigning an Inherited Rights Mask (IRM) to the subdirectory.

An IRM lets you specify which rights a user can inherit from parent directories and filter out rights the user shouldn't inherit. By default, the IRM permits all available trustee rights to be inherited. However, even though the IRM allows all rights to be inherited, users can still inherit only those rights they actually had in the parent directory. The only right the IRM cannot mask is the Supervisory right. The only way to revoke the Supervisory right is to remove it at the original assignment.

The rights a user can ultimately exercise in a directory are called the user's "effective rights." Effective rights are calculated in two ways:

- The rights the user inherits from the parent directory, minus the rights blocked by the IRM

- The sum of all individual and group trustee assignments and security equivalences (Neither of these assignments is affected by the IRM.)

Table 4.1 lists each of the trustee rights available in NetWare 3.12 and describes what that right allows a user to do to the affected file or directory. It also lists the abbreviation NetWare uses for each trustee right.

File and Directory Attributes

Attributes are another major tool that NetWare provides for protecting your network directories and files. Attributes, which are sometimes called flags, control whether users can share a file or directory, delete it, rename it, change it, and so on.

Attributes differ from rights in the following ways:

- Attributes are assigned directly to files and directories; rights are assigned to users.

- Attributes control the actions of all users, including the SUPERVISOR; rights affect only the user to whom the rights are assigned.

- Attributes override rights. For example, if you have the Write right to a file but that file has the Read Only attribute, you won't be able to change the file. Your Write right is ineffective because the Read Only attribute is dominant.

▶ **T A B L E 4.1** *Trustee Rights in NetWare 3.12*

RIGHT	ABBREVIATION	EXPLANATION
Read	R	In a directory, allows you to open and read files in the directory. In a file, allows you to open and read the file
Write	W	In a directory, allows you to open and write to (change) files in the directory. In a file, allows you to open and write to the file
Create	C	In a directory, allows you to create subdirectories and files and write to files in the directory. In a file, allows you to salvage the file if it is deleted
Erase	E	In a directory, allows you to delete the directory and its files and subdirectories. In a file, allows you to delete the file
Modify	M	In a directory, allows you to change the name, directory attributes, and file attributes of the files and subdirectories in the directory. In a file, allows you to change the name or file attributes of the file
File Scan	F	In a directory, allows you to see the names of all files and subdirectories in the directory. In a file, allows you to see the name of the file
Access Control	A	In a directory, allows you to change the directory's Inherited Rights Mask and trustee assignments. In a file, allows you to change the file's Inherited Rights Mask and trustee assignments
Supervisory	S	In a directory, gives you all rights to files and subdirectories in the directory. In a file, gives you all rights to the file. The Supervisory right cannot be taken away

▶ Attributes do not grant rights. Regardless of the attributes a file or directory may have, you still must have been assigned a right to be able to exercise that right. For example, if a file has the Read Write attribute, which permits users to change the file, only users who have the Write right will actually be able to change the file.

▶ Attributes control some features that rights do not, such as whether a file (such as a utility or an application's executable file) can be used by more than one user at the same time.

▶ To change a file or directory's attributes, you must have the Modify right to that file or directory. To change a user's rights to a file or directory, you must have the Access Control right to that file or directory.

Some attributes can be assigned to directories, some can be assigned to files, and some can be assigned to either. Table 4.2 lists the file attributes available in NetWare 3.12 and shows the letters used to indicate those attributes. Table 4.3 lists the directory attributes.

▶ **T A B L E** 4.2 *NetWare 3.12 File Attributes*

FILE ATTRIBUTE	LETTERS	EXPLANATION
Read Only	Ro	Allows users to read the file but not change it. Read Only can be changed to Read Write. All NetWare files in SYS:SYSTEM, SYS:PUBLIC, and SYS:LOGIN are Read Only. Assigning Read Only automatically assigns Delete Inhibit and Rename Inhibit
Read Write	Rw	Allows users to read and change the file. Read Write can be changed to Read Only. Most files are set to Read Write by default when the file is created

▶ T A B L E 4.2   *NetWare 3.12 File Attributes (continued)*

FILE ATTRIBUTE	LETTERS	EXPLANATION
Shareable	S	Allows several users to open the file at the same time. It is useful for utilities, commands, application files, and some database files. All NetWare files in SYS:SYSTEM, SYS:PUBLIC, and SYS:LOGIN are Shareable. Most data files should not be Shareable so users do not conflict with each other's work
Archive Needed	A	Automatically assigned to files that have been changed since the last time they were backed up
Execute Only	X	Use with caution. Must be assigned by a supervisor-equivalent user. Prevents executable files from being copied, changed, or deleted. Once assigned, this attribute cannot be removed, so assign it only if you have a backup copy of the file. It is a good idea to assign the Read Only attribute to executable files instead of Execute Only
Hidden	H	Hides files and prevents them from being copied or deleted. They do not appear when you use DOS's DIR command to list files, but they do appear when you use NetWare's NDIR utility. You must remove the Hidden attribute before you can delete the file
System	Sy	Indicates system files (such as DOS files). Protects files by hiding them and preventing them from being copied or deleted. They do not appear when you use DOS's DIR command to list files, but they do appear when you use NetWare's NDIR utility. You must remove the System attribute before you can delete the file.

▸ **T A B L E 4.2**   *NetWare 3.12 File Attributes (continued)*

FILE ATTRIBUTE	LETTERS	EXPLANATION
Transactional	T	Use on database files to allow NetWare's Transactional Tracking System (TTS) to protect the files from being corrupted if, for example, the power goes out during a transaction
Purge	P	Purges the file as soon as the file is deleted. Purged files cannot be restored with the SALVAGE utility
Read Audit	Ra	Not used (It appears in the list of available attributes but is not supported.)
Write Audit	Wa	Not used (It appears in the list of available attributes but is not supported.)
Copy Inhibit	CI	Prevents Macintosh files from being copied. It does not apply to DOS files
Delete Inhibit	DI	Prevents users from deleting the file
Rename Inhibit	RI	Prevents users from renaming the file
Normal	N	Use the Normal attribute to flag a file to the normal default attribute (which is Read Write, with all other attributes cleared)
All	ALL	Use ALL to assign all available attributes to the file
Subdirectory	SUB	Use SUB to work with attributes in directories and their subdirectories

▸ **T A B L E 4.3**   *NetWare 3.12 Directory Attributes*

DIRECTORY ATTRIBUTE	LETTERS	EXPLANATION
System	Sy	Indicates system directories (such as DOS directories). Protects directories by hiding them and preventing them from being copied or deleted. They do not appear when you use DOS's DIR command to list files, but they do appear when you use NetWare's NDIR utility. You must remove the System attribute before you can delete the directory
Hidden	H	Hides directories and prevents them from being copied or deleted. They do not appear when you use DOS's DIR command to list files, but they do appear when you use NetWare's NDIR utility. You must remove the Hidden attribute before you can delete the directory
Delete Inhibit	DI	Prevents users from deleting the directory
Purge	P	Purges all files in the directory as soon as they are deleted. Purged files cannot be restored with the SALVAGE utility
Rename Inhibit	RI	Prevents users from renaming the directory
Normal	N	Use Normal to clear all other attributes from the directory

NCP Packet Signature

NCP Packet Signature is a feature designed to prevent unauthorized intruders from forging packets and accessing network resources. Workstations and servers sign each NCP packet with a signature and change the signature for every packet.

There are four levels of NCP Packet Signature. If the levels set on the server and workstations don't comply with each other's settings, the workstations and server won't be able to communicate.

NCP Packet Signature is an optional security feature. Using packet signatures can slow down network performance on busy networks. Therefore, you may not want to implement NCP packet signing if your network is operating in a trusted environment with little or no access for intruders or if the data on your server is not sensitive enough to warrant the extra protection. Another option is to implement NCP Packet Signature only on workstations that are accessing sensitive information.

Table 4.4 shows the levels of NCP Packet Signature you can set on the workstation. To set the signature level on a workstation, add the SIGNATURE LEVEL = x command to the workstation's NET.CFG file.

▸ T A B L E 4.4   *NCP Packet Signature Levels for Workstations*

LEVEL	DESCRIPTION
0	No signing
1	Workstation signs packets only if server asks for signature
2	Workstation signs packets if the server can handle signatures (whether or not the server actually requires signatures)
3	Workstation and server are both required to sign packets

Table 4.5 shows the signature levels you can set on the server. To set the level on the server, use the SET NCP Packet Signature Option = *number* command in the server's STARTUP.NCF or AUTOEXEC.NCF file. After the server has been booted, you can execute this SET command

from the server's console, but only to increase the signature level. To decrease the level you must modify STARTUP.NCF or AUTOEXEC.NCF and reboot the server.

▶ **T A B L E** 4.5   *NCP Packet Signature Levels for Servers*

LEVEL	DESCRIPTION
0	No signing
1	Server signs packets only if workstation asks for signature
2	Server signs packets if the workstation can handle signatures (whether or not the workstation actually requires signatures)
3	Server and workstation are both required to sign packets

Figure 4.1 illustrates how the signature levels on workstations and servers match up to allow unsigned packets, force signed packets, or deny login.

▶ **F I G U R E** 4.1   *How NCP Packet Signature levels on the server and the workstation match up*

Server Level

Workstation Level	0	1	2	3
0	Unsigned	Unsigned	Unsigned	**Login fails**
1	Unsigned	Unsigned	Signed	Signed
2	Unsigned	Signed	Signed	Signed
3	**Login fails**	Signed	Signed	Signed

Securing the File Server

An important but often overlooked element of network security is the physical security of the file server itself. The network can be only as secure as the file server. If the file server is sitting out in the open with no keyboard lock or password enabled, an intruder can easily tamper with the server and do harm.

Therefore, it is important that you take steps to safeguard the file server and its data. There are several things you can do to protect the server:

> ▶ Put the file server in a locked room. Locking up your file server protects it from both malicious and accidental tampering. Malicious tampering is more theatrical: disgruntled employees trying to derail projects when they get fired, competing employees tampering with each other's files to get an advantage, corporate spies trying to steal the plans for Project X. Accidental tampering is less exciting but a lot more common: a curious employee typing commands at the file server console "to see what happens," another employee tripping and pulling the file server plug out of the wall socket, the custodian turning the file server off over the weekend because he thought no one was using it. By locking the file server in its own room, you can prevent many problems.

> ▶ Protect the server from electrical problems by installing a UPS (uninterruptible power supply). A UPS has its own battery, which allows it to keep the file server (not all the workstations and peripherals) running during a power outage. When the UPS's battery begins to run down, the UPS tells the file server to close all its open files and shut itself down. By allowing the server time to shut itself down properly, the UPS can prevent excessive damage to the network files.

▶ Lock the file server console with MONITOR.NLM. If you lock the console with MONITOR, you need to enter a password to unlock it. There are two passwords that will work: one is user SUPERVISOR's password, and the other is the password that you give MONITOR when you lock the console. You can use a different password each time (which is probably a good idea). To lock the console, type LOAD MONITOR at the file server keyboard. Then, from the Available Options menu, choose the Lock File Server Console option and type in the password to lock the console. To unlock the console, press any key to remove the screen saver (if necessary) and then type the console password.

▶ Use the SECURE CONSOLE utility at the server's console to prevent loadable modules from being loaded from anywhere but SYS:SYSTEM. If loadable modules can be loaded from other directories where users have more rights than SYS:SYSTEM, an intruder could create an NLM that breaches security and load that NLM from an unprotected directory. SECURE CONSOLE also prevents intruders from accessing the OS debugger from the server's keyboard, and it removes DOS from the server so that no one can get to the DOS partition and access data.

▶ Assign a password to the Remote Console feature so that anyone who tries to use RCONSOLE or ACONSOLE will be prompted for the password. When you load REMOTE.NLM on the server to enable Remote Console, you are asked for a password. You can assign any new password you like, and then that password will be required whenever anyone runs RCONSOLE or ACONSOLE to access that server. (The SUPERVISOR's password also works, however.)

▶ Use disk mirroring or disk duplexing to ensure that all network data exists on two identical disks, in case one disk crashes.

▶ Keep to a strict backup schedule and make sure your backup library is in good order.

▶ Maintain up-to-date virus protection software for your server and workstations, and use it regularly.

Taking these precautions can help protect your file server and network resources from numerous evils.

Checking for Security Holes with SECURITY

NetWare's SECURITY command-line utility allows you to see how secure your network is. You must have supervisor equivalency to run the SECURITY utility.

The SECURITY utility checks your entire network setup for possible security violations in the following areas:

▶ **Passwords:** Shows which users don't have passwords, which have passwords that are the same as their user names, and which do not have adequate password restrictions (such as minimum length and grace logins).

▶ **Supervisor equivalence:** Lists users who have a security equivalence to the SUPERVISOR.

▶ **Rights to the root directory:** Shows which users have trustee rights in the root directory of any volume. Any user who has rights at the root of a volume inherits those rights throughout the entire directory structure unless you block those rights with an Inherited Rights Mask or new trustee assignments. Avoid granting users any more than Read and File Scan rights at the root directory.

▸ **Login scripts:** Lists users who don't have user login scripts. If a user doesn't have a login script, an intruder could create one and place it into that user's MAIL directory, thus gaining illegal access to the network. For this reason, every user should have a login script, no matter how minimal.

▸ **Rights in NetWare directories:** Displays the rights users have in the four NetWare system directories. All users should have only Read and File Scan rights in SYS:PUBLIC and SYS:LOGIN, the Create right to SYS:MAIL, and the Write and Create rights to their own MAIL subdirectories. Only the SUPERVISOR should have any rights at all in SYS:SYSTEM.

Troubleshooting Common Problems

If your users are having trouble working on the network and you suspect the problem is related to security, check the following areas:

▸ If the user can open a file but cannot save changes to it, the user may not have enough rights to work with the file. To make changes to a file, the user usually must have the Create, Write, and Erase rights. When saving a changed file, many applications delete the old version. If the user doesn't have the Erase right, the application won't be able to delete the old version of the file, so it will stop the saving process.

▸ If a user can't use an application to create or save files, make sure the user has enough rights in both the application's directory (generally File Scan and Read) and the directories where files created with the application are stored (at least Create, Write, and Erase).

- Are the application's files flagged with the wrong file attributes? Most applications' executable files should be flagged Read Only and Shareable, but the application's data files should probably be flagged Normal (which is the same as Read Write).

- If the user tries to list the files within a directory and the directory looks empty, the user probably has no rights to the directory. Without the File Scan right, a user cannot see the names of any files in the directory.

- A user who cannot log in to the network may be typing either the wrong password or the wrong username. Only the network supervisor can give a new password to a user who has forgotten the old one. Use the SYSCON utility to assign passwords and also to verify the spelling of the user's username.

- If the user is using the right password and username but still can't log in, the user's account may be locked. To see whether the user's account is locked (and to unlock it), use the SYSCON utility. From the main SYSCON menu, select User Information ➤ *Username* ➤ Account Restrictions. The option Account Disabled will show either Yes or No. If the account is disabled, you can reenable it by changing the Yes to No.

- If a user's username, password, or rights cannot be changed, the server's bindery may have become corrupted. You can use the NetWare BINDFIX utility to try to repair the bindery, as explained in Chapter 2.

CHAPTER 5

The User's Environment

Whenever you add a new user to the network, there are several things you can do to increase the user's productivity. First, you assign account restrictions, if necessary, and grant the user trustee rights to the necessary files and directories, as explained in Chapter 4.

Next, you can use login scripts to automate much of the user's routine workstation setup, such as mapping drives, logging in to the right server, executing a CAPTURE command, and so on.

You can also create menu programs so that your users never have to execute DOS commands. A menu program allows the user to select tasks, such as opening word processing or spreadsheet files, from a menu.

This chapter explains how to create login scripts and menu programs for your users.

Login Scripts

A login script runs automatically when a user logs in to the network. Login scripts save users time by executing commands that those users would otherwise need to repeat every time they logged in. The commands in a login script can map drives to network directories, display messages on the user's screen, and even launch an application.

There are three types of login scripts:

- ▶ The system login script, which the network administrator must create, is the first script that executes.

- ▶ User login scripts, which either the network administrator or the user can create, execute after the system login script.

- ▶ The default login script, which is part of the LOGIN utility, executes only if there is no user login script.

THE THREE TYPES OF LOGIN SCRIPTS

The default login script is a very simple login script that is built into the LOGIN utility. It executes for any users who don't have their own user login scripts.

The default login script contains a few basic commands that perform the following tasks:

- ▶ Display a greeting to the user.

- ▶ Map a drive to the user's home directory (as long as the home directory is located in the SYS volume).

- ▶ Map a search drive to the SYS:PUBLIC directory so that the user can access the NetWare utilities.

- ▶ Map a drive to the SYS:SYSTEM directory if the user who logged in is SUPERVISOR. If the user is not SUPERVISOR, the default script will not map a drive to SYS:SYSTEM.

This login script will work adequately in many cases, but it is rather limited. Although you can't delete the default login script, you can prevent it from executing by creating user login scripts customized to your users' needs.

Every file server can have a system login script, which executes for every user who logs in to the server. The system login script allows you to set up common drive mappings and set other options for everyone on the network. It gives you a single point of administration for controlling common elements of your workstations' environments. This is a good place to put drive mappings to application directories that are available to all your users. The system login script is a text file called NET$LOG.DAT, located in the SYS:PUBLIC directory.

Finally, all users can have their own user login scripts. A user login script contains commands that apply only to a single user, such as specific drive mappings to his or her personal work directories. The user login script executes after the system login script and adds to any drive mappings the system login script has already set up. Each user's login script is a text file called LOGIN, located in that user's ID directory under SYS:MAIL. The user login script replaces the default script.

Figure 5.1 is a flowchart showing the order in which the system login script, the user login script, and the default login script execute.

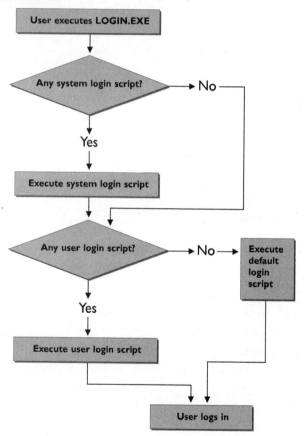

FIGURE 5.1 *The order in which login scripts execute*

Although you do not have to create either system or user login scripts, it's a very good idea to create both. By creating your own system login script and user login scripts, you can automate some of the tasks your users perform to begin using their workstations every day.

PLANNING LOGIN SCRIPTS

You should create the system login script first, before you create user login scripts. Put any commands that all your users need, such as drive mappings to commonly used application directories, in the system login script. Having the common commands in the system login script makes it easier to maintain your login scripts. For example, if you put an application drive mapping into the system login script and then later need to change that mapping, you can make one change to the system login script instead of making the same change to every user login script.

After you create the system login script, create a user login script for each user. A user's login script should include commands that are particular to that user, such as a drive mapping to that user's personal project directory or to an application that only that person uses.

Since the user login script executes after the system login script, it is possible for the user login script to overwrite some of the commands executed by the system login script. Be careful to plan your drive mappings so that you don't inadvertently map a drive letter to one directory in the system login script and then to another directory in the user login script.

If you don't create user login scripts, the default login script executes after the system login script. If you've created drive mappings in your system login script, the default login script might overwrite some of those drive mappings. This is one of the reasons it's a good idea to create user login scripts. If you don't need to put any commands in the user login script but you want to prevent the default login script from running, you can create a blank user login script or use the EXIT command at the end of the system login script. (The EXIT command is explained later in this chapter.)

To create both the system and the user login scripts, use the SYSCON utility. You create the system login script through the Supervisor Options option and user login scripts through the User Information option.

Before you begin creating login scripts, you should plan which commands you will include. The following sections describe the login script commands and variables you can use.

LOGIN SCRIPT COMMANDS

There are numerous commands you can put in login scripts, all of which can be used in both system and user login scripts. Of these commands, the following nine are probably the most common:

- ▸ #: Executes an external command or program, such as CAPTURE

- ▸ COMSPEC: Tells the workstation where COMMAND.COM is located

- ▸ EXIT: Exits the login script, and can be used to send the user directly from the end of the login script into a menu or application

- ▸ FIRE PHASERS: Makes a phaser sound emit from the workstation

- ▸ IF...THEN: Executes part of the script only if a certain condition is met; otherwise that part of the script is ignored

- ▸ MAP: Maps drives and search drives to directories

- ▸ PCCOMPATIBLE: Used only if you've changed the long machine name in NET.CFG to something other than IBM_PC

- ▸ REMARK: Allows you to add comments to the login script that do not display or execute

- ▸ WRITE: Displays messages on the workstation screen

These commands, as well as all the others, are explained on the following pages.

Command

You can execute an external command, such as a NetWare utility, from a login script. To execute this type of command from within a login script, you must precede the command with the # symbol. When the command is finished executing, the login script takes over again and continues running.

One of the most common uses of the # command is to execute the CAPTURE command, which sets up a workstation's printing capabilities. For example, the following line executes a CAPTURE command that will send the user's print jobs to a queue named LASERJET (with a timeout at 10 seconds and no banner page):

```
#CAPTURE Q=LASERJET TI=10 NB
```

If an external command or application is executed from within the login script, LOGIN.EXE and the login script are held in memory until the external command finishes and the login process continues.

It is possible to run out of conventional memory when executing commands inside the login script if several TSRs are loaded on the workstation.

ATTACH Command

Use the ATTACH command to attach to additional file servers during the login process. ATTACH doesn't execute another login script on an additional server; it just connects you to that server so that you can map drives to its directories and access its files, printers, and so on.

To attach to a server, add the following command to the login script:

```
ATTACH server/username
```

For example, if user Bob wants to attach to server PARIS, the command in the login script would be

```
ATTACH PARIS/BOB
```

BREAK Command

The BREAK ON command lets the user abort the progress of the login script while it's executing by pressing Ctrl+C or Ctrl+Break. The default is BREAK OFF. (BREAK ON does not affect the DOS BREAK command, which lets you break out of programs other than the login script.)

To enter this command in a login script, type

    BREAK ON

COMSPEC Command

If your workstations are running DOS from the network, you can use the COMSPEC command to tell the workstation where the DOS command processor (COMMAND.COM) is located.

If your users are running DOS from their local drives instead of from a network directory, you do not need the COMSPEC command in the login script. By default, the workstation will look for the COMMAND.COM file in the root directory on the boot disk.

OS/2 users running virtual DOS sessions cannot use this command in the login script but must use it in the CONFIG.SYS file instead, to point to DOS on the local hard disk.

To put a COMSPEC command in the login script, use the following format:

    COMSPEC=path COMMAND.COM

For *path*, type the path of the directory that contains DOS (or the drive that is mapped to the DOS directory).

For example, suppose you map the second search drive to the directory that contains DOS by using the following MAP command in your login script:

    MAP INS S2:=SYS:PUBLIC\%MACHINE\%OS\%OS_VERSION

Since the DOS COMMAND.COM file is located in this directory, you need to tell the workstation where to find it. Use the COMSPEC command like this:

```
COMSPEC=S2:COMMAND.COM
```

You use S2 for the path because that is the second search drive, which has already been mapped to the DOS directory.

DISPLAY Command

The DISPLAY command displays an ASCII text file on the workstation screen. To display such a file, put the following command in the login script:

```
DISPLAY path\filename
```

For example, if you want to display the file READTHIS.TXT that is located in the VOL1:DATA\SALES directory, the command would be

```
DISPLAY VOL1:DATA\SALES\READTHIS.TXT
```

Do not use this command to display word processor files, because the word processing and printer codes will also display. To display word processor files, use FDISPLAY instead.

DOS BREAK Command

The DOS BREAK ON command lets a user abort a program (other than the login script) by pressing Ctrl+Break. The default is DOS BREAK OFF. (DOS BREAK ON does not affect the BREAK command, which lets you break out of the login script.)

This command does not work on OS/2 workstations.

To enter this command in the login script, type

```
DOS BREAK ON
```

DOS VERIFY Command

The DOS VERIFY ON command makes the DOS COPY command verify that the copied data can be read after the copy. NetWare's NCOPY utility verifies the success of the copy automatically, so if you use only NCOPY, you do not need to use this command. This command applies only to DOS's COPY command. The default is DOS VERIFY OFF.

To enter this command in the login script, type

```
DOS VERIFY ON
```

DRIVE Command

Use the DRIVE command to specify a default drive to use instead of the first network drive, which is usually set to your home directory.

Place this command after a MAP command that maps a drive to the directory you want to use. For example, to make the directory VOL1:TEST\RESULTS the default directory after login, you would put the following commands in the login script:

```
MAP G:=VOL1:TEST\RESULTS
DRIVE G:
```

EXIT Command

Normally, when the user login script finishes executing, it returns the user to the DOS prompt. From there the user can start up an application and begin working in it. However, with the EXIT command, you can automate this step so that instead of the DOS prompt, the application or menu appears on the workstation screen, and the user can begin working immediately.

To do this, put the EXIT command, followed by the name of the application or menu in quotation marks, at the end of the login script. This command does not work on OS/2 workstations.

For example, to send the user into a menu program you created called DP, add the following line to your login script:

```
EXIT "NMENU DP"
```

If you want members of the group ADMIN to enter the DP menu and members of the group ARTISTS to enter the application CAD, put the following lines at the end of the login script:

```
IF MEMBER OF "ADMIN" THEN
EXIT "NMENU DP"
END
IF MEMBER OF "ARTISTS" THEN
EXIT "CAD"
END
```

Users who are not members of ADMIN or of ARTISTS would return to the DOS prompt when the login script finished running.

Note that if you put the EXIT command at the end of the system login script, the user login scripts will *not* execute.

Creating menu programs and using NetWare's NMENU utility to run them are described in the section "Menu Programs" later in this chapter.

FDISPLAY Command

The FDISPLAY command displays a word-processed file on the workstation screen. To display such a file, put the following command in the login script:

```
FDISPLAY path\filename
```

For example, if you want to display the file READTHIS.DOC that is located in the VOL1:DATA\SALES directory, use the command

```
FDISPLAY VOL1:DATA\SALES\READTHIS.DOC
```

To display ASCII text files, you can use DISPLAY instead.

FIRE PHASERS Command

The FIRE PHASERS command may not be the most important login script command you could use, but it does have its appeal. This command makes a phaser sound emit from the workstation, and you can specify how many times (up to nine) the phaser sound occurs.

Although the command may sound frivolous, it can actually be useful when you want to draw attention to a message displayed with the WRITE command. For example, to make the phaser sound happen three times when you display a message reminding your users about an important sales meeting, add the following two lines to your system login script:

```
FIRE PHASERS 3 TIMES
WRITE "Come to the sales meeting today at 3:00!"
```

GOTO Command

The GOTO command lets you execute a portion of the login script out of sequence. To use this command, label the portion of the script you want to execute with a single word, and then type the following command in the login script:

```
GOTO label
```

For *label*, substitute the label you gave the portion of the script you want to execute.

IF...THEN Command

IF...THEN lets you specify that a command execute only at certain times. For example, you could use the IF...THEN command in combination with the WRITE command to have the message "Status meeting is today at 3:00" display only on Tuesdays.

By using IF...THEN, you can make commands execute only on certain days, during specific times of day, when a particular user logs in, or only when a user belongs to a certain group.

The command uses the following basic format:

```
IF something is true THEN
execute this command
ELSE execute a different command
END
```

The ELSE part of the command is optional. You use ELSE only when you have two or more different commands you want to execute, based on different circumstances. For example, if you want "Status report is due today" to appear on Fridays and "Have a nice day" to appear on all other days, use the ELSE command like this:

```
IF DAY_OF_WEEK="Friday" THEN
WRITE "Status report is due today."
ELSE
WRITE "Have a nice day!"
END
```

If you don't want any message to appear on the other days of the week, include just the following lines instead:

```
IF DAY_OF_WEEK="Friday" THEN
WRITE "Status report is due today."
END
```

The "IF *something is true*" part of the command is called a conditional statement because this is the condition that causes the rest of the command to execute. To use a conditional statement, specify the variable you need, such as the day of the week, and the value you want that variable to have, such as "Tuesday". Then, whenever the value of the variable matches the one you specified in the command (in other words, on every Tuesday), the command executes.

Using Identifier Variables with IF...Then   You can use many different variables (called identifier variables) in an IF...THEN command, and you can specify how the identifier variable matches the value in six ways:

VARIABLE	DESCRIPTION
=	Equals (Example: IF DAY_OF_WEEK = "Tuesday" means *If it's Tuesday.*)
<>	Doesn't equal (Example: IF AM_PM <> "AM" means *If it isn't morning.*)
>	Is greater than (Example: IF HOUR > "8" means *If the hour is 9:00 or later.*)
>=	Is greater than or equal to (Example: IF HOUR >= "8" means *If the hour is 8:00 or later.*)
<	Is less than (Example: IF HOUR < "8" means *If the hour is 7:00 or earlier.*)
<=	Is less than or equal to (Example: IF HOUR <= "8" means *If the hour is 8:00 or earlier.*)

In a conditional statement you must enclose the value in quotation marks. For a list of the most common identifier variables and more rules on using them, see the section "Using Identifier Variables in Login Script Commands" later in this chapter.

Examples of Using IF...THEN The following are examples of ways
you can use the IF...THEN command in login scripts:

```
IF DAY_OF_WEEK = "Monday" THEN
WRITE "Welcome back!"
END
```

In this example the message "Welcome back!" appears on the user's
screen whenever the user logs in on Monday. On other days of the week
no message is displayed.

```
IF MEMBER OF "ADMIN" THEN
MAP *5:=VOL1:APPS\RECORDS
END
```

In this example, if the user who logs in happens to belong to the group
called ADMIN, the user's fifth available network drive is mapped to the
RECORDS subdirectory under the APPS directory, which is located on
the VOL1 volume. If the user who logs in does not belong to the group
ADMIN, that user will not get this drive mapping. The login script will
simply skip to the next command in the script.

```
IF DAY <= "5" THEN
FIRE PHASERS 2 TIMES
WRITE "Is your monthly sales report completed yet?"
MAP *6:=VOL1:APPS\ACCT\REPORTS
ELSE
WRITE "Find a new client today!"
END
```

This example has an ELSE command in it. This means that one of two
different series of commands will execute, depending on whether or not
the condition in the first line is true. The conditional in the first line

```
IF DAY <= "5"
```

means *If the day of the month is less than or equal to 5,* or in other words, *If today is the first, second, third, fourth, or fifth day of the month.* Therefore, the commands that execute in this example depend on the day of the month.

Whenever a user logs in on the first five days of the month, three things happen: a phaser sound occurs twice, the message "Is your monthly sales report completed yet?" appears on the screen, and the user's sixth available network drive is mapped to VOL1:APPS\ACCT\REPORTS.

When the user logs in on any day after the fifth of the month, a different message appears: "Find a new client today!" There will not be any phaser sounds or drive mapping on those days.

INCLUDE Command

The INCLUDE command lets you call and execute login script commands contained in a separate text file (referred to as a subscript). The commands in this subscript are normal login script commands, which are executed in addition to the main login script.

To call a subscript during the main login script's execution, use the following command:

```
INCLUDE path\filename
```

MACHINE Command

The MACHINE command sets the workstation's DOS machine name to something other than the default, which is IBM_PC. For example, to set a Hewlett-Packard's name, use the following command:

```
MACHINE=HE_PAC
```

The machine name cannot be longer than 15 characters.
This command does not work on OS/2 workstations.

MAP Command

The MAP command allows you to map drives to network directories. By putting MAP commands in a login script, you ensure that those drive mappings will automatically be set up for your users every time they log in.

Use the MAP login script command to map drives to network directories just as you use the MAP utility at the DOS prompt. Type

```
MAP letter:=path
```

For example, to map drive F to the VOL1:USERS\MARY directory, type

```
MAP F:=VOL1:USERS\MARY
```

Instead of using the exact drive letters in login script drive mappings, you can map each available drive in order. This allows drive mappings to be more dynamic; if you delete a drive mapping, the other mappings adjust automatically.

To assign available network drives to directories, use an asterisk, followed by a number. For example, type

```
MAP *1:=VOL1:HOME\%LOGIN_NAME
```

The *1 indicates that you want the first available network drive to be assigned to this directory. Use *2 to indicate the second available drive, and so on.

To delete the mapping for a drive (in this example, drive F), type

```
MAP DEL F:
```

Handling MAP's Display   If you don't turn off MAP's display, each MAP command will appear on the screen as it is executed in the login script. Although it is not a problem for these mappings to appear on the screen, they can be distracting to the user. (They scroll off the screen as other commands are executed.) You can keep the screen from being cluttered during the login process by placing this command at the beginning of your login scripts:

```
MAP DISPLAY OFF
```

After all your drive mappings are complete, you can turn the display back on. Toward the end of the login script, add the following two commands:

```
MAP DISPLAY ON
MAP
```

The first command turns on the display of drive mappings. The second command, MAP, displays a list of all the current drive mappings. When the login script is finished executing, the complete list of the user's drive mappings remains on the screen. This way, the user can see at a glance which drive mappings are available.

• **Mapping Search Drives** Search drives are special drive mappings to directories that contain applications, utilities, or other program files. By using search drives, you can allow users to execute an application regardless of the directory they are currently in.

You use the MAP utility to map a search drive to a directory, but instead of indicating a drive letter, you specify a number preceded by an "S". The search drive will assign its own letter. (Search drives assign drive letters in reverse order, starting with Z and working backward.) For example, to map your first search drive to the PUBLIC directory, which contains the NetWare utilities, type the following command:

```
MAP S1:=SYS:PUBLIC
```

Search drive mappings are added to the workstation's DOS PATH environment variable. Therefore, by typing the MAP S1 command shown above, you overwrite the first PATH that may have been specified in your AUTOEXEC.BAT file. If you want to preserve the paths set in your AUTOEXEC.BAT file but still make the first search drive mapped to SYS:PUBLIC, use the MAP INS S1 command instead. MAP INS inserts the search drive into the rest of the path commands or search drives you may have already set, instead of overwriting them. Whichever path was first before you used the MAP INS command gets moved to the second position.

In your login scripts, it is important to map some search drives in a particular order. In your system login script, map the following two search drives before you create additional search drives:

- Map INS S1 (the first search drive) to the SYS:PUBLIC directory. SYS:PUBLIC contains the NetWare utilities and other files users need.

- Map INS S2 (the second search drive) to the DOS directory you created if your users will be running DOS from the network instead of from their local drives.

After you map these two search drives, you can map additional search drives in any order you want. For example, if you map a third search drive to the directory that contains a database application and a fourth one to the directory that contains a word processing application, the search drive mappings in your system login script might appear similar to the following:

```
MAP INS S1:=SYS:PUBLIC
MAP INS S2:=SYS:PUBLIC\%MACHINE\%OS\%OS_VERSION
MAP INS S3:=VOL1:APPS\DB
MAP INS S4:=VOL1:APPS\WORD
```

Instead of mapping search drives in sequential order (S3, S4, S5, and so on), you can use the last available search drive number (S16) for each mapping. By mapping S16, you append the drive mapping to the end of the list of search drives. This way, if you delete a search drive later, NetWare adjusts the order of the remaining search drives automatically. For example, instead of mapping S3 and S4 to your application directories, you could have the following commands in your login script:

```
MAP INS S1:=SYS:PUBLIC
MAP INS S2:=SYS:PUBLIC\%MACHINE\%OS\%OS_VERSION
MAP S16:=VOL1:APPS\DB
MAP S16:=VOL1:APPS\WORD
```

Mapping Users' Home Directories A common practice is to map the first network drive (not search drive) to the user's home directory. For example, suppose your users' home directories are located in the VOL1 volume, under the parent directory HOME. Since the first network drive is usually drive F, add the following command to your system login script so that every user's first network drive is mapped to his or her home directory:

```
MAP F:=VOL1:HOME\%LOGIN_NAME
```

%LOGIN_NAME is an identifier variable that automatically substitutes the user's login name. For example, if user Ray logged in, his name would be substituted for the %LOGIN_NAME, and his first network drive would be mapped to VOL1:HOME\RAY. You can use this variable in your system login script instead of entering an individual drive mapping in every user's personal login script. Using identifier variables in login scripts is described in more detail in the section "Using Identifier Variables in Login Script Commands" later in this chapter.

Mapping a Fake Root Some applications require that they be executed at the root of the volume. If you would rather install the application in a subdirectory, you can use MAP to map a fake root to the subdirectory that contains the application.

For example, suppose you have an application called JobMaker that needs to be installed at the root. However, you would rather install it in a directory called JOBMAKER under the parent directory APPS, which is on volume VOL1. To map a fake root to this directory and map a search drive to it at the same time, you could add the following MAP command to your login script:

```
MAP ROOT S16:=VOL1:APPS\JOBMAKER
```

Then the application will think it is located at the root of the volume instead of in a subdirectory, and your users will have a search drive to that directory, too.

PAUSE Command

The PAUSE command makes the login script pause in the middle of its execution (wherever you put the command). The message "Strike any key when ready…" appears on the screen when the pause occurs. When the user presses any key, the login script resumes its execution. This can be a helpful command if, for example, you want the user to have time to read a message you display using DISPLAY or WRITE.

To use this command, simply type the following command at the point in the login script where you want the pause to occur:

```
PAUSE
```

PCCOMPATIBLE Command

You need to use the PCCOMPATIBLE login script command only if you are using the EXIT command *and* have changed the workstation's long machine name in the NET.CFG file to something other than IBM_PC. For example, if your Hewlett-Packard workstations have the machine name HE_PAC in their NET.CFG files and you want those users to go directly to an application, add the PCCOMPATIBLE command to the login script before the EXIT command.

If you use the EXIT command without the PCCOMPATIBLE command and the workstations are not compatible with IBM PCs, the EXIT command won't execute.

This command does not work on OS/2 workstations.

To use the PCCOMPATIBLE command in your login script, type

```
PCCOMPATIBLE
```

REMARK Command

The REMARK command lets you add notes to yourself (or to anyone else who might be editing your login scripts) in a login script. These remarks do not display on the users' screens, nor do they execute any tasks. You use remarks merely to remind yourself why you put certain commands in the login script or to explain what the command is doing.

You can indicate that a line in a login script is simply a remark rather than a command in one of four ways: use the whole word REMARK, the shortened word REM, an asterisk (*), or a semicolon (;). You must put one of these words or symbols at the beginning of any line you want included as a note to yourself.

For example, the remark in this login script provides information about a drive mapping:

```
REM The next mapping is to the students' tutorial program.
IF MEMBER OF "Students" THEN
MAP S16:=VOL1:APPS\TRAINING
END
```

In this example, if the user who logs in belongs to the group STUDENTS, a search drive is mapped to the TRAINING directory. The remark indicates that this directory contains a tutorial program that students may need to access.

SET Command

You use the SET command to set DOS and OS/2 environment variables. (For OS/2 workstations, these variables are in effect only during the login script's execution.)

You can use any of the regular DOS environment variables, such as the prompt setting or a path. The only difference between using SET at the DOS command line or in AUTOEXEC.BAT and using it in a login script is that in the login script, the value you are setting must be enclosed in quotation marks.

For example, to set the prompt to display the current directory, add the following line to the login script:

```
SET PROMPT="$P$G"
```

If you use SET PATH in the login script, the path you set will overwrite any paths or search drives already set in the AUTOEXEC.BAT or earlier in the login script.

SHIFT Command

The SHIFT command specifies the order in which %n variables are interpreted. You can use %n variables in login script commands as placeholders for values users enter when they type the LOGIN command. The %0 variable is always the name of the file server and the %1 variable is always the name of the user, because those are the first two (and often the only) parameters the user specifies during the login.

Any additional parameters the user types at the command line are substituted, in order, for any other %n variables used in login script commands.

For example, the following LOGIN command contains three variables:

```
LOGIN SERVER\ERICA SPREAD
```

The first parameter, SERVER, which is the name of the file server, will replace %0 in any login script command that contains that variable. The second parameter, ERICA, which is the username, will replace %1 in any login script command that uses that variable. The third parameter, SPREAD, is a keyword that will replace the variable %2 in any login script command that contains it.

In this case, Erica has a command in her login script that will map a search drive to the spreadsheet application directory if she enters the SPREAD parameter during LOGIN. The command would look like this:

```
IF "%2"="SPREAD" THEN
MAP INS S3:=VOL1:APPS\123
```

The SHIFT command, used with the GOTO command in a loop, lets a user enter several parameters without worrying about their order. For example, suppose Erica's login script contains the following lines:

```
START
IF "%2"="SPREAD" THEN
MAP INS S3:=VOL1:APPS\123
IF "%2"="WP" THEN
SET WP="\u-ebw"
MAP INS S4:=VOL1:APPS\WP6
IF "%2"="DRAW" THEN
MAP INS S5:=VOL1:APPS\ADOBE
SHIFT 1
IF "%2" <> " " THEN GOTO START
```

Now Erica types the following line when she logs in:

```
LOGIN SERVER\ERICA SPREAD WP DRAW
```

Ordinarily, "SPREAD" would be %2, "WP" would be %3, and "DRAW" would be %4. However, the last two lines in the login script make it so that each of the three parameters, in turn, becomes the %2 variable. On each loop through the script (beginning at the START label), the %2 variable is moved one parameter to the right, causing the appropriate MAP command to be executed. This makes it so that Erica can log in and use any one or more of the three parameters, in any order, and the correct mappings will still occur.

You can shift the parameters up to nine spaces either forward (positive numbers) or backward (negative numbers). The default is SHIFT 1.

WRITE Command

The WRITE command allows you to display brief messages on users' workstation screens when they log in. To use the WRITE command, you type the word WRITE, followed by the text you want to appear on the user's screen. The text must be enclosed in quotation marks.

For example, to display the message "It's a great day to make widgets!" on your users' screens every time they log in, put the following command in your system login script:

```
WRITE "It's a great day to make widgets!"
```

Displaying Multiline Messages   To display a message that takes up several lines, it generally works best to start each line with the command WRITE. For example, suppose you added the following lines to your login script:

```
WRITE "Don't forget to turn in your budget report by"
WRITE "the first Friday of the month, or you will need to"
WRITE "file an amendment and serve on the committee!"
```

The message that appears on the users' screens will appear on three lines, similar to the following:

```
Don't forget to turn in your budget report by
the first Friday of the month, or you will need to
file an amendment and serve on the committee!
```

Using Identifier Variables for User-Specific Messages   To display specific messages for each user, you can use identifier variables with the WRITE command. Identifier variables allow you to put a generic variable, such as DAY_OF_WEEK or LOGIN_NAME, in a login script command. Then when the user logs in, the login script substitutes real values for the variable.

To use an identifier variable to display only the value of the variable, without an additional message, put just the identifier variable after the command WRITE. For example, the following command displays only the name of the user:

```
WRITE LOGIN_NAME
```

You can display the value of the variable and a message in either of two ways:

- ▸ Include the variable with the text of the message inside the quotation marks.

- ▸ Use a semicolon (;) to join the variable to the text.

Generally, the easiest method is to put the variable inside the quotation marks with the rest of the message.

To put a variable inside the quotation marks, you must add a percent sign (%) to the beginning of the variable and be sure to type the variable in uppercase letters. For example, to display the message "Hello Ian!" when user IAN logs in, use the command

```
WRITE "Hello, %LOGIN_NAME!"
```

You can display the same message by joining the variable to the text using a semicolon:

```
WRITE "Hello, "; LOGIN_NAME; "!"
```

But with this method, be careful to type the elements in the correct order to make the spaces and punctuation appear where you want them. Notice that the WRITE command has three elements that must be joined with semicolons. The first element is the text "Hello, ". The comma and a space are enclosed in the quotation marks so that the words are spaced correctly when displayed. The second element is the variable LOGIN_NAME, which is joined to the first text by a semicolon. Finally, to get the exclamation point to display after the name, you need to add another semicolon and then the text "!".

Using identifier variables in login scripts is discussed in more detail in the next section.

USING IDENTIFIER VARIABLES IN LOGIN SCRIPT COMMANDS

You can use special variables, called identifier variables, in some login script commands to make those commands more flexible. Identifier variables can be a user's login name, the day of the week, the time of day, the current month, and so on.

By using identifier variables, you can put generic commands into your system login script instead of entering nearly identical commands in each user's login script. Then, when a user logs in, the login script inserts the specific values into the generic command and executes the command using those values.

For example, if you put the identifier variable DAY_OF_WEEK in a command, the login script would substitute the real value (Monday, Tuesday, and so on) for the variable, depending on which day it is that the login script is executed.

Another advantage of using identifier variables is that you can display current information, such as the day's date, on users' workstation screens when they log in. You can also place identifier variables in IF...THEN commands to allow different commands to be executed depending on the current circumstances.

Identifier variables fall loosely into six categories:

- ▸ Date

- ▸ Time

- ▸ Workstation

- ▸ Network

- ▸ User

- ▸ Miscellaneous

Tables 5.1 through 5.6 list the many identifer variables by category. You must type the variable exactly as shown in the tables, including underscore characters (_).

▸ **T A B L E 5.1** *Date Identifier Variables for Login Script Commands*

VARIABLE	EXPLANATION
DAY	Represents: Day's date Values: 01 through 31 Example: IF DAY="15"
DAY_OF_WEEK	Represents: Day's name Values: Monday, Tuesday, etc. Example: WRITE "Today is %DAY_OF_WEEK"
MONTH	Represents: Month's number Values: 01 through 12 Example: IF MONTH>"11"
MONTH_NAME	Represents: Month's name Values: January, February, etc. Example: IF MONTH_NAME="October"
NDAY_OF_WEEK	Represents: Day's number Values: 1 through 7 (1=Sunday) Example: IF NDAY_OF_WEEK="2"

▸ **T A B L E   5.1**   *Date Identifier Variables for Login Script Commands (continued)*

VARIABLE	EXPLANATION
SHORT_YEAR	Represents: Last two numbers of the year Values: 94, 95, 96, etc. Example: WRITE "Today is %MONTH-%DAY-%SHORT_YEAR"
YEAR	Represents: All four numbers of the year Values: 1994, 1995, 1996, etc. Example: IF YEAR>='2000'

▸ **T A B L E   5.2**   *Time Identifier Variables for Login Script Commands*

IDENTIFIER VARIABLE	EXPLANATION
AM_PM	Represents: Before noon or after noon Values: AM or PM Example: WRITE "%HOUR:%MINUTE %AM_PM"
GREETING_TIME	Represents: General time of day Values: Morning, Afternoon, or Evening Example: WRITE "Good %GREETING_TIME, %LOGIN_NAME."
HOUR	Represents: Hour on a 12-hour clock Values: 1 through 12 Example: IF HOUR <"7 "
HOUR24	Represents: Hour on a 24-hour clock Values: 00 through 24 (00=midnight) Example: IF HOUR >="20"
MINUTE	Represents: Minute Values: 00 through 59 Example: WRITE "It's %HOUR:%MINUTE %AM_PM."
SECOND	Represents: Second Values: 00 through 59 Example: WRITE "The exact time is %HOUR24:%MINUTE:%SECOND."

▸ **T A B L E** 5.3 *Workstation Identifier Variables for Login Script Commands*

IDENTIFIER VARIABLE	EXPLANATION
DOS_REQUESTER	Represents: Version of the workstation's NETX shell Values: 1.02, etc. Example: IF DOS_REQUESTER="3.32"
MACHINE	Represents: Type of computer Values: IBM_PC, HE_PAC, etc. (Default=IBM_PC) Example: MAP INS S2:= SYS:PUBLIC\%MACHINE\%OS\%OS_VERSION
NETWARE_RE-QUESTER	Represents: Version of the NetWare Requester for OS/2 Values: 2.01, etc. Example: WRITE "You are using Requester for OS/2 version %NETWARE_REQUESTER."
OS	Represents: Type of DOS running on the workstation Values: MSDOS, etc. (Default=MSDOS) Example: MAP INS S2:= SYS:PUBLIC\%MACHINE\%OS\%OS_VERSION
OS_VERSION	Represents: Version of DOS on the workstation Values: 3.30, 5.0, etc. Example: MAP INS S2:= SYS:PUBLIC\%MACHINE\%OS\%OS_VERSION
P_STATION	Represents: Workstation's node address Values: 12-digit hex number Example: WRITE "This workstation's address is %P_STATION."
SHELL_TYPE	Represents: Version of the workstation's NETX shell Values: 1.02, etc. Example: IF SHELL_TYPE ="3.32"

▸ **T A B L E 5.3**   *Workstation Identifier Variables for Login Script Commands (continued)*

IDENTIFIER VARIABLE	EXPLANATION
SMACHINE	Represents: Short machine name Values: IBM, etc. (Default=IBM) Example: IF SMACHINE <> "IBM"
STATION	Represents: Workstation's connection number Values: Connection number Example: WRITE "This station is using connection %STATION."

▸ **T A B L E 5.4**   *Network Identifier Variables for Login Script Commands*

IDENTIFIER VARIABLE	EXPLANATION
FILE_SERVER	Represents: NetWare server name Values: The name of the server Example: WRITE "You are connected to server %FILE_SERVER."
NETWORK_ADDRESS	Represents: Network number Values: 8-digit hex number Example: WRITE "You are on network %NETWORK_ADDRESS."

▸ **T A B L E 5.5**   *User Identifier Variables for Login Script Commands*

IDENTIFIER VARIABLE	EXPLANATION
FULL_NAME	Represents: The user's full name Values: The user's full name as listed in SYSCON Example: WRITE "This is user %FULL_NAME."
LOGIN_NAME	Represents: The user's login name Values: The name the user uses to log in to the network Example: WRITE "Hello, %LOGIN_NAME."

IDENTIFIER VARIABLE	EXPLANATION
MEMBER OF "*group*"	Represents: Group the user belongs to Values: A group name Example: IF MEMBER OF "sales" (You can also use the word NOT with this variable. Example: IF NOT MEMBER OF "sales")
PASSWORD_EXPIRES	Represents: How many days before password expires Values: The number of days left before the user's password expires Example: WRITE "Your password expires in %PASSWORD_EXPIRES days."
USER_ID	Represents: Number assigned to each user Values: User's ID number (as shown in SYSCON) Example: IF USER_ID="12345678"

►T A B L E 5.6   *Miscellaneous Identifier Variables for Login Script Commands*

IDENTIFIER VARIABLE	EXPLANATION
<DOS variable>	Represents: A DOS environment variable Values: Any DOS environment variable (PATH, PROMPT, etc.) Must be enclosed in angle brackets. If in a MAP command, must also be preceded by a percent sign Example: MAP INS S16:=%<path>
ACCESS_SERVER	Represents: Whether access server is online Values: TRUE or FALSE (TRUE=functional, FALSE=not functional) Example: IF ACCESS_SERVER="TRUE"

▸ **T A B L E** 5.6 *Miscellaneous Identifier Variables for Login Script Commands (continued)*

IDENTIFIER VARIABLE	EXPLANATION
ERROR_LEVEL	Represents: An error number Values: Any error number (0=no errors) Example: IF ERROR_LEVEL<>"0"
%n	Represents: Variable for LOGIN command parameters Values: File server name, user name, etc. See the section "SHIFT Command" for more information Example: IF %3="ACCOUNT" THEN GOTO START

AN EXAMPLE LOGIN SCRIPT

Figure 5.2 shows an example login script. Each of the commands in this script is explained below.

The first line in the script,

```
MAP DISPLAY OFF
```

turns off the MAP command's display so that drive mappings don't appear on the screen as they are created.

The next command,

```
MAP *1:=VOL1:HOME\%LOGIN_NAME
```

maps the first network drive to the user's home directory, which is located under HOME on volume VOL1.

An IF...THEN command follows:

```
IF "%1"="SUPERVISOR" THEN MAP *1:=SYS:SYSTEM
```

If the user who logs in is SUPERVISOR, this command maps the first network drive to the SYS:SYSTEM directory instead of to a home directory. Because this command fits on one line, you can omit the END command.

FIGURE 5.2 *System login script*

```
MAP DISPLAY OFF

MAP*1:=VOL1:HOME\%LOGIN_NAME

IF "%1"="SUPERVISOR" THEN MAP*1:=SYS:SYSTEM

MAP INS S1:=SYS:PUBLIC

MAP INS S2:=SYS:PUBLIC\%MACHINE\%OS\%OS_VERSION

COMPSPEC=S2:COMMAND.COM

MAP S16:=VOL1:APPS\WP

MAP S16:=VOL1:APPS\DB

IF MEMBER OF "ACCTS" THEN

MAP ROOT S16:=VOL1:APPS\COUNTER

MAP*2:=VOL1:WORK\PROJECTS\NEW

MAP*3:=VOL1:WORK\PROJECTS\STATUS

END

IF MEMBER OF "ARTISTS" THEN

MAP S16:=VOL1:APPS\DRAW2

MAP*4:=VOL1:GRAPHICS

END

#CAPTURE Q=LASER_Q NB TI=10

MAP DISPLAY ON

MAP

WRITE "Good %GREETING_TIME, %LOGIN_NAME."

IF DAY_OF_WEEK="Friday" THEN

WRITE "Hang in there! The weekend is coming!"

FIRE PHASERS 2 TIMES

END
```

The next two lines map search drives:

```
MAP INS S1:=SYS:PUBLIC
```

maps the first search drive to the SYS:PUBLIC directory, which contains NetWare utilities, and

```
MAP INS S2:=SYS:PUBLIC\%MACHINE\%OS\%OS_VERSION
```

maps the second search drive to the DOS directory. When you use identifier variables with percent signs instead of the name of the DOS directory, workstations can find the particular type of DOS they need if there is more than one version of DOS on the network.

The command

```
COMSPEC=S2:COMMAND.COM
```

tells the workstation where to find the COMMAND.COM file for DOS. In this case COMMAND.COM is located in the DOS directory, which is mapped to the second search drive, S2.

Then the script continues with two search drive mappings:

```
MAP S16:=VOL1:APPS\WP
MAP S16:=VOL1:APPS\DB
```

which map the next two available search drives to a word processing directory and to a database directory, both under the APPS parent directory on volume VOL1.

The next five lines

```
IF MEMBER OF "ACCTS" THEN
MAP ROOT INS S16:=VOL1:APPS\COUNTER
MAP *2:=VOL1:WORK\PROJECTS\NEW
MAP *3:=VOL1:WORK\PROJECTS\STATUS
END
```

execute only if the user who logs in is a member of the group ACCTS. If the user is a member of that group, the user's next available search drive is mapped as a fake root to the COUNTER directory. In this case the application in the COUNTER directory requires that it be installed in the root of the volume. Then the next two available network drives are mapped to the NEW directory and the STATUS directory, where the user can store work files. END signals that this is the end of the IF...THEN command.

The next four commands

```
IF MEMBER OF "ARTISTS" THEN
MAP S16:=VOL1:APPS\DRAW2
MAP *4:=VOL1:GRAPHICS
END
```

execute only if the user who logs in is a member of the group ARTISTS. If the user is a member of that group, the user's next available search drive is mapped to the DRAW2 directory. Then the next available network drive is mapped to the GRAPHICS directory, where the user can store work files. END signals that this is the end of the IF...THEN command.

The command

```
#CAPTURE Q=LASER_Q NB TI=10
```

executes the NetWare utility CAPTURE, which directs the user's print jobs to the print queue called LASER_Q, specifies that no banner be printed, and assigns a timeout of 10 seconds.

The next two MAP commands

```
MAP DISPLAY ON
MAP
```

turn back on the display of drive mappings and list all the drive mappings that are now in effect.

The WRITE command

```
WRITE "Good %GREETING_TIME, %LOGIN_NAME."
```

displays a greeting to the user, with the appropriate time of day and user name inserted. For example, when Andy logs in at 8:00 a.m., the message on his screen will be "Good morning, ANDY."

The last four lines in the script

```
IF DAY_OF_WEEK = "Friday" THEN
WRITE "Hang in there! The weekend is coming!"
FIRE PHASERS 2 TIMES
END
```

display the message "Hang in there! The weekend is coming!" and fire two phaser blasts, but only on Fridays.

Menu Programs

NetWare 3.12 includes a menu-creation utility called NMENU that is actually a trimmed-down version of the Saber Menu System for DOS, created by Saber Software Corporation.

Using NMENU, you can create your own menu programs for your users. If you are upgrading an existing NetWare network to NetWare 3.12 and you already have menu programs that you created using the earlier MENU utility, you can use NMENU to convert those older menus.

To create a menu program in NetWare 3.12, you first use a text editor to create a text file containing the commands you want the menu program to execute. Then you use the MENUMAKE utility, which takes the text file and compiles it into a program file. To execute the menu program file, use the NMENU utility.

MENU PROGRAM COMMANDS

The commands you can use in the text file to create your menu program are described in the following sections.

MENU Command

The MENU command identifies the heading of a menu or submenu. The format for the command is

```
MENU number,name
```

Each menu or submenu of a program must have a unique *number* so that other commands in the program can reference that menu. The *name* is the title that will appear at the top of the menu. A menu name can be up to 40 characters long. An example of this command is

```
MENU 1,Customer Service
```

ITEM Command

The ITEM command indicates an option that will be displayed in the menu. The format for the command is

```
ITEM name {option option ...}
```

The *name* is the text that will appear on this line of the menu. You can also include one or more *options* inside a single pair of braces, separating the options with a space. You can use the following options:

OPTION	DESCRIPTION
BATCH	Removes the menu program from the workstation's memory before executing the item called for in this option. This option automatically sets the CHDIR option as well (Do not use the EXEC DOS command with this option.)

OPTION	DESCRIPTION
CHDIR	After the program executed by the ITEM command is closed, the CHDIR option changes the workstation back to the drive and directory from which the menu program was originally running
PAUSE	Pauses the executing program so the user can read any messages displayed at the DOS prompt. The message "Press any key to continue" appears and waits for the user to press a key before continuing
SHOW	Displays the name of the DOS command being executed by this ITEM command

For example, to display an option called Word Processing and to make sure that when the word processor is closed, the user is returned to the original directory from which the menu program was running, use the following command:

```
ITEM Word Processing {CHDIR}
```

EXEC Command

The EXEC command executes the commands necessary to complete an ITEM option when the user selects it. The format for this command is

```
EXEC command
```

For *command*, insert the command necessary to execute the program being called. For example, to execute WordPerfect, the command would be

```
EXEC WP
```

You can use the executable for any application in this command. In addition, three commands are available that are specific to the menu program:

COMMAND	DESCRIPTION
EXEC DOS	Takes users out of the menu program temporarily and sends them to DOS. When finished working at the DOS command prompt, users type EXIT to return to the menu program
EXEC EXIT	Exits the menu program and sends the user to DOS
EXEC LOGOUT	Logs the user out of the network

SHOW Command

The SHOW command calls a submenu to be displayed when the user selects this option. The format for this command is

```
SHOW number
```

The SHOW command calls submenus by their numbers.

LOAD Command

The LOAD command calls and displays a submenu from an entirely different menu program. The format for this command is

```
LOAD filename
```

Use the file name of the NMENU file. Make sure the NMENU file being called is in the workstation's current directory or in a directory that has a search drive mapped to it.

GETx Command

The GETx command requests input from the user to execute a menu item. This command has three variations:

COMMAND	DESCRIPTION
GETR	Requests input that is required
GETO	Requests input that is optional. Can also be used to allow the user to press any key to continue
GETP	Requests input and assigns a variable to that input so it can be reused.

The format for this command is

```
GETx text {prepend} length,default, {append}
```

For *text,* insert the text you want displayed, asking the user for input. The message can be up to 40 characters long.

Prepend and *append* are values that should be automatically added by the menu program to the beginning and the ending of the user's input. If no values are needed, simply put a space in between the braces.

Length is the maximum number of characters the user can input. Enter 0 if you just want the user to press any key to continue.

Default is a default response that will be displayed, which users can either select or replace with their own response. If you do not want to supply a default, use a comma instead of the default value.

CREATING A NEW MENU PROGRAM

Using the commands explained in the previous sections, you can create a source file for a menu program. Figure 5.3 shows an example menu program as it should appear on a user's screen.

Choose a Spreadsheet File

B.   Budget

I.   Inventory

Select a Task

S.   Spreadsheet

W. Word Processing

M. Mail

E.   Exit to DOS

L.   Logout

To build this menu, first create two directories to hold the program and the temporary files the menu program will generate. The temporary directories can be on the network or on the user's hard disk. Then use a text editor to create the menu source file. The text file has to be named with the extension .SRC or it cannot be compiled by the MENUMAKE utility. Figure 5.4 shows the text file, called MANAGERS.SRC, for the example menu program.

Notice that the sections of the file pertaining to each menu or sub-menu are separated from each other by a space and the commands for each item within a menu are indented. Each ITEM command, which in-dicates an option on a menu, is followed by the EXEC command that executes that option.

In this menu you want users to be able to select an item from the menu by typing the first letter of the option. To accomplish this, add a caret (^) and the letter that should be typed to the beginning of the ITEM command.

Under the Mail ITEM, the following GETR command appears:

```
GETR Enter your email name: { } 8,, { }
```

Source file for the example menu program

```
MENU 1, Select a Task
     ITEM ^SSpreadsheet
          SHOW 2
     ITEM ^WWord Processing
          EXEC WP
     ITEM ^MMail
          GETR Enter your email name: { } 8,, { }
          EXEC EMAIL
     ITEM ^EExit to DOS
          EXEC DOS
     ITEM ^LLogout
          EXEC LOGOUT


MENU 2, Choose a Spreadsheet File
     ITEM ^BBudget
          EXEC COUNT BUDGET
     ITEM ^IInventory
          EXEC COUNT INV
```

This command asks users for their email user name before the option executes the command to load the email application. The syntax for the GETR command is

```
GETR text {prepend} length, default, {append}
```

In this example the *text* is the statement "Enter your email name:". No value is needed for the *prepend,* so a blank space is placed inside the brackets. A user's email name can be up to eight characters long, so the number 8 is entered for the *length.* The next field in the command lets you enter a default value the user can select. However, for this menu there is no default user name, so you enter no value here. The two commas, however, are necessary; they show that there is no default value. The last field, *append,* lets you enter any value that should be added to the end of the user's input. Again, in this example there is no value needed, so the brackets contain only a space.

After the text file is created and saved as MANAGERS.SRC, it's time to compile the file. To compile the MANAGERS.SRC file, use the MENUMAKE utility, and type the following command:

```
MENUMAKE MANAGERS
```

It is not necessary to type the .SRC extension in the command. The MENUMAKE utility compiles the file and creates a data file called MANAGERS.DAT. This is the file that will execute when a user runs NMENU.

To allow users to access this new menu program, set up drive mappings in the user or system login script to the program and temporary directories. However, if you created the directories under SYS:PUBLIC, you do not need to add these drive mappings to the login scripts because a search drive is already mapped to SYS:PUBLIC.

Next, if users' temporary files will be stored in network directories, add DOS SET commands to the user or system login script that point to the directories and indicate the workstation's ID number. For example, if the temporary directory is called MENUTEMP and you created it in SYS:PUBLIC, you would add the following commands to the user or system login script:

```
SET S_FILEDIR="Z:\PUBLIC\MENUTEMP\"
SET S_FILE="%STATION"
```

Finally, if you want users to enter the menu program automatically after their login scripts have finished executing, add the command to execute the new menu program to the end of the login script. For example, to make a user enter the MANAGERS menu automatically, add the following line to the login script:

```
EXIT "NMENU MANAGERS"
```

CONVERTING OLD MENU PROGRAMS

The NMENU utility is a different menu-creation utility than was used in previous versions of NetWare. If you have a menu program you created using earlier versions of NetWare's MENU utility, you can convert that menu program into an NMENU program. The older menu files have the .MNU extension, such as CLERKS.MNU.

To convert a menu file, complete the following steps:

1 · Create two directories to hold the program and the temporary files the menu program will generate. The temporary directories can be on the network or on the user's hard disk. If you already have menu directories for your existing menu programs, you can use those directories.

2 · Use the MENUCNVT utility and specify the name of the menu file you wish to convert. The utility will create a new file with the .SRC file name extension and will leave the old .MNU file unchanged. For example, to convert the CLERKS.MNU file, type

```
MENUCNVT CLERKS
```

3 · Edit the new .SRC file if necessary.

4 · Use the MENUMAKE utility to compile the new .SRC file. For example, to compile the CLERKS.SRC file, type the following command:

```
MENUMAKE CLERKS
```

5 · Make sure there are drive mappings in the user or system login script to the program and temporary directories.

6 · Add DOS SET commands to the user or system login script to point to the temporary subdirectories and indicate the workstation's ID number. For example, if the temporary directory is called MENUTEMP and you created it in SYS:PUBLIC, add the following commands to the login script:

```
SET S_FILEDIR="Z:\PUBLIC\MENUTEMP\"
SET S_FILE="%STATION"
```

7 · Finally, if you want users to go into the menu program automatically after their login scripts have finished executing, add the command to execute the new menu program to the end of the login script. For example, to make a user go into the CLERKS menu automatically, add the following line to the login script:

```
EXIT "NMENU CLERKS"
```

For more information about the commands and format for creating .SRC files, see the previous section.

Troubleshooting Common Problems

If you're having trouble with login scripts or menus, check the following areas:

▸ If a command in a login script or menu doesn't seem to execute, check the command for misspelled words or directories. If the command uses an identifier variable, make sure the variable is spelled correctly and that you used the appropriate punctuation (percent sign or quotation marks as necessary, and so on). Make sure commands in a menu program are indented correctly.

► If a MAP or CAPTURE command can't find the right directory or queue, make sure the commands are spelled correctly and that the directory or queue really exists where you specified it does. Make sure volume names are followed by a colon instead of a backslash and that directories are separated by backslashes in MAP commands. Also make sure the user has the necessary trustee rights to the directory.

► If a workstation's DOS paths are specified in AUTOEXEC.BAT but are gone after the user logs in, check both the system and user login scripts for search drive mappings that use the MAP S*x*: command instead of the MAP INS S*x*: command. Without the INS keyword, the search drive mapping for S1, for example, overwrites the user's first DOS path. INS inserts the search drive mapping in front of the workstation's defined path instead of overwriting it. MAP S16: always appends the search drive mapping to the *end* of the path.

► If submenus don't execute or execute in the wrong place, verify that the menu source file calls the submenu by the correct number.

► If an application doesn't execute correctly from a menu, make sure the correct executable commands are in the menu source file. If the commands are correct, check to see whether the user has rights to the directory where the application is stored and whether the user has a search drive mapped to the application's directory.

Network Printing

NetWare printing provides all network users with access to the same printers. To control how the users access the printers, NetWare includes regulating features, called the print server and the print queue. These features help ensure that print jobs are printed in the correct order.

A print server is a software program you can install in either the file server or a workstation. The print server controls how print queues and printers work together. When users send files, those files are placed in a special directory, called a print queue, in first-come/first-served order. The print jobs wait in the print queue until the printer is ready to print the next one; then the print server takes a job from the print queue and directs it to the printer.

Setting up printing services on a NetWare network involves the steps shown in Figure 6.1. Each of these steps is explained in more detail in the following sections.

Where Should the Printers and Print Servers Be Located?

With NetWare you can run a print server in either a file server or a workstation. If you run the print server in a workstation, you must dedicate the workstation to being the print server; an employee cannot use it as a regular workstation.

The advantage of running the print server in a workstation is that it can improve the performance of both the print server and the file server. You can use any PC-compatible computer as a dedicated print server. For example, an older 8088 or 286 PC will work well as a print server. The advantage of running the print server in the file server is that you save the expense of an extra workstation.

I. **Decide where you want the printers and print servers to be located, and connect the printers to the network.**

2. **Run the PCONSOLE utility to set up print queues, print servers, and printers.**

- Choose Print Queue Information and press Ins to create a new queue.

- Choose Print Server Information and press Ins to create a new print server.

- Choose Print Server Configuration ➤ Printer Configuration to configure a printer.

- Choose Queues Serviced by Printer, select a printer, and press Ins to assign a queue to the printer.

3. **Load the print server software (PSERVER.NLM on a file server or PSERVER.EXE on a dedicated workstation).**

4. **If the printer will be a remote printer (attached to a workstation that is not running the print server), run RPRINTER.EXE on that workstation.**

5. **Configure your application for network printing, specifying queues, and so on.**

6. **If your users will be using the NPRINT and CAPTURE utilities, create a spooler assignment to specify a default queue for these utilities.**

7. **If you have applications that aren't designed for network printing or if your users need to print screens using the Shift+PrtScrn key combination, put a CAPTURE command in your login scripts or in a batch file.**

8. **If your applications aren't designed for network printing or if your printer doesn't reset correctly after some print jobs, you may need to use the PRINTDEF and PRINTCON utilities to simplify your network printing.**

With NetWare 3.12 you have two choices for the print server:

- ▶ Load PSERVER.NLM on the file server to run the print server in the file server.

- ▶ Run PSERVER.EXE on a DOS workstation to run the print server in the workstation.

Some printers are preconfigured with both a network board and print server software already installed in the printer itself. These printers function as their own print server, and you can attach them to the network cabling instead of to a file server or workstation.

The next step in planning your printing setup is to decide which computers you want your printers attached to. This will determine which software you need to run on the network.

You do not necessarily need to attach your printers to the computer that is running the print server (either the file server or a dedicated workstation); you can attach them to any DOS workstation on the network. If a printer is attached directly to the print server, it is called a local printer. If the printer is attached to a workstation that is not running the print server (a workstation that is not dedicated to running the printer and that an employee can use for regular work), it is called a remote printer.

For remote printers you need to run an extra software program, called RPRINTER.EXE, on the computer to which the remote printer is attached. RPRINTER allows the print server to find and communicate with the remote printer. Figure 6.2 illustrates remote and local printers.

To summarize, you can attach a printer to the network in three different places:

- ▶ To the file server that is running PSERVER.NLM. You don't need to run RPRINTER.EXE.

- ▶ To a dedicated print server (a workstation that is running PSERVER.EXE). You don't need to run RPRINTER.EXE.

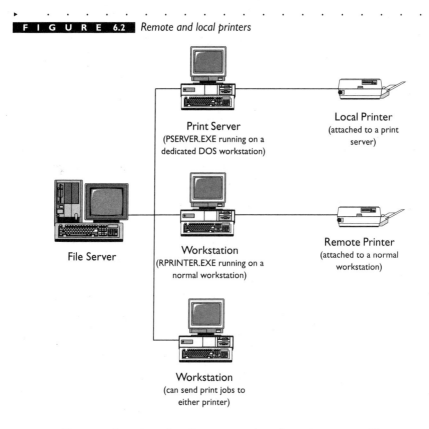

Remote and local printers

Print Server
(PSERVER.EXE running on a
dedicated DOS workstation)

Local Printer
(attached to a print
server)

File Server

Workstation
(RPRINTER.EXE running on a
normal workstation)

Remote Printer
(attached to a normal
workstation)

Workstation
(can send print jobs to
either printer)

▶ To a workstation that is *not* running the print server. You must
run RPRINTER.EXE on this workstation. A print server must
be running somewhere else on the network.

After deciding where to run the print server and printers, connect
each printer and test the printers to make sure they work.

Often, network printing problems stem from a printer that wasn't configured correctly to begin with, not from its network connections. You
should ensure that the printer is working correctly in stand-alone mode
before you install that printer on the network.

Following the instructions in the printer documentation, connect the printer to a DOS workstation's port and try to print directly from the workstation. If the printer works in stand-alone mode (without communicating with the network), it should work on the network.

Record all configuration information about the printer and archive this information with the rest of your network information.

Setting Up Print Queues and Printers

You use the PCONSOLE menu utility to set up print queues and printers. Remember to record the information about your printing setup, such as the names of print queues and printers, the users who are assigned to operate them, which queues are assigned to which printers, and so on.

To run PCONSOLE, you must be logged in to a workstation as SUPERVISOR or as a print server operator. Follow these steps to set up for printing:

I · To start the utility, type

    PCONSOLE

and press the Enter key.

2 · Select Available Topics ➤ Print Queue Information to create a print queue and assign users and an operator to that queue. (Press the Ins key to create a new queue.)

3 · Select Available Topics ➤ Print Server Information to create a print server account and assign a password, an operator, and users to the print server. (Press the Ins key to create a new print server.)

4 · Select Print Server ➤ Print Server Configuration to add a printer to the print server. Then define the printer by specifying whether it will be local or remote and by specifying the port number. If the printer is serial (connected to the COM1 or COM2 port of a file server or workstation), you must also specify its baud rate, data bits, stop bits, parity, and XON/XOFF protocol. See the printer documentation for this information.

5 · Select Print Server Configuration ➤ Queues Serviced by Printer to assign the print queue to its printer.

Optionally, you can also assign the queue a priority from the Print Server Configuration menu. If you have more than one queue assigned to the same printer, you can assign one queue priority 1 and another priority 2, for example. To assign a priority, press the Ins key at the File Server/Queue/Priority box. The default is priority 1.

Next you must load the print server.

Loading the Print Server Software

Load the print server software onto the computer that will be running the print server:

➤ On a file server, load PSERVER.NLM.

➤ On a workstation, modify the workstation's NET.CFG file to add the line

```
SPX CONNECTIONS=60
```

Then reboot the workstation, log in to the network, and run PSERVER.EXE.

Running **RPRINTER** for a Remote Printer

If the printer will be a remote printer (attached to a workstation that is not running the print server), change the workstation's NET.CFG file to add the line

```
SPX CONNECTIONS=60
```

and delete the line

```
LOCAL PRINTERS=0
```

Then reboot the workstation, log in to the network, and then run RPRINTER.EXE.

If you will attach two remote printers to the same workstation, you must run RPRINTER twice. Each remote printer needs its own copy of RPRINTER.

SETTING UP APPLICATIONS FOR NETWORK PRINTING

Set up your applications for network printing by following the instructions in the application's documentation. Many applications today have been configured to take advantage of networking.

If your application asks for network printer numbers instead of print queues, you need to set up spooler assignments. Spooler assignments give a print-queue name a corresponding printer number (0 through 4) so that the application and NetWare can communicate.

To create a spooler assignment, you type a SPOOL command at the file server console. You can also put spooler commands in the file server's AUTOEXEC.NCF file so they will automatically be in place whenever the file server is rebooted. The command format you use for creating spooler assignments is

```
SPOOL n queuename
```

Replace *n* with the printer number you want (0 to 4). Replace *queuename* with the name of the queue you want assigned to that printer number. Note that the printer numbers for spooler assignments are not the same as the printer numbers shown in the PCONSOLE utility.

CREATING A SPOOLER ASSIGNMENT FOR NPRINT AND CAPTURE

If your users will be using the NPRINT and CAPTURE utilities, create a spooler assignment to specify a default queue for these utilities to use. Set Spool 0 to the queue where you want NPRINT and CAPTURE to send print jobs. This allows users to execute NPRINT and CAPTURE commands without needing to specify a queue. For example, if you want CAPTURE and NPRINT to automatically send jobs to the queue named LASER_Q, type this command at the file server console:

```
SPOOL 0 LASER_Q
```

Then add this same command to the file server's AUTOEXEC.NCF file.

ADDING CAPTURE TO LOGIN SCRIPTS OR BATCH FILES

If you will be using applications that aren't designed for network printing or if your users need to print screens using the Shift+PrtScrn key combination, you may want to put a CAPTURE command in your login scripts or in a batch file. A stand-alone application expects a printer to be attached to a port on the workstation. Therefore, the application tries to send print jobs to that port. CAPTURE simply redirects the print jobs from the port to a network print queue.

You can include a CAPTURE command in login scripts if you want the command to be in effect all the time. Otherwise, you can place the CAPTURE command in a batch file in the user's home directory (or in the PUBLIC directory if all users need the same batch file) or in a menu as an option. (Creating login scripts and menus for users is discussed in Chapter 5.)

USING THE PRINTDEF AND PRINTCON UTILITIES

If your applications aren't designed for network printing, you may need to use two additional NetWare utilities to simplify your network printing: PRINTDEF and PRINTCON.

Use PRINTDEF to specify the brand of printer you are using and the types of paper (called forms) on which you want to print. This is helpful if you use applications that print on different types of paper, such as paychecks, invoices, and so on, and the printer doesn't reset correctly after each type of job.

Use PRINTCON to tell the printer how the print job should be printed on the form you set up in PRINTDEF. With PRINTCON you set up print job configurations, which specify items such as whether or not a banner page will be printed and to which queue the job should be sent.

Troubleshooting Common Problems

If you're having trouble with network printing, check the following areas:

- Is the problem with a single workstation or several? If the problem is with several workstations, it may be a problem with the network cabling or related cabling hardware.

▸ Is the printer configured correctly? Double-check the documentation for any configuration information, especially about interrupt conflicts. Serial printers cannot be configured to use IRQ 7 if you want them to use COM ports. Use IRQ 4 for COM1 and IRQ 3 for COM2. Also, if a local printer is configured to use interrupts, try switching it to not use interrupts.

▸ Is the cable that connects the printer to the workstation or file server functioning?

▸ If you just installed or upgraded the printer, did you follow the instructions in the documentation exactly? Check for missed steps, shortcuts that may have bypassed an important step, and so on.

▸ Are the print queues, print servers, and printers all assigned to each other correctly? Use PCONSOLE to see the status of print queues and print servers.

▸ Is the application using the correct printer driver for the printer? Check the manufacturer's documentation for instructions on using the right driver.

▸ Does the printer have a printer definition file?

▸ If the printer is attached to a workstation running RPRINTER.EXE, make sure the workstation's NET.CFG file does not contain the command LOCAL PRINTERS=0.

▸ Does the workstation hang when the user presses the Shift and PrtScrn keys? If so, make sure the line LOCAL PRINTERS=0 is in the workstation's NET.CFG file.

CHAPTER 7

Installing and Using Novell's Online Documentation

When NetWare 3.12 was first released, the CD-ROM version of the product included most of the documentation in electronic form, viewed through an online documentation viewer called Novell ElectroText. When the international version of NetWare 3.12 (which contains translated documentation) was released in June 1994, the ElectroText viewer was replaced with an updated viewer, called DynaText.

Both ElectroText and DynaText include all the NetWare 3.12 documentation in online format. The content of the manuals was not changed; merely the viewer. Therefore, this chapter explains how to install and use both types of viewers. (The updated DynaText version of the documentation is available on NetWire if you would like to update your ElectroText files, but it isn't required.)

If you have Microsoft Windows 3.1 installed on a workstation, you can access the complete set of NetWare 3.12 documentation online using either viewer. If you do not have Microsoft Windows 3.1 or if you want printed manuals in addition to the online versions, you can purchase a set of the printed manuals separately. The printed manuals are identical to the electronic documentation.

To order the printed manuals, you can use the order form that came in your NetWare 3.12 box or call 800-336-3892 (in the United States) or 512-834-6905.

Installing the Online Documentation

If you purchased the CD-ROM version of NetWare 3.12, use the following instructions to install the online documentation. These instructions work for both ElectroText and DynaText.

Because the instructions for installing a workstation are in the online documentation, you may first have to install the documentation on a stand-alone computer. (For an installation quick path, see Chapter 3 of this book.) You can either load the ElectroText or DynaText files onto the computer's hard disk or run them directly from the CD-ROM attached to the computer. After you have workstations set up and running on the network, you can install the documentation into a network directory on the server. Then the documentation can be accessed from any workstation on the network.

You install the online documentation on the network server as part of the INSTALL.NLM procedure. The instructions in Figure 7.1 explain how to install the documentation onto the network so that all network users can access it. Note that with ElectroText, you copy only one set of files during the installation process; with DynaText you have to repeat

F I G U R E   7.1   *Online documentation installation quick path*

1. **Load INSTALL.NLM by typing LOAD INSTALL.**

2. **Select Product Options.**

3. **Press the Ins key.**

4. **(ElectroText only) Specify the CD-ROM's drive letter and path for the directory that contains the documentation files: NETWARE.312\ENGLISH\DOC.**

5. **(DynaText only) Enter the CD-ROM's drive letter and path for the directory that contains the viewer files: INSTALL\IBM_PC\NETWARE\312\ENGLISH\VIEWER (For a different language, specify FRANCAIS, DEUTSCH, ITALIANO, or ESPANOL instead of ENGLISH.)**

6. **(DynaText only) Press the Ins key again to copy the documentation files. Enter the CD-ROM's drive letter and INSTALL\IBM_PC\NETWARE\312\ENGLISH\312DOC. (Specify a different language if necessary.)**

the copying process to copy two sets of files: the viewer files and the documentation files.

The INSTALL.NLM program will copy all of the online documentation files onto the network. Next you must set up workstations to run the viewer.

Setting Up a Workstation for Novell ElectroText

To set up a workstation to view the ElectroText documentation, follow the instructions in Figure 7.2.

After the documentation is installed, double-click on the Novell Electro-Text icon to start up the viewer.

Novell ElectroText is arranged like a set of bookshelves. By clicking on icons you select the bookshelf you want to access and the book you want to read.

Once you've opened a book, you can read the text from the beginning of the book, using the ↑ and ↓ keys or the scroll bar to move through the text. You can also click on headings in the book's outline (Table of Contents) to move instantly between chapters and sections of the book. If a plus sign appears next to a heading in the Table of Contents, click on the plus sign to expand the Table of Contents under that heading.

In the book's text, you can click on icons to see graphics and tables, or you can click on cross-references to move to related information in other sections of the book or even in other books. The Search field at the bottom of the window lets you search for specific words or phrases in the book.

1. Map a fake root to the Novell ElectroText directory (SYS:DOC). For example, to use drive P, type
MAP ROOT P:=SYS:DOC

2. Copy the ET.INI file from the SYS:DOC\DATA\CONFIG directory to the workstation's WINDOWS directory.

3. Edit ET.INI so it will find ElectroText files in the fake root you mapped. There are several places in the ET.INI file where you must substitute the correct drive letter (in the example, drive P) for the letter that exists in the commands.

4. If the workstation has an LCD display, add the command "DISPLAY=WLCDVGA" to the Preferences section of ET.INI.

5. Edit the workstation's AUTOEXEC.BAT file to include the following command:
SET NWLANGUAGE=ENGLISH

6. Type the same command at the command line or reboot the computer so the language setting will take effect.

7. Start Windows.

8. Select (make active) the program group in which you want to place the ElectroText icon.

9. Choose File ➤ New ➤ Program Item.

10. Enter a description for the icon, such as "Novell ElectroText."

FIGURE 7.2 *Setting up a workstation for Novell ElectroText (continued)*

11. **For the command line, enter the path to the ET.EXE file, which executes ElectroText. For example, enter P: PUBLIC\ET.EXE**

12. **For the working directory, enter the path to the directory that contains ET.EXE. For example, enter P:\PUBLIC**

13. **Select OK.**

Setting Up a Workstation for DynaText

To set up a workstation to use DynaText, see Figure 7.3.

DynaText can contain more than one collection of documentation. A collection is a set of documentation; for example, all the manuals for NetWare 3.12 are contained in one collection. All the manuals for NetWare 4 are contained in a separate collection. It is possible to have several collections stored on a server or workstation so that you can access whichever collection you choose.

In most cases, installing a single collection of DynaText documentation in a single language into the default network directories is adequate. However, in some cases, you might need to install multiple collections, allow multiple languages, or install the files into a different directory.

FIGURE 7.3 *Setting up a workstation for DynaText*

1. Map a search drive to the online documentation directory (SYS:DOCVIEW).

2. Edit the workstation's AUTOEXEC.BAT file to add the following command (substitute another language for ENGLISH, if necessary):
SET NWLANGUAGE=ENGLISH

3. Type the same command at the command line or reboot the computer so the language setting will take effect.

4. Start Windows.

5. Select (make active) the program group in which you want to place the DynaText icon.

6. Choose File ➤ New ➤ Program Item.

7. Enter a description for the icon, such as "NetWare Documentation."

8. For the command line, enter the path to the DTEXTRW.EXE file, which executes DynaText. For example, enter X:\DOCVIEW.

9. For the working directory, enter the path for the directory that contains DTEXTRW.EXE, such as X:\DOCVIEW

10. Select OK.

11. Edit SYSDOCS.CFG and DYNATEXT.INI if necessary to allow for multiple languages or collections.

In these cases you must edit two files to configure your setup:

- ▸ SYSDOCS.CFG allows you to specify a name and location for a documentation collection. To add multiple collections to the default file, edit the Windows Collection line. Separate each collection reference with a semicolon and no space between references.

- ▸ DYNATEXT.INI is the DynaText initialization file. It contains various installation and configuration commands. This file is a text file, and it contains all the necessary editing instructions right in the text of the file itself.

After the documentation is installed, double-click on the DynaText icon to start up the viewer.

When you select a collection and the name of a book from that collection, the book appears on the workstation screen, with part of the screen showing the book's text and another part of the screen showing the book's Table of Contents.

Once you've opened a book, you can read the text from the beginning of the book, using the ↑ and ↓ keys or the scroll bar to move through the text. You can also click on a heading in the book's Table of Contents to move instantly between chapters and sections of the book. If a plus sign appears next to a heading in the Table of Contents, click on the plus sign to expand the Table of Contents under that heading.

In the book's text you can click on icons to see graphics and tables, or you can click on cross-references to move to related information in other sections of the book or even in other books. The Find field lets you search for specific words or phrases in the book.

Troubleshooting Common Problems

If you're having trouble with the online documentation, check the following areas:

► Are you running Microsoft Windows 3.1? Both Novell Electro-Text and DynaText require Microsoft Windows 3.1.

► Does the workstation's AUTOEXEC.BAT file include the SET NWLANGUAGE=ENGLISH command? (For DynaText, a different language can be specified, but that language's documentation files must have been installed for this command to work.) If the command exists, did you reboot the computer or type the same command at the command line to make the language setting take effect?

► Are the command line and working directory specified for the online documentation correct? To check, click on the online documentation's icon, and then choose File ► Properties. Compare the directory paths listed with those in the instructions.

► (ElectroText only) Is a fake root mapped to the directory that contains the Novell ElectroText files? This mapping cannot be a regular mapping or even a search drive mapping. It must be a fake root.

► (ElectroText only) Is the ET.INI file in the WINDOWS directory on the workstation's hard disk? Has ET.INI been edited so that it will look for the ElectroText files in the directory to which you mapped the fake root? There are several places in the ET.INI file where you must substitute the correct drive letter for the letter that exists in the commands.

- ▶ (ElectroText only) If the workstation you're using has an LCD display, did you add the command DISPLAY=WLCDVGA to the Preferences section of the ET.INI file?

- ▶ (DynaText only) Is a search drive (X, by default) mapped to the directory that contains the online documentation files (usually SYS:DOCVIEW)?

- ▶ (DynaText only) If necessary, did you edit the DYNATEXT.INI file and the SYSDOCS.CFG file to specify multiple collections, multiple languages, or different directory locations?

CHAPTER 8

NetWare
for Macintosh 3.12

NetWare 3.12 includes a five-user version of NetWare for Macintosh. With this product you can connect up to five Macintosh workstations to your NetWare 3.12 network. Those Macintosh users can then work on the network and take advantage of NetWare's file-sharing, security, and printing features. In addition, DOS users can share files with Macintosh users and can access Apple printers, such as LaserWriters and ImageWriters. This chapter explains how NetWare for Macintosh allows Macintosh and DOS workstations to work together on the same network.

NetWare for Macintosh 3.12 is not a network operating system by itself. You cannot use a Macintosh file server for your NetWare network, nor can you have a Macintosh-only NetWare network. NetWare for Macintosh allows you only to add Macintoshes to a PC-based NetWare network. Your file server must be a PC, and you must have at least one PC workstation to set up your network.

NetWare for Macintosh includes a set of NLMs that are loaded onto the file server. These NLMs enable the server to store Macintosh files and manage Macintosh communications. NetWare for Macintosh 3.12 also contains an application called NetWare Tools that is loaded onto the workstations. NetWare Tools lets the network supervisor (and, to a lesser extent, users) work with print queues, send messages, change passwords, create users, assign trustee rights and file attributes, and so on.

How NetWare for Macintosh Works

NetWare for Macintosh is basically a set of NLMs that, when loaded on a NetWare network, create an AppleTalk router in the file server and provide file and print services for the Macintosh workstations. The AppleTalk router allows AppleTalk traffic to be routed between two network boards in the file server and it communicates with any other AppleTalk routers on the network.

As long as an AppleTalk router exists on a file server, Macintosh workstations can communicate with the server and with other Macintoshes or AppleTalk printers on the other side of the file server.

There are five NLMs that you use to set up NetWare for Macintosh. The first four are copied to the file server by default during NetWare's installation process.

- ▸ **APPLETLK.NLM:** This is the main AppleTalk router and protocol stack.

- ▸ **AFP.NLM:** (AppleTalk Filing Protocol 2.0) This module lets workstations running AppleShare workstation software work with NetWare's file services.

- ▸ **ATPS.NLM:** (AppleTalk Print Services) This module makes AppleTalk and NetWare printing services work together. This allows Macintosh users to use NetWare print queues and lets NetWare print queues send jobs to AppleTalk printers.

- ▸ **ATCON.NLM:** (AppleTalk Console) The network supervisor can use this module to see information about AppleTalk networks, the AppleTalk router, and the AppleTalk protocol stack.

- ▸ **ATTOKLLC.NLM:** This module is necessary for running Macintosh workstations on a Token-Ring network. It is not copied to the server by default; to use it, you must copy it from the NW-MAC diskette (or the NetWare for Macintosh directory on the CD) to SYS:SYSTEM.

Installing NetWare for Macintosh 3.12

Before you install NetWare for Macintosh, select the type of network boards (such as Ethernet, Token-Ring, or LocalTalk) and the cabling system you want to use to connect your Macintoshes to your network. LocalTalk is already built in to all Macintoshes. If you use LocalTalk, you won't need to install network boards in your Macintoshes. However, you need to buy one LocalTalk network board to install in your file server so the server can communicate with the Macintosh workstations. You also need LocalTalk cabling.

Using LocalTalk is generally the least expensive option. Its major disadvantage is that network communication is much slower than with other types of cabling.

After you've selected the hardware, you follow the steps shown in Figure 8.1 to install NetWare for Macintosh. Refer to the NetWare for Macintosh installation manual for specific details about each step.

TIPS ON INSTALLATION

You probably want to create a separate volume on the file server just for Macintosh files. Having this volume often simplifies backing up and restoring Macintosh files separately from DOS files, and it may make it easier to repair volumes without worrying about the different types of files stored on them.

After creating one or more volumes for the Macintosh files, load the MAC name space module on the file server and add the MAC name space to each volume that will contain the Macintosh files. The Macintosh name space allows the server and volumes to store the longer Macintosh file names.

After preparing the volumes, you copy the NetWare for Macintosh files on the server by using INSTALL.NLM. After the files are copied, you load the NetWare for Macintosh NLMs and then load and configure the Apple-Talk router, which lets the Macintoshes communicate with the NetWare file server.

To configure the AppleTalk router, you assign it a network number and zone name (or names) for its internal network and another network number and zone name (or names) for its external network.

FIGURE 8.1 *NetWare for Macintosh installation quick path*

1. Install network boards in all Macintosh workstations (not necessary if you're using LocalTalk) and cable the workstations to the network.

2. Install a corresponding network board in the file server.

3. (Optional) Create a separate volume on the file server for the Macintosh files.

4. Load the MAC name space module on the file server by typing the following command at the console prompt:
   LOAD MAC

5. Add the MAC name space to each volume that will contain the Macintosh files by typing the following command at the console prompt:
   ADD NAME SPACE MAC TO *volume*

6. Load INSTALL.NLM ➤ Product Options, press the Ins key, and insert the NetWare for Macintosh diskette or specify the path to the NetWare for Macintosh NLMs on the CD-ROM.

7. Select the path to the STARTUP.NCF file (or enter a new path if you don't want to edit the existing file), and then choose Install NW-MAC.

8. After the files are installed, choose Currently Installed Products ➤ NW-MAC.

9. Edit the STARTUP.NCF file to add the following two lines:
   LOAD MAC
   SET MINIMUM PACKET RECEIVE BUFFERS = 100

FIGURE 8.1 *NetWare for Macintosh installation quick path (continued)*

10. **Edit the AUTOEXEC.NCF file to add the following commands:**

- Load the AppleTalk protocol and router module (APPLETLK) on the file server and specify a network number and zones for the AppleTalk router's internal network.

- Load the appropriate LAN driver and bind the AppleTalk protocol to the driver, specifying another network number (or range of numbers) and zones for this.

- Load AFP.NLM (file services module) and ATPS.NLM (print services module), specifying configuration options if necessary.

11. **Edit the ATPS.CFG file to configure print services.**

12. **Reboot the server, or retype the commands in steps 9 and 10 at the server's console.**

What Are Internal and External Networks?

In NetWare for Macintosh, the AppleTalk router is software that runs in the file server. This AppleTalk router contains its own internal network, which doesn't actually encompass any hardware. The internal network is just a software feature of the router.

Besides the internal network, the AppleTalk router is aware of at least one external network—the "real" network that contains all the Macintosh workstations.

The internal and the external networks have to be configured with separate, unique network numbers (or ranges of numbers), which you assign when you load the AppleTalk router and when you bind the AppleTalk protocol to the LAN driver. (These network numbers don't exist before you assign them in the LOAD and BIND commands in the AUTOEXEC.NCF file.) At the same time, you specify which zones you want the internal and external networks to belong to.

What Are Zones?

A zone is a collection of devices on a network that users can access through the Chooser. For example, you might group related printers and file servers in the same zone so everyone in that area can easily find them.

You don't have to set up zones before installing NetWare for Macintosh. In fact, you set up zones at the same time you assign network numbers, in the LOAD and BIND commands for configuring the AppleTalk router.

An extended AppleTalk network (explained in the section "Extended AppleTalk Networks" later in this chapter) can have more than one zone assigned to it (up to 255, in fact), so users in different zones can access it. To assign multiple zones to a network, you can list all the zones in the LOAD and BIND commands. For NetWare for Macintosh, the default zone is the first zone in the list.

If there are more zones than will fit on a single command line in the AUTOEXEC.NCF file, you can create a separate global file, called ATZONES.CFG, that contains a zone list (the names of all the zones assigned to that network). Then you load the APPLETLK module with the −z option and omit the zones list from the LOAD and BIND commands. This is explained in the section "Configuring the Appletalk Router" later in this chapter.

Nonextended AppleTalk Networks

EtherTalk 1.0, Arcnet, and LocalTalk are all nonextended AppleTalk networks. These networks can support only up to 254 nodes, all of which which are contained in a single zone.

For a nonextended network, the network number can be any integer you want to assign, from 1 to 65,279. (These are 16-bit numbers.) This number helps identify the AppleTalk network. If you have more than one such network connected to a NetWare network, each AppleTalk network must have a unique network number.

The zone name can be any name, up to 32 characters long.

Nodes (workstations, and so on) on a nonextended network have 8-bit addresses, which means the node addresses can range from 1 to 254.

Extended AppleTalk Networks

Ethernet and Token-Ring networks are extended AppleTalk networks because they allow far more than 254 nodes to be connected to the network (theoretically, up to more than 16 million nodes).

To allow more than 254-node addresses, extended networks add the 16-bit network number to the 8-bit node number, which makes up a 24-bit number. This 24-bit number is then assigned as the node's full address. There are over 16 million 24-bit numbers available.

To configure an extended network to allow more than 254 nodes, you can assign the network a range of network numbers instead of a single number. For example, if you assign an extended network a network number of 1 digit, that network will support only 254 nodes (1 × 254). If you assign the network a network number range of, say 6–10, the total possible number of nodes on that network would be 1270 (5 × 254). You can combine each number in the network's range with the same 8-bit node number to give five different variations of that number.

Extended networks can also belong to up to 255 zones. As explained earlier in this chapter, to make a network a member of multiple zones you can either list the zones in the LOAD and BIND commands or create an ATZONES.CFG file, which contains the zones list.

Configuring the AppleTalk Router

You configure the AppleTalk router by using commands to load the LAN driver, load the AppleTalk module, and bind AppleTalk to the LAN driver. During this process you also assign network numbers and zones. (If there is already another AppleTalk router on the network, your new AppleTalk can learn its configuration information from that router. This is referred to as "learning the configuration from a seed router." Using seed routers is explained in the section "Using Seed Routers" later in this chapter.)

The commands you use for this process are LOAD and BIND. First you load the LAN driver and bind the IPX protocol to it for the PC side of the network. Then you load the AppleTalk module and configure its internal router. Finally, you load another LAN driver (or the same LAN driver with a different frame type), bind the AppleTalk protocol to the LAN driver, and configure the external network. Use the following command formats:

```
LOAD driver parameters NAME=name1
BIND IPX name1 NET=number1
LOAD APPLETLK NET=number2 ZONE={"zonename"}
LOAD driver parameters NAME=name2
BIND APPLETLK name2 NET=number3 ZONE={"zonename"}
```

The following is an example AUTOEXEC.NCF file that might be used by a nonextended AppleTalk network:

```
LOAD NE2000 INT=2 PORT=300 FRAME=ETHERNET_802.2 NAME=IPXBRD
BIND IPX IPXBRD NET=65
LOAD APPLETLK NET=3000 ZONE={"GRAPHICS"}
LOAD NE2000 INT=2 PORT=300 FRAME=ETHERNET_SNAP NAME=MACBRD
BIND APPLETLK MACBRD NET=10015 ZONE={"GRAPHICS"}
LOAD AFP
LOAD ATPS
```

In this example:

▸ The first line loads the NE2000 LAN driver for the NE2000 board that is installed in the file server.

▸ The second line binds IPX to the NE2000 driver for the PC-based side of the network.

▸ The third line loads the AppleTalk module and configures its internal network with a network number of 3000 and a zone named GRAPHICS.

▸ The fourth line loads the NE2000 LAN driver again, but this time with a different frame type for the AppleTalk side of the network. This line names this board/driver combination MACBRD.

▸ The fifth line binds AppleTalk to the MACBRD board/driver combination. It also configures the external network with a network number and a zone.

▸ The remaining two lines load AFP.NLM and ATPS.NLM, which are the file services and print services modules, respectively.

The following example shows how AUTOEXEC.NCF might look if this were an extended AppleTalk network with multiple zones.

```
LOAD NE2000 INT=2 PORT=300 FRAME=ETHERNET_802.2 NAME=IPXBRD
BIND IPX IPXBRD NET=65
LOAD APPLETLK NET=3000 ZONE={"GRAPHICS"}
LOAD NE2000 INT=2 PORT=300 FRAME=ETHERNET_SNAP NAME=MACBRD
BIND APPLETLK MACBRD NET=20-25 ZONE={"GRAPHICS","PR","MKTG"}
LOAD AFP
LOAD ATPS
```

In this example the first four and the last two lines are the same as in the previous example. The difference is in the fifth line, which binds

AppleTalk to the MACBRD board/driver combination and configures the external AppleTalk network.

In this case the network number is specified to be a range of numbers, from 20 to 25. In addition, three zones are listed.

The BIND command can contain only up to 82 characters. If you need to list more zones than will fit on the command, create an ATZONES.CFG file. (You can create and edit the ATZONES.CFG file from within INSTALL.) In this case the AUTOEXEC.NCF file would look like this:

```
LOAD NE2000 INT=2 PORT=300 FRAME=ETHERNET_802.2 NAME=IPXBRD
BIND IPX IPXBRD NET=65
LOAD APPLETLK -Z NET=3000
LOAD NE2000 INT=2 PORT=300 FRAME=ETHERNET_SNAP NAME=MACBRD
BIND APPLETLK MACBRD NET=20-25
LOAD AFP
LOAD ATPS
```

In the third line the APPLETLK module is loaded with the -z option instead of specifying a zone name, which tells the module to look for the ATZONES.CFG file in SYS:SYSTEM. In the fifth line, which binds the APPLETLK protocol to the LAN driver, the ZONE= parameter is again omitted so that the ATZONES.CFG file will be used. If you specify a zone in either of these commands, that zone will override any zones listed in ATZONES.CFG.

To create ATZONES.CFG you specify network numbers and the zones assigned to them, similarly to the way you specify them in the BIND commands. (Make sure the network numbers in ATZONES.CFG match the network numbers you use in the BIND command.) The following is an example of an ATZONES.CFG file:

```
NET=20-25 ZONE={"ZONE1","ZONE2","ZONE3"}
NET=26-30 ZONE={"ZONE4","ZONE5","ZONE6"}
```

ATZONES.CFG ignores blank lines and spaces, so you can list each zone name on a different line, if desired, such as

```
NET=20-25 ZONE={
"ZONE1",
"ZONE2",
"ZONE3"
}
NET=26-30 ZONE={
"ZONE4",
"ZONE5",
"ZONE6"
}
```

Using ATTOKLLC.NLM on Token-Ring Networks

In most situations, if you are running Macintosh workstations on a Token-Ring network, you will need to use the ATTOKLLC.NLM module. This module is not copied to the server by default; you must copy it from the NW-MAC diskette (or the NetWare for Macintosh directory on the CD) to SYS:SYSTEM.

The following example shows how AUTOEXEC.NCF might look if this were a Token-Ring network.

```
LOAD TOKEN INT=2 SAPS=4 LS=32 NAME=IPXBRD
BIND IPX IPXBRD NET=65
LOAD APPLETLK NET=3000 ZONE={"GRAPHICS"}
LOAD TOKEN INT=2 SAPS=4 LS=32 FRAME=TOKEN-RING_SNAP
  NAME=MACBRD
BIND APPLETLK MACBRD NET=20-25 ZONE={"GRAPHICS","PR","MKTG"}
LOAD ROUTE BOARD=1
LOAD ATTOKLLC
BIND ATTOKLLC TO IPXBRD
LOAD AFP
LOAD ATPS
```

In this example:

▸ The first two commands load the Token-Ring driver and bind IPX to it, for the PC-based side of the network.

▸ The third command loads the AppleTalk module and configures its internal network.

▸ The fourth command loads the Token-Ring driver again, but this time for the AppleTalk side of the network, using the TOKEN-RING_SNAP frame type. This line also names this board/driver combination MACBRD. (Although this command is printed on two lines in this book, it must be entered on one line.)

▸ The fifth command binds AppleTalk to the MACBRD board/driver combination and configures the external Apple-Talk network.

▸ The sixth command loads the Token-Ring Source Routing NLM (ROUTE.NLM) for the Token-Ring board.

▸ The seventh command loads the ATTOKLLC module.

▸ The eighth command binds ATTOKLLC to the IPXBRD board/driver combination. Note that ATTOKLLC is bound to the IPX board/driver combination rather than to the APPLETLK board/driver combination.

▸ The final two commands load AFP.NLM and ATPS.NLM.

Using Seed Routers

If you already have one AppleTalk router configured on the network with network numbers and zones, you do not have to explicitly assign network numbers and zones to additional AppleTalk routers' external networks if you don't want to. Instead, the new routers can learn their external network configuration from the original AppleTalk router, called the seed router.

To make a non-seed router learn its configuration from a seed router, you still use the BIND command to bind AppleTalk to the LAN driver.

However, instead of specifying a network number or range, specify NET=0–0 and omit the ZONE= parameter. For example, the command would look like this:

```
BIND APPLETLK MACBRD NET=0-0
```

However, if the seed router ever goes down and the non-seed router is rebooted, the non-seed router will not function correctly because it will attempt to use 0 as a network number, which isn't valid in AppleTalk.

SETTING UP MACINTOSH WORKSTATIONS

To set up Macintosh workstations you run an Installer program from the NetWare 3.12 CD-ROM or from the NetWare for Macintosh Client diskette.

The following software is copied to the workstation by the Installer:

- ▸ NetWare Notify, which lets Macintosh users send and receive short messages

- ▸ NetWare UAM (User Authentication Module), which encrypts the user's password before sending it across the cabling

- ▸ NetWare Tools, which allows the network supervisor to work with users, groups, security, and printing

There are two installation scripts you can use for this installation:

- ▸ The Admin installation script, which is the default. This script installs all workstation software, including the NetWare Tools application.

- ▸ The User installation script, which installs all workstation software except the NetWare Tools application.

Most of the features provided by NetWare Tools can be used only by the network supervisor. Therefore, you may not want to install this application on all users' workstations.

To use the User installation script instead of the default Admin script, open the User Install Script folder and double-click on the file named NWM User Install Script. To make an install disk that runs only the User script, move the NWM User Install Script out of its folder to the same level as the Installer program, and remove the NWM Admin Install Script.

After you've selected the script you want to use, you can execute the Installer.

Figure 8.2 shows the simple steps involved in setting up a Macintosh workstation.

FIGURE 8.2 *Macintosh workstation installation quick path*

1. **Make sure the LAN driver is loaded on each workstation, in the System folder for System 6.0.5 or in the Extensions folder for System 7.**

2. **Select the correct LAN driver icon in the Network Control Panel.**

3. **Run the Installer program from the CD-ROM or NetWare for Macintosh Client diskette.**

- Use the Admin installation to install all client software, including NetWare Tools.

- Use the User installation to install all client software, except for NetWare Tools.

Using the NetWare Tools Application

The NetWare Tools application consists of five different utilities.

To use NetWare Tools you select a utility. Then you select an entity, such as a user, a print queue, or a volume. Every time you use a utility to work with an entity, you have activated a session.

To use NetWare Tools, doubleclick on the NetWare Tools icon, and choose one of the utilities from the Utilities menu. Then you can select the entity with which you want to work.

Most of the features of the NetWare Tools application can be used only by the network supervisor. The five utilities are explained in Table 8.1.

When you first open the NetWare Tools application, a workspace appears on your screen. This workspace has two panels: a Connected Items panel and a Saved Items panel.

▸ **T A B L E 8.1** *NetWare Tools Utilities*

UTILITY	DESCRIPTION
Print Queue	Lets you view the print jobs in a queue and lets you delete them, delay them, change their position in the queue, and so on
Users and Groups	Lets you create and delete users and groups, change passwords, assign trustees, and assign security equivalences
Messaging	Lets you send short messages to other users on the network
NetWare Rights	Lets you view your effective rights, assign trustee rights to users, and modify the Inherited Rights Mask
File and Folder Flags	Lets you set flags (attributes) for files and folders

The Connected Items panel shows the volumes and print queues with which you currently have a session. You can use the Saved Items panel to specify entities with which you often have sessions. If an item appears in either panel, you can double-click on that item as a quick way to re-open the utility session with that entity.

To add a session with a particular entity to your workspace, choose File ➤ Add to Workspace. To copy a session from the Connected Items panel to the Saved Items panel, choose File ➤ Add to Saved Items. To delete a session from the Saved Items panel, highlight the item and press the Del key.

You can have more than one Saved Items session file if you like. To save items to a different session file, choose File ➤ Export Workspace to File. Then, to use the new file the next time you use the NetWare Tools application, double-click on the new session file's icon to launch NetWare Tools.

Sharing Files between PCs and Macintoshes

NetWare for Macintosh makes it possible for PC and Macintosh users to see the names of each other's files, but whether or not the users can open those files depends on the applications being used. NetWare doesn't control how applications open and create files.

PC applications cannot be used on a Macintosh, and vice versa, because PC and Macintosh files have different formats. Macintosh files consist of two parts:

- **Data fork:** Contains the text of the file

- **Resource fork:** Contains information about the file, such as the name of the application that created the file and the icon that should be displayed for the file

DOS and OS/2 files don't have resource forks. They contain only information that corresponds to the Macintosh file's data fork. However, even though Macintosh and PC files are different, there are ways to share their files. The two most common are to

- Use an application that has both a PC-based (DOS, Windows, or OS/2) version and a Macintosh version. These types of applications usually can convert files from one version's format to the other version's format.

- Convert the files into a format the other workstation can use. For example, if a Macintosh application allows you to save a file in an ASCII format, you can then open the file from a DOS application that also supports ASCII. However, this process converts only the text in a file; any graphic or formatting elements will be lost.

Another difference between Macintosh and DOS files is the rules that govern file names. DOS files can be up to eight characters long plus an optional three-character extension, such as FILENAME.NEW. Macintosh names can be much longer—up to 31 characters—and can contain spaces and punctuation, which are invalid in DOS names.

When Macintosh file names are displayed on a PC, those names are truncated (shortened) to the DOS format. This is for PC display purposes only; the names are not actually changed, and they will still appear in their original form when displayed on a Macintosh. If your PC and Macintosh users will share files often, encourage the Macintosh users to use DOS-type file names so the names are comprehensible to the PC users.

Can PC and Macintosh Users Share Printers?

With NetWare for Macintosh, DOS and Macintosh users can share printers, such as Apple LaserWriters and ImageWriters, on the network.

Macintosh users can take advantage of NetWare's print server and print queue features so they don't need to wait until the printer is free before they can continue working.

As explained in Chapter 6, when PC workstations send files to be printed on a NetWare network, the print jobs are sent first to a NetWare print queue, which then funnels the jobs to the printer. This process works well for PC workstations because the PCs can recognize NetWare print queues.

Macintosh workstations do not recognize print queues. Macintoshes are designed to send print jobs directly to printers. To get a print job to the queue, NetWare for Macintosh adds a step to the printing process, called an AppleTalk print spooler (formerly called an AppleTalk Queue Server). To the Macintosh, the print spooler appears to be a regular Apple printer, so the workstation sends the print job to it. Then the print spooler sends the job to the NetWare print queue, where the Macintosh's print job joins any other print jobs from other Macintosh or DOS workstations and waits its turn to be printed. When a printer is available, the print server takes the job from the queue and sends it to the printer.

Another feature, called an AppleTalk print server, takes print jobs from a NetWare queue and sends those jobs to an AppleTalk printer on the AppleTalk network.

In NetWare 3.12 the NetWare print server (PSERVER) handles PC print jobs, and you can decide whether Macintosh print jobs are handled by the NetWare print server or by a separate AppleTalk print server.

Setting Up Printing with NetWare for Macintosh

The steps in Figure 8.3 outline the basic procedure for adding Apple printers to a NetWare network so that both PC and Macintosh workstations can use them. Refer to the NetWare for Macintosh installation manual for more specific information. After you have installed NetWare for Macintosh printing, both PC and Macintosh users can easily send print jobs to Apple printers.

INSTALLING LASERWRITERS

LaserWriter printers must be attached to a network cabling segment that supports the AppleTalk protocol so that ATPS.NLM can find and communicate with it and set up the AppleTalk print spooler. If a Laser-Writer is attached to a Macintosh workstation via LocalTalk and the Macintosh is connected to the network via Ethernet cabling, ATPS.NLM will not find the LaserWriter. This is because, by default, the Macintosh can communicate through only one of its ports at a time. Therefore, even the Macintosh running on Ethernet can't see a LaserWriter that is attached to it via LocalTalk.

USING THE ATPS.CFG FILE

The ATPS.CFG file is a configuration file the ATPS module uses to see the list of queues for AppleTalk printers it must service. You can create and edit this file from within INSTALL.NLM. To specify a queue for an AppleTalk printer in this file, use the format

```
"printername:zonename" parameters
```

Macintosh printing installation quick path

1. **Connect the printer to the cabling segment that supports the AppleTalk protocol.**

2. **Make sure each Macintosh workstation has the correct Apple printer driver software installed.**

3. **Use the PRINTDEF utility from a DOS-based workstation to import the Apple printer's device definition files into the NetWare printer database. These files describe the printer to the file server.**

4. **Run INSTALL.NLM to edit the ATPS.CFG file so that it will create print spoolers (queues). Enter commands in the following format (see Table 8.2 for an explanation of the available parameters):**
   "printername:zonename" parameter

5. **Use PCONSOLE from a DOS-based workstation to set up print queues, print queue operators, and so on, just as you do for a PC-based printer (see Chapter 6). The queue names should be identical to the AppleTalk print spooler names you specified in ATPS.CFG using the –o parameter.**

6. **Load the regular NetWare print server software (PSERVER) onto the file server and configure it.**

7. **Use PRINTDEF to set up a print form called Normal that defines 8.5- by 11-inch sheets of paper.**

8. **If the printer is a LaserWriter, use PRINTCON to set up PostScript and PostText print job configurations that PC users can use.**

9. **Load ATPS.NLM onto the file server to create the AppleTalk Queue Server and manage Macintosh print jobs. (If ATPS is already loaded, unload it and reload it to make the new settings take effect.) To load APTS, type LOAD ATPS.**

For example, to specify a queue that will service the printer LaserFast, which is in the zone Graphics, type

```
"LASERFAST:GRAPHICS"
```

This will advertise a queue called NW_LASERFAST to the Macintoshes. By default, the queue name is simply the printer's name with NW_ added to the beginning. If the printer is located in the internal network's default zone, the zone name can be omitted from the command.

You can also use the parameters listed in Table 8.2 with these queue commands. For example, if you wanted a different queue name (such as MYQUEUE) to appear in the Chooser instead of the default NW_LASER-FAST, use the −o option, as in

```
"LASERFAST:GRAPHICS" −o MYQUEUE
```

▸ **T A B L E** 8.2 *ATPS.CFG Parameters*

PARAMETER	DESCRIPTION
−A	Lets Macintosh users spool print jobs to this queue only if they are logged in through AFP and are designated Queue Users
−B	Prints a banner page
−C	Causes an AppleTalk print spooler to appear like an ImageWriter or ImageWriter LQ with a color ribbon loaded, so Macintoshes will generate color codes
−E	Turns off PostScript error banner pages
−F *filename*	Specifies a PostScript font list file
−H	Hides the AppleTalk printer by changing its NBP type. Use this option to prevent Macintosh users from sending jobs directly to printers; the printers don't appear in the Chooser; only print queues (actually, the AppleTalk print spoolers) appear

▶ **T A B L E 8.2** *ATPS.CFG Parameters (continued)*

PARAMETER	DESCRIPTION
–L	Includes the necessary Macintosh Laser Prep file in each print job
–N *number*	Specifies how many concurrent print jobs can print to an AppleTalk print spooler (1–50)
–O *spooler:zonename*	Specifies what the AppleTalk print spooler's name will be in the Chooser (its object name, which is the same as the queue name). If you include a zone name, the spooler appears in the specified zone of the internal network. If you omit the zone name, the spooler appears in the internal network's default zone
–T *type*	Specifies the NBP type of the printer. The default type is LaserWriter, so if you are using an ImageWriter, you must use this parameter (for example, "–T IMAGEWRITER")
–S	Specifies that you are using a PostScript printer (not necessary if you're using a LaserWriter)
–WB	(Without back end) Turns off the AppleTalk print server. PSERVER will service the queue instead
–WF	(Without front end) Turns off the AppleTalk print spooler so PC users can use the queue but Macintosh users cannot

SENDING PRINT JOBS TO AN APPLE PRINTER FROM A PC

In most situations, sending print jobs to an Apple printer from a PC workstation is the same as sending print jobs to any other type of printer. Users simply select the print queue to which they want to send print jobs.

If users have an application that supports network printing, they select the print queue from the application. If the application does not support network printing, they can specify the print queue by using the CAPTURE and NPRINT utilities, as explained in Chapter 6.

SENDING PRINT JOBS TO AN APPLE PRINTER FROM A MACINTOSH

The steps for sending a file from a Macintosh to a network print queue are the same as the steps for sending the file directly to the printer. To send files directly to an Apple printer, open the Chooser, select the printer icon (such as the LaserWriter icon), choose a zone if necessary, and select the Apple printer you want to use. Then print from your application, and the file is sent directly to the printer.

To send the file to a network print queue, open the Chooser and select a print queue (which is actually the AppleTalk print spooler) instead of a printer. Make sure the AppleTalk button in the Chooser is set to Active and turn off Background Printing. Then print the file from the application. The file is sent to the AppleTalk print spooler, then to the print queue, and finally to the printer. Meanwhile, you can continue your work at the Macintosh workstation.

Sending jobs to print queues is almost always more efficient because it leaves the workstation free for other tasks. In addition, if other users are sending print jobs to the same printer, the print queue manages the printing traffic and ensures that the jobs are printed in the correct order.

You can hide printers so that users will see only print queues in the Chooser. To hide a printer, use the –h parameter in the ATPS.CFG file. For example, to hide the LaserFast printer, which is located in the Graphics zone, type

```
"LASERFAST:GRAPHICS" -h
```

Troubleshooting Common Problems

If you're having trouble running Macintosh workstations on your NetWare network, you can use a diagnostic utility called ATCON.NLM to check on the AppleTalk network's condition. To use this module, type the following command at the file server's console:

```
LOAD ATCON
```

When this module loads, you can select one of the following seven options from the main menu:

- **Lookup and Echo Services:** Lets you verify that services are available on the AppleTalk network. You can look up all services, services of a particular type, or a service of a specified name. You can also use the Echo test to verify that a particular node is communicating on the network.

- **View AppleTalk Statistics:** Lets you see statistics about the AppleTalk router's receipt and delivery of packets.

- **View Logs:** Lets you display the system and volume error log files so you can read any messages received from the file server or from the NetWare for Macintosh loadable modules.

- **View Router Interfaces:** Lets you see the network numbers for the AppleTalk router's internal network and external networks.

- **View RTMP Table:** Lets you see the AppleTalk router's router table, which shows you the status of all other AppleTalk networks that this router can access.

- **View Stack Interface:** Displays the configuration (network number and zones list) of the AppleTalk router's internal network.

- **View Zones List:** Lists the AppleTalk zones that are available to the AppleTalk router.

After using ATCON, you may also need to check the following areas:

▸ Is the problem with a single workstation or several? If the problem is with several workstations, it may be caused by the network cabling or related hardware.

▸ Is the cable that connects the Macintosh workstation to the rest of the network functioning?

▸ Are all the cables correctly connected or terminated? Check for any loose connections and tighten them.

▸ Are the network boards and any other boards (video, and so on) seated firmly in their slots?

▸ Do any of the cable segments exceed the length limits for your type of networking hardware?

▸ Is the file server using the SNAP frame type (ETHERNET_SNAP, TOKEN-RING_SNAP, or FDDI_SNAP)? The server must use the SNAP frame type to work with AppleTalk.

▸ Is the network board configured correctly? Are the board settings conflicting with any other boards or printers attached to the workstation? Check the boards' documentation for instructions on avoiding conflicts with other boards.

▸ Does the LAN driver loaded on the workstation match the network board?

▸ Is AppleTalk bound to the LAN driver in the file server?

▸ Did you configure network numbers and zones for both the AppleTalk router's internal and external networks?

▸ If you did not specify a zone or zone list in the LOAD and BIND commands for the AppleTalk router, does an ATZONES.CFG file exist in SYS:SYSTEM?

- If you just installed or upgraded the workstation, did you follow the instructions in the documentation exactly? Check for missed steps, shortcuts that may have bypassed an important file, and so on.

- Is the workstation running on a Token-Ring network? If so, you may need to load ATTOKLLC.NLM on the file server. This module is necessary in some situations for running Macintosh workstations on a Token-Ring network. It is not copied to the server by default; you must copy it from the NW-MAC diskette (or the NetWare for Macintosh directory on the CD) to SYS:SYSTEM.

- If the image on the monitor's screen is rolling or bouncing, make sure the video cable isn't loose. Also make sure no other monitors are situated near the monitor; monitors in close proximity can cause interference with each other.

CHAPTER 9

NetWare 3.12
NLMs

In NetWare 3.12, two types of utilities can be executed at the file server (or from Remote Console). One type of file server utility is a NetWare Loadable Module (NLM). NLMs are modules you can load into the NetWare operating system and unload at any time. These modules add functionality to NetWare. The other type of utility is called a console utility (or console command). Console utilities are built in to the NetWare operating system.

This chapter lists the NLMs included with NetWare 3.12. Other companies also produce NLMs you can add to NetWare, such as database engines and backup systems, but those are not listed here. Console utilities are described in Chapter 10.

NetWare Loadable Modules

Four types of NLMs can be loaded onto the file server:

- **Disk drivers:** Have the extension .DSK. They load drivers to support the disk controllers installed in the file server.

- **LAN drivers:** Have the extension .LAN. They load LAN drivers for the network boards installed in the file server.

- **Name space modules:** Have the extension .NAM. They load name spaces so that the volume can handle the file system conventions supported by non-DOS operating systems (Macintosh, OS/2, and NFS).

- **NLM utilities:** Have the extension .NLM. They can be of many different types. NLMs can configure the server or let you load protocols, database engines, backup capabilities, UPS support, CD-ROM support, and so on.

You can use the MODULES console utility to see a list of all loadable modules that are already loaded on the file server. To use MODULES, type

```
MODULES
```

To load an NLM, type

```
LOAD module
```

substituting the name of the NLM for *module*. You do not need to include the file name extension.

To unload an NLM, type

```
UNLOAD module
```

Some modules depend on other NLMs already being loaded. Often, NLMs automatically load the modules they need if those modules aren't already loaded. Similarly, if you try to unload a module that has another NLM depending on it, that module won't unload; it will tell you which NLM is depending on it so you can unload that one first.

If you have multiple modules (which create their own system screens) loaded at once, you can switch console screens among the modules. There are two ways to switch between screens:

- ▶ Press Alt+Esc to switch through the activated modules' screens.

- ▶ Press Ctrl+Esc and select the number of the screen you want from the menu that appears.

LOADING DISK DRIVERS

To load a disk driver, use the following command format:

```
LOAD driver parameter parameter
```

For *driver,* substitute the file name of the disk driver. You do not need to include the file name's extension (.DSK). For *parameter,* substitute any pertinent values for items such as interrupts, DMA addresses, and so on. Each disk driver may have different parameters. See the manufacturer's documentation for the correct parameters to use. Common parameters are listed here:

PARAMETER	DESCRIPTION
DMA=*number*	Specifies a DMA (Direct Memory Access) channel
INT=*number*	Specifies an interrupt (in hex)
MEM=*number*	Specifies a memory address
PORT=*number*	Specifies an I/O port
SLOT=*number*	Specifies the slot in which the applicable board is installed

LOADING LAN DRIVERS

When you load a LAN driver, you load the software that allows the file server to send and receive packets on the network. After you load a LAN driver, you must use the BIND command to bind a protocol (such as IPX or AppleTalk) to the driver. (See Chapter 10 for information about the BIND command.)

To load a LAN driver, use the following command format:

```
LOAD driver parameter parameter
```

For *driver,* substitute the file name of the LAN driver. You do not need to include the file name's extension (.LAN). For *parameter,* substitute any pertinent values for items such as interrupts, DMA addresses, frame types, and so on. Each LAN driver may have different parameters. See the manufacturer's documentation for the correct parameters to use. Common parameters are listed here:

PARAMETER	DESCRIPTION
DMA=*number*	Specifies a DMA channel
FRAME=*name*	Specifies which frame type to use (Ethernet or Token-Ring only). Ethernet frame types: Ethernet_802.2 (default), Ethernet_802.3, Ethernet_II, Ethernet_SNAP. Token-Ring frame types: Token-Ring (default), Token-Ring_SNAP
INT=*number*	Specifies an interrupt (in hex)
LS=*number*	Specifies the number of 802.5 link stations for a Token-Ring driver
MEM=*number*	Specifies a memory address
NAME=*name*	Specifies a unique name for the board's configuration. Use this parameter to simplify the BIND command, which comes after the LOAD *LAN driver* command; you can bind a protocol to the board's name rather than having to specify the board's configuration again in the BIND command
NODE=*number*	Specifies a different node address than that set on the board
PORT=*number*	Specifies an I/O port
RETRIES=*number*	Specifies how many times the driver should try to resend a packet after the packet transmission has failed
SAPS=*number*	Specifies the number of 802.2 service access point stations for a Token-Ring driver

PARAMETER	DESCRIPTION
SLOT=*number*	Specifies which slot the applicable board is installed in
TBC=*number*	Specifies the transmit buffer count for a Token-Ring driver
TBZ=*number*	Specifies the transmit buffer size for a Token-Ring driver. (The default is the maximum size allowed by the operating system or the board.)

LOADING NAME SPACE MODULES

To allow a network volume to store non-DOS files and preserve their names (which can often be longer than DOS allows), you can add what's called a name space to the volume. To do this, you load a name space module and then type a command to tell the server the volume in which you want to store the name space.

To load a name space module, you use the command format

```
LOAD namespace
```

Replace *namespace* with the module name for the name space, such as MAC, OS2, or NFS. After you load the name space module, add the name space to a specific volume by typing the following console command:

```
ADD NAME SPACE namespace TO volume
```

For example, the following two commands load the Macintosh name space and add it to a volume named MINE:

```
LOAD MAC
ADD NAME SPACE MAC TO MINE
```

If the volume to which you're adding the name space is volume SYS, the name space module must be on the server's boot disk, and the LOAD *namespace* command must be in the server's STARTUP.NCF file. If the volume is not SYS, the name space module must be in SYS:SYSTEM, and the LOAD *namespace* command must be in the AUTOEXEC.NCF file. (If you are installing NetWare for Macintosh by using the Product Options menu in INSTALL.NLM, the installation procedure will automatically take care of putting the name space module in the correct directory and adding the load command to the appropriate .NCF file.)

The ADD NAME SPACE command doesn't have to be added to either .NCF file, because once you've added the name space to the volume by typing this command once at the console, the only way to remove it is to run VREPAIR.

NLMs in NetWare 3.12

The following sections describe the NLMs available in NetWare 3.12.

APPLETLK.NLM

APPLETLK.NLM is the main AppleTalk router and protocol stack, used with NetWare for Macintosh.

AFP.NLM

AFP.NLM (AppleTalk Filing Protocol 2.0) is the NetWare for Macintosh module that lets workstations running AppleShare workstation software work with NetWare's file services.

ATPS.NLM

ATPS.NLM (AppleTalk Print Services) is the NetWare for Macintosh module that makes AppleTalk and NetWare printing services work together. This allows Macintosh users to use NetWare print queues and lets NetWare print queues send jobs to AppleTalk printers.

ATCON.NLM

The network supervisor can use the ATCON.NLM (AppleTalk Console) NetWare for Macintosh module to see information about AppleTalk networks, the AppleTalk router, and the AppleTalk protocol stack.

ATTOKLLC.NLM

The ATTOKLLC.NLM NetWare for Macintosh module is necessary for running Macintosh workstations on a Token-Ring network. It is not copied to the server by default; to use it, you must copy it from the NW-MAC diskette (or the NetWare for Macintosh directory on the CD) to SYS:SYSTEM.

CDROM.NLM

The CDROM.NLM module lets you mount a CD-ROM as a volume on a NetWare network. After you've loaded CDROM.NLM, you can use the console commands in Table 9.1 to work with CD-ROMs.

CLIB.NLM

The CLIB.NLM module contains libraries and functions that many other modules require and have in common. Most dependent modules will automatically load CLIB if they need it.

EDIT.NLM

Use EDIT.NLM to edit text files on the server, such as STARTUP.NCF and AUTOEXEC.NCF. You can edit these or other text files on either the

►**T A B L E** 9.1 *CDROM.NLM Console Commands*

COMMAND	DESCRIPTION
CD HELP	Displays a help screen for using this module
CD DEVICE LIST	Lists the CD-ROM drives that are already connected to the file server and displays the volume labels and device numbers of the CD-ROMs in the CD-ROM drives
CD VOLUME LIST	Lists the volumes on each CD-ROM device and shows whether or not they are mounted
CD MOUNT *device volume*	Mounts a CD-ROM volume so it can be accessed by network users
CD DISMOUNT *device volume*	Dismounts a CD-ROM volume
CD DIR *device volume*	Lists the directories and files at the root of the CD-ROM volume
CD CHANGE *device volume*	Lets you remove the CD-ROM and replace it with another

server's DOS partition or the NetWare partition. After loading EDIT, you are prompted for the file to edit. Enter the directory path and file name for the file you want. If you prefer, you can specify a file name when you load EDIT. For example, to edit the AUTOEXEC.NCF file, type

```
LOAD EDIT SYS:SYSTEM\AUTOEXEC.NCF
```

After you've edited or created the file, press Esc to save and exit the file.

INSTALL.NLM

The INSTALL.NLM module is a menu-based utility that lets you install a new file server or modify the configuration of an existing one. The main INSTALL menu contains four options:

- ▶ **Disk Options:** Lets you add or replace hard disks, partition and format hard disks, set up or modify the Hot Fix redirection information, and mirror or duplex disks

- ▶ **Volume Options:** Lets you create, delete, rename, or increase the size of volumes

- ▶ **System Options:** Lets you copy SYSTEM and PUBLIC files and create or edit the STARTUP.NCF and AUTOEXEC.NCF files

- ▶ **Product Options:** Lets you install another product on the file server, such as NetWare for Macintosh or the online documentation files

IPXS.NLM

The IPXS.NLM module provides STREAMS-based IPX protocol services to other modules. IPXS must be used with three other NLMS, and the order in which all four are loaded is important. They should be loaded in the following order:

1 · STREAMS

2 · CLIB

3 · TLI

4 · IPXS

KEYB.NLM

The KEYB.NLM module lets you specify the type of keyboard being used on your file server. Keyboard layouts vary from country to country and from language to language. NetWare's default keyboard type is the type used in the United States with English, so if you are using a different keyboard layout, use KEYB to set the correct type of keyboard. To use KEYB, type

```
LOAD KEYB country
```

For *country*, substitute the name of the country in which your keyboard is used. To see a list of all supported countries, load KEYB without specifying any country.

MATHLIB.NLM

Use the MATHLIB.NLM module if a math coprocessor is installed in your computer. Math coprocessors are contained in all 486 computers and can be installed as a chip in 386 computers.

To use this module, you must also use two additional modules. The order in which all three are loaded is important. They should be loaded in the following order:

1 · STREAMS

2 · CLIB

3 · MATHLIB

MATHLIBC.NLM

Use the MATHLIBC.NLM module if your computer does not have a math coprocessor.

To use this module, you must also use two additional modules. The order in which all three are loaded is important. They should be loaded in the following order:

1 · STREAMS

2 · CLIB

3 · MATHLIBC

MONITOR.NLM

The MONITOR.NLM module allows you to track the perform-ance of your server and network. It also allows you to run a screen saver on the server and to lock the server's console so unauthorized users can't access it.

When you load MONITOR, there are three parameters you can use, in the format

```
LOAD MONITOR parameter
```

The three parameters are listed here:

PARAMETER	DESCRIPTION
ns	(No Screen Saver) Turns off the screen saver feature
nh	(No Help) Loads MONITOR without loading the help files, which take up memory you might want to preserve for something else
−p	(Processor Utilization) Provides the Processor Utilization option on the Available Options menu

On the initial screen that appears, the top window shows some com-mon statistics about the server. The bottom window lists several options. The options are explained in the following list:

▸ **Connection Information:** Shows information about specific workstations' connections, such as the number of open files and the number of physical record locks being used. This option also lets you clear a workstation connection from the server.

▸ **Disk Information:** Lets you see the server's hard disks and their volume segments, activate or deactivate disks, mount or dis-mount volumes, and lock or unlock removable media devices (such as tapes or CD-ROMs).

▶ **LAN Information:** Lists the LAN drivers and displays information about them.

▶ **System Module Information:** Lists the NLMs on the server and lets you display each module's name, size, and resource tags. Resource tags show the types of server resources the module is using, such as memory, event locks, and processes.

▶ **Lock File Server Console:** Lets you lock the server console so that any user who wants to use the server's keyboard must enter the correct password. Two passwords are acceptable: the SUPERVISOR password and the password that was entered when the console was locked.

▶ **File Open/Lock Activity:** Lets you display the current activity for a specific file. It shows you how many connections currently have the file open, how many have it open for writing, and so on. It also shows whether the file is locked.

▶ **Resource Utilization:** Displays statistics about the server's memory usage.

▶ **Process Utilization:** Appears only if you loaded MONITOR with the −p option. It shows you how the server's CPU is being used. To list the currently loaded processes and interrupts, press F3. The percentage listed in the Load column for each process shows the percentage of the CPU's time that process is using.

NLICLEAR.NLM

The NLICLEAR.NLM module periodically clears "not-logged-in" user connections from the server so you can reuse those connections. "Not-logged-in" user connections occur when the user establishes a connection with the server but doesn't actually log in, when a user logs out without logging in to another server, when the workstation client is not removed from memory, or if the user does not turn off the workstation after logging out of the network.

You can use three parameters with NLICLEAR, in the following format:

```
LOAD NLICLEAR parameter
```

The parameters are listed here:

PARAMETER	DESCRIPTION
NOTIFY	Displays a message on the server's screen whenever a connection is cleared
POLL=number	Sets the time NLICLEAR waits between checks for user connections. Default: 60 seconds. Range: 15 to 3600 seconds
CONN=number	Lets you tell NLICLEAR to check only workstation connections above a certain number. Workstation connections are numbered from 1 to the maximum number of allowable licensed connections. For example, on a 100-user version of NetWare, connection numbers will range from 1 to 100. If you set CONN=25 on a 100-user version, NLICLEAR will check only connection numbers 75 through 100

NMAGENT.NLM

The NMAGENT.NLM module lets LAN drivers register three types of resources that network management software can track. This module must be loaded before the LAN drivers are loaded. (In most cases, this module is automatically loaded.) The three tracked resources are

- ▸ Network management triggers
- ▸ Network management managers
- ▸ Network management objects

You can see these tracked resources in MONITOR.

NUT.NLM

The NUT.NLM module contains libraries and routines that Net-Ware 3.11 NLMs require. If you are using NetWare 3.11 NLMs, you must load this module. In most cases, NetWare 3.11 modules that require NUT.NLM will automatically load it.

NWSNUT.NLM

The NWSNUT.NLM module contains libraries and routines that Net-Ware 4 NLMs require. If you are using NetWare 4 NLMs, you must load this module. In most cases, NetWare 4 modules that require NWSNUT will automatically load it.

PSERVER.NLM

The PSERVER.NLM module loads the print server software on the file server. Before using this module, you must have used the PCONSOLE workstation utility to set up the printing environment. See Chapter 6 for more information. To load the print server, use this command format:

```
LOAD PSERVER name
```

REMOTE.NLM

The REMOTE.NLM module enables the Remote Console feature to be used with this file server. Once this module and the communication module (either RSPX.NLM or RS232.NLM) have been loaded, you can execute RCONSOLE or ACONSOLE from a workstation and turn that workstation into the file server's console.

When you load REMOTE, you must specify a password to be used at the workstation to gain access to the Remote Console. (The only other acceptable password is the SUPERVISOR password.) To load REMOTE and set the password, type

```
LOAD REMOTE password
```

ROUTE.NLM

The ROUTE.NLM module allows NetWare to send data through IBM bridges on a Token-Ring network using Source Routing. You load this module once for every Token-Ring board installed in the server. The format for loading this module is

```
LOAD ROUTE parameter
```

The parameters you can use are listed here:

PARAMETER	DESCRIPTION
BOARD=number	Specifies the board number if the Token-Ring driver was not the first LAN driver loaded (The first board is number 1.)
CLEAR	Clears the Source Routing table so it can be rebuilt

PARAMETER	DESCRIPTION
DEF	Prevents frames (packets) that have unknown destination addresses from being sent across Single Route IBM bridges. Without this parameter, frames with unknown addresses are forwarded as Single Route Broadcast frames. If this parameter is set, frames with unknown addresses are forwarded as All Routes Broadcast packets
GBR	Sends General Broadcast frames as All Routes Broadcast frames (instead of Single Route Broadcast frames)
MBR	Sends Multicast Broadcast frames as All Routes Broadcast frames (instead of Single Route Broadcast frames)
REMOVE=*number*	Deletes a node address (a 12-digit hex number) from the server's Source Routing table. Use this parameter if a bridge has gone down to force the server to determine a new route
RSP=*value*	Specifies how the server should respond to a request. Values: NR=Not Required (default: respond to all broadcast requests directly); AR (respond to broadcast requests with an All Routes Broadcast frame); and SR (respond to broadcast requests with a Single Route Broadcast frame)

PARAMETER	DESCRIPTION
TIME=*number*	Specifies how often the Source Routing table is updated. Updates a new route if the current route was not used within the specified time. Default: 03 seconds. Range: 03 to 255
UNLOAD	Removes source routing from a board. Use the board= parameter first and then this one to remove source routing from this board

RPL.NLM

The RPL.NLM module lets the file server allow diskless workstations to boot from the server instead of from a local hard or floppy disk.

RS232.NLM

The RS232.NLM module allows asynchronous communication (via modem) between a workstation running the asynchronous Remote Console utility (ACONSOLE) and the file server. REMOTE.NLM must also be loaded on the server for the workstation to be able to access the server.

To load RS232, use the following format:

```
LOAD RS232 port baud
```

Replace *port* with the communications port number (1 or 2) being used by the modem and *baud* with the modem's baud rate (speed).

RSPX.NLM

The RSPX.NLM module allows direct communication between a workstation running Remote Console (RCONSOLE) and the file server. REMOTE.NLM must also be loaded on the server for the workstation to be able to access the server. Use this module instead of RS232 if the workstation is directly connected to the file server's network (in other words, if you don't have to use a modem). There are no parameters with this module.

SBACKUP.NLM

The SBACKUP.NLM module lets you back up and restore data from the network. To use SBACKUP, a target service agent (TSA) must be loaded on the server or workstation you're trying to back up. To load this module, use the following format:

```
LOAD SBACKUP SIZE=number BUFFERS=number
```

For SIZE=, put the size of buffers (default: 64K; range: 16, 32, 64, 128, or 256). For BUFFERS=, put the number of buffers (default: 4; range: 2 to 10).

SPXCONFG.NLM

The SPXCONFG.NLM module lets you configure SPX. You can either load this module and select the values to set from a menu or put the load command in the AUTOEXEC.NCF file and include the values as parameters on the command line in that file. To specify these parameters in the AUTOEXEC.NCF file, use the following format:

```
LOAD SPXCONFG option=value option=value
```

To select the values from the SPXCONFG menu, load SPXCONFG with no parameters. The menu that appears shows each option and its current value. To change a value, select the option you want by typing the letter displayed next to it. The default and acceptable values for that option will then be displayed, and you can specify the value you want.

Table 9.2 shows the parameters you can choose from the menu and the parameters to use if you include the value in the AUTOEXEC.NCF file. In addition to the parameters listed in the table, there are two others you can specify on the command line:

PARAMETER	DESCRIPTION
H	Displays help screens for SPXCONFG
Q=1	(Quiet Mode) Prevents messages about changed values from being displayed

▶ T A B L E 9.2   *SPXCONFG Parameters*

OPTION	COMMAND-LINE PARAMETER
SPX Watchdog Abort timeout (in ticks)	A=*value*
SPX Watchdog Verify timeout (in ticks)	V=*value*
SPX Ack wait timeout (in ticks)	W=*value*
SPX Default Retry count	R=*value*
Maximum Concurrent SPX Sessions	S=*value*

SPXS.NLM

The SPXS.NLM module provides STREAMS-based SPX protocol services to other modules. SPXS must be used with three other NLMS, and the order in which all four are loaded is important. They should be loaded in the following order:

1 · STREAMS

2 · CLIB

3 · TLI

4 · SPXS

STREAMS.NLM

The STREAMS.NLM module provides STREAMS-based protocol services to other modules, and it must be loaded if you are using CLIB.NLM. (STREAMS must be loaded before CLIB. However, CLIB automatically loads STREAMS.)

TLI.NLM

The TLI.NLM module provides Transport Link Interface (TLI) communication services to other modules. TLI must be used with STREAMS, CLIB, and at least one protocol service, such as IPXS or SPXS, and the order in which the modules are loaded is important. They should be loaded in the following order:

1 · STREAMS

2 · CLIB

3 · TLI

4 · Protocol service module (IPXS, SPXS, and so on)

UPS.NLM

The UPS.NLM module allows an uninterruptible power supply (UPS) to communicate with the file server. To load this module, use the following format:

```
LOAD UPS TYPE=name PORT=number DISCHARGE=number RECHARGE=number
```

For the TYPE parameter, enter the type or name of the communication board being used by the UPS, such as stand-alone or mouse. For PORT, enter a hex number for the board's jumper setting. Table 9.3 shows the available board types and the allowable port numbers. (If you try STANDALONE and it doesn't work, try KEYCARD.)

▸**T A B L E** 9.3   *UPS Boards and Ports*

BOARD TYPE	PORTS
DCB (default)	346, 34E, 326, 32E, 286, 28E
ECDB	380, 388, 320, 328
KEYCARD	230, 238
MOUSE	No port required
STANDALONE	240, 231
OTHER	See manufacturer's documentation

VREPAIR.NLM

The VREPAIR.NLM module can repair minor problems with the volume, such as corrupted File Allocation Tables (FATs) or Directory Entry Tables. VREPAIR is also used to remove name spaces from a volume.

Each name space has a support module that VREPAIR can use. These modules are named V_*namespace*.NLM—for example, V_MAC.NAM. You should copy VREPAIR and these name space support modules to the DOS boot partition of the server so you can get to them if volume SYS has a problem.

VREPAIR will repair only dismounted volumes.

CHAPTER 10

NetWare 3.12
Console Utilities

In NetWare 3.12, console utilities (or console commands) are utilities that can be executed at the file server or from Remote Console. These utilities are a built-in part of the NetWare operating system. This chapter lists the console utilities included with NetWare 3.12.

Another type of file server utility is a NetWare Loadable Module (NLM). NLMs are modules that can be loaded into the NetWare operating system or unloaded at any time and that add functionality to NetWare. NLMs are listed in Chapter 9.

Console Utilities in NetWare 3.12

To execute a console utility, simply type the command at the server's keyboard (or through Remote Console).

The available console utilities are described in the following sections.

ABORT REMIRROR

The ABORT REMIRROR command stops the remirroring of logical disk partitions. To use this command, use the format

```
ABORT REMIRROR number
```

Replace *number* with the number of the logical partition you want to stop from remirroring.

ADD NAME SPACE

Use the ADD NAME SPACE command to add support for a non-DOS name space, such as Macintosh or OS/2, to a volume. You must have loaded the name space module (using the LOAD *namespace* command) before you can actually add the name space to the volume.

Once you've added name space support to a volume, you must run VREPAIR.NLM to remove it.

To use this command, use the format

```
ADD NAME SPACE name TO volume
```

Replace *name* with the name space module (such as MAC, OS2, or NFS) and replace *volume* with the name of the volume to which you are adding the name space.

To display the name spaces that are already loaded, just type

```
ADD NAME SPACE
```

BIND

Use the BIND command after you've loaded a LAN driver, to link (or "bind") a protocol, such as IPX or AppleTalk, to the LAN driver or board. If you have more than one board of the same type installed in the server, you will use the BIND command more than once. (See Chapter 9 for information about loading LAN drivers.)

Any configuration parameters (such as DMA or frame type) you specified when you loaded the LAN driver must also be added to the BIND command so the BIND command knows exactly which board you are binding the protocol to. Alternatively, in the LOAD command for the LAN driver, you can assign each LAN driver/board combination a name and then use that name in the BIND command. If you specify a name in this way, you don't need to specify board parameters.

The format for this command is

```
BIND protocol driver parameters
```

Replace *protocol* with the protocol, such as IPX or APPLETLK (for Apple-Talk). Replace *driver* with the LAN driver name, the name of the network board, or the name you assigned the driver/board combination when you loaded the LAN driver.

Replace *parameters,* if necessary, with the driver parameters and/or protocol drivers needed for your protocol or driver. The most common driver parameters are

PARAMETER	DESCRIPTION
DMA=*number*	Specifies a DMA channel
FRAME=*name*	Specifies which frame type to use (Ethernet or Token-Ring only). Ethernet frame types: Ethernet_802.2 (default), Ethernet_802.3, Ethernet_II, Ethernet_SNAP. Token-Ring frame types: Token-Ring (default), Token-Ring_SNAP
INT=*number*	Specifies an interrupt (in hex)
MEM=*number*	Specifies a memory address
PORT=*number*	Specifies an I/O port
SLOT=*number*	Specifies the slot in which the applicable board is installed

The protocol parameters depend on the protocol being bound. IPX has only one parameter:

PARAMETER	DESCRIPTION
NET=*number*	A unique network number for the network this board is running on. If two network boards are installed in a file server or if one board has two frame types loaded, the boards will have two different network numbers

The AppleTalk protocol has two protocol parameters:

PARAMETER	DESCRIPTION
NET=*number*	A unique network number for the network this board is running on. If two network boards are installed in a file server or if one board has two frame types loaded, the boards will have two different network numbers. On an extended AppleTalk network, this number may be specified as a range of numbers, such as 1–10 or 25–33
ZONE={"*name*"}	(Or -Z) Within the braces and quotation marks, which are required, list the zones assigned to the network. Nonextended AppleTalk networks can belong to only one zone. Extended AppleTalk networks can belong to more than one zone. To list more than one zone, separate each zone name with a comma, and enclose each zone name in quotation marks, (such as ZONE={"ZoneA","ZoneB","ZoneC"}). If you have more zones than will fit on one BIND command line, list the zones in a global file called ATZONES.CFG, load the AppleTalk router with the −Z option, and omit the ZONE= parameter .

For example, to bind IPX to an NE2000 network board, you might use the following commands to load the driver and then bind IPX to it:

```
LOAD NE2000 INT=2 PORT=300 FRAME=ETHERNET_SNAP NAME=SNAP-IPX
BIND IPX SNAP-IPX NET=111
```

To load another NE2000 driver and bind AppleTalk to it, you must first load the APPLETLK protocol loadable module and assign it its own internal network number and zones. Then you can bind APPLETLK to the LAN driver. For example, you might use the following commands:

```
LOAD APPLETLK NET=5 ZONE={"Office","Warehouse"}
LOAD NE2000 INT=2 PORT=300 FRAME=ETHERNET_SNAP NAME=SNAP-AT
BIND APPLETLK SNAP-AT NET=10-15 ZONE={"Office","Warehouse"}
```

BROADCAST

Use the BROADCAST command to send a message from the console to users on the network. Use the following command format:

```
BROADCAST "message" user
```

The message you specify can be up to 55 characters long, and it must be enclosed in quotation marks. For *user,* you can specify either a user-name or a connection number. To send a message to more than one user, separate each username or connection number with a space or comma. To send a message to all users, omit the *user* parameter entirely.

CLEAR STATION

Use the CLEAR STATION command when a workstation has crashed and cannot log out of the server and has left files open. This command closes all of the workstation's open files and removes the workstation's connection to the server. Use the following command format:

```
CLEAR STATION n
```

Replace the *n* with the workstation's connection number.

CLS

Use the CLS command to clear the screen of the file server. This command works the same way the DOS CLS command works on a workstation.

CONFIG

Use the CONFIG command to display the following configuration information about the file server and network:

- ▶ The server's name
- ▶ The server's internal network number
- ▶ The loaded LAN drivers
- ▶ Hardware settings for all installed network boards
- ▶ The node address assigned to each network board
- ▶ The protocol bound to each network board
- ▶ The network number for each network board
- ▶ The frame type for each network board
- ▶ The name assigned to each network board

DISABLE LOGIN

Use the DISABLE LOGIN command to prevent users from logging in to the server. Any users who are already logged in are not affected, but once those users log out, they will not be able to log back in. To allow users to log in again, use the command ENABLE LOGIN.

DISABLE TTS

Use the DISABLE TTS command to turn off TTS (Transaction Tracking System). To turn TTS back on, use the command ENABLE TTS.

DISKSET

Use the DISKSET command to install and configure Novell or ADIC external disk subsystems and place the configuration information on the host bus adapter's (or DCB's) EEPROM chip.

DISMOUNT

Use the DISMOUNT command to dismount a volume so users cannot access it. You must dismount a volume before repairing it, upgrading its disk drivers, and so on. Use the following command format:

```
DISMOUNT volume
```

Replace *volume* with the name of the volume you wish to dismount. To remount the volume, use the MOUNT command.

DISPLAY NETWORKS

Use the DISPLAY NETWORKS command to display a list of all the networks (identified by their network numbers). This command also shows how many hops away those networks are and the number of ticks ($\frac{1}{18}$ of a second) it takes for a packet to reach the network.

DISPLAY SERVERS

Use the DISPLAY SERVERS command to list all the file servers this server knows about and has recorded in its router table. This command also shows how many hops away those networks are.

DOWN

Use the DOWN command to bring down the file server cleanly before turning its power off. This command closes all open files, writes all data in the cache buffers to the disk, and so on, before shutting down the server. After using the DOWN command, you can use the

EXIT command to go to DOS and access files on the server's DOS partition, such as SERVER.EXE.

ENABLE LOGIN

Use the ENABLE LOGIN command to allow users to log in to the network after you've used the DISABLE LOGIN command.

ENABLE TTS

Use the ENABLE TTS command to turn TTS (Transaction Tracking System) back on after the server has disabled TTS or after you've used the DISABLE TTS command. The server automatically disables TTS if volume SYS gets full or if the server lacks enough memory to run TTS.

EXIT

Use the EXIT command to return to DOS after you've brought down the file server. If you have removed DOS from the server using the REMOVE DOS command before bringing down the server, the EXIT command will reboot the server instead of going to DOS.

LIST DEVICES

Use the LIST DEVICES command to list all the storage devices, such as tape drives, CD-ROM drives, and disk drives, that are attached to the file server.

MAGAZINE

Use the MAGAZINE command to tell the server you have inserted or removed a media magazine. (The server prompts you when it wants you to insert a new magazine during some activity.) Use the following command format:

```
MAGAZINE parameter
```

Replace *parameter* with one of the following:

PARAMETER	DESCRIPTION
INSERTED	Indicates that you have inserted the media magazine
NOT INSERTED	Indicates that you have not inserted the media magazine
REMOVED	Indicates that you have removed the media magazine
NOT REMOVED	Indicates that you have not removed the media magazine

MEDIA

Use the MEDIA command to tell the server you have inserted or removed a specified storage medium. (The server prompts you when it wants you to insert new media during some activity.) Use the following command format:

```
MEDIA parameter
```

Replace *parameter* with one of the following:

PARAMETER	DESCRIPTION
INSERTED	Indicates that you have inserted the specified medium
NOT INSERTED	Indicates that you have not inserted the specified medium
REMOVED	Indicates that you have removed the specified medium
NOT REMOVED	Indicates that you have not removed the specified medium

MEMORY

Use the MEMORY command to show how much of the server's installed memory the operating system can address.

MIRROR STATUS

Use the MIRROR STATUS command to list all the logical disk partitions and show their mirroring status. The following states are possible:

STATUS	DESCRIPTION
Being Remirrored	The partition is being synchronized with another and will soon be mirrored
Fully Synchronized	The partitions are mirrored and functioning correctly. Both partitions contain identical data
Not Mirrored	The partition has not been mirrored with any other partition
Orphaned State	The partition was mirrored with another, but this is no longer true. The integrity of the data in this partition is not ensured
Out of Synchronization	The two mirrored partitions do not have the same data; therefore, they are out of synchronization and need to be remirrored

MODULES

Use the MODULES command to list all the NetWare Loadable Modules (NLMs) currently loaded on this file server.

MOUNT

Use the MOUNT command to mount a volume so it can be accessed by network users. Use the command format

```
MOUNT volume
```

For *volume,* you can substitute a specific volume name, or you can specify ALL so that all available volumes are mounted.

NAME

Use the NAME command to display the name of the file server.

OFF

Use the OFF command to clear the file server console's screen. You can also use the command CLS.

PROTOCOL

Use the PROTOCOL command to list all the protocols that are currently registered on the file server or to register a new protocol. To list the current protocols, simply type

```
PROTOCOL
```

To register a new protocol (which should happen only in unusual cases, since most protocols register themselves automatically), use the format

```
PROTOCOL REGISTER protocol frame id#
```

Replace *protocol* with the name of the new protocol. Replace *frame* with the name of the frame type, and replace *id#* with the Protocol ID (PID) number assigned to the protocol. (This can usually be found in the manufacturer's documentation, although it may be called an Ethernet Type, E-Type, or SAP.)

REGISTER MEMORY

On microchannel and ISA (AT bus) computers, NetWare cannot automatically register memory above 16MB. Use the REGISTER MEMORY command to register memory above 16MB so NetWare can address it. (This command is not necessary for EISA computers because NetWare automatically registers memory above 16MB on EISA computers.)

Use the command format

```
REGISTER MEMORY start length
```

Replace *start* with the hex address of where the memory above 16MB begins. (In most cases this starting address is 16MB, or address 0x1000000.) Replace *length* with the hex length of the memory installed above 16MB. This number must be on an even paragraph boundary (a number divisible by 10h). The following table shows the start and length values for computers that begin addressing memory above 16MB:

TOTAL MEMORY INSTALLED (MB)	START ADDRESS (HEX)	LENGTH (HEX)
20	1000000	400000
24	1000000	800000
28	1000000	C00000
32	1000000	1000000
36	1000000	1400000
40	1000000	1800000

REMIRROR PARTITION

Use the REMIRROR PARTITION command to remirror a logical disk partition to its original mirrored partition. Use the command format

```
REMIRROR PARTITION number
```

Replace *number* with the number of the disk partition you want to remirror.

REMOVE DOS

Use the REMOVE DOS command to remove DOS from the server's memory so commands and files on the DOS partition cannot be accessed and to free up the memory that DOS was using. After DOS is removed, loadable modules located in the DOS partition cannot be loaded. Only loadable modules in network directories, such as SYS:SYSTEM, can be loaded.

RESET ROUTER

Use the RESET ROUTER command to rebuild a new router table for the server. The server updates its router table every two minutes anyway, adjusting it for any servers or routers that have gone down, but this command allows you to update the table faster, without having to wait two minutes.

SCAN FOR NEW DEVICES

Use the SCAN FOR NEW DEVICES command to have the server look for any new storage devices, such as CD-ROM drives or disk drives, that have been added since the last time the server was booted.

SEARCH

Use the SEARCH command to tell the server which directories to search when looking for loadable modules or .NCF files. If volume SYS is not mounted, the default search path is the DOS directory from which the file server booted. If volume SYS is mounted, the default search path is SYS:SYSTEM.

To see which search paths are already set and the order in which they are searched, type

```
SEARCH
```

To add a search path, type

```
SEARCH ADD path
```

Replace *path* with the directory or path you want the operating system to search, such as A:, C:, or SYS:PUBLIC\MODULES.

When you add a search path, it is searched last. If you want to specify that this path be searched in a different order, you can add a number to the command. For example, to search drive C first, before SYS:SYSTEM is searched, type

```
SEARCH ADD 1 C:
```

To delete a search drive, use the number of the drive (displayed when you just type SEARCH) in the following command:

```
SEARCH DEL number
```

SECURE CONSOLE

Use the SECURE CONSOLE command to prevent loadable modules from being loaded from anywhere but SYS:SYSTEM. If loadable modules can be loaded from other directories where users have more rights than SYS:SYSTEM, an intruder could create an NLM that breaches security and load that NLM from an unprotected directory.

SECURE CONSOLE also prevents intruders from accessing the OS debugger from the server's keyboard, and it removes DOS from the server so no one can get to the DOS partition and access data. In addition, it prevents anyone but the supervisor from changing the server's date and time (which affects accounting and auditing features).

To disable this command, you must reboot the file server.

SEND

Use the SEND command to send a message from the console to users on the network. Use the following command format:

```
SEND "message" user
```

The message you specify can be up to 55 characters long, and it must be enclosed in quotation marks. For *user,* you can specify either a user name or a connection number. To send a message to more than one user, separate each user name or connection number with a space or comma. To send a message to all users, omit the *user* parameter entirely.

SET

Use the SET command to display and change many configuration parameters for the operating system. For a list of all the SET parameters and values, see Chapter 2.

SET TIME

Use the SET TIME command to set the date, the time, or both for the file server. Use the following command format:

```
SET TIME month/day/year hour:minute:second
```

After the time, you can specify AM or PM, or the operating system will supply it for you based on usual working hours.

SET TIMEZONE

Use the SET TIMEZONE command to specify the time zone you're in so CLIB and the programs that use CLIB will be set correctly. Use the following command format:

```
SET TIMEZONE zone hours daylight
```

Replace *zone* with the three-letter abbreviation for your time zone (such as EST, CST, MST, or PST). Replace *hours* with the number of hours you are ahead of or behind Greenwich Mean Time (or Universal Coordinated Time). If you are currently on daylight savings time, add the three-letter abbreviation for the daylight time. If you are on standard time, you do not need to enter anything for *daylight*.

The default time zone is Eastern Daylight Savings Time, which is five hours earlier than Greenwich Mean Time. This is written as EST5EDT. If you live east of London (Greenwich), you add a plus sign to the beginning of the *hours* parameter.

For example, to set the time zone to Eastern Standard Time, type

```
SET TIMEZONE EST5
```

To set the time zone to Pacific Daylight Savings Time, type

```
SET TIMEZONE PST8PDT
```

To set the time zone to Germany's standard time (Germany is one hour ahead of Greenwich Mean Time), type

```
SET TIMEZONE MEZ+1
```

SPEED

Use the SPEED command to display the speed rating of the file server.

SPOOL

Use the SPOOL command to display or create a spooler mapping so applications that print to printer numbers will direct their print jobs to print queues instead. This command also specifies the default print queue for NPRINT and CAPTURE.

Use the command format

```
SPOOL n TO queue
```

Replace *n* with the printer number (which will become the spooler number), and replace *queue* with the name of the print queue to which you want that printer number spooled.

TIME

Use the TIME command to display the file server's current date and time. To change the date and time, use the SET TIME command instead.

TRACK OFF

Use the TRACK OFF command to turn off the router table display being shown by the TRACK ON command.

TRACK ON

Use the TRACK ON command to make the server's router display all incoming and outgoing server and network advertising packets on the file server's screen. This display allows you to see the advertising traffic that servers and routers send to keep track of the network routers.

UNBIND

Use the UNBIND command to remove a protocol, such as IPX or Apple-Talk, from a LAN driver or board. If you want to unbind more than one board of the same type installed in the server, you must use the UNBIND command separately for each one.

Any configuration parameters (such as DMA or frame type) you specified when you loaded the LAN driver can also be added to the UNBIND command so the UNBIND command knows exactly which board you are unbinding the protocol from. If you don't specify these parameters, you are prompted for the board you want. Alternatively, in the LOAD command for the LAN driver, you can assign each LAN driver/board combination a name, and then you can use that name in the UNBIND command. If you specify a name in this way, you don't need to specify board parameters.

The format for this command is

```
UNBIND protocol FROM driver parameters
```

Replace *protocol* with the protocol, such as IPX or AppleTalk. Replace *driver* with the LAN driver name, the name of the network board, or the name you assigned the driver/board combination when you loaded the LAN driver.

Replace *parameters*, if necessary, with the driver parameters you originally specified when you loaded the driver. The most common driver parameters are

PARAMETER	DESCRIPTION
DMA=*number*	Specifies a DMA channel
INT=*number*	Specifies an interrupt (in hex)
MEM=*number*	Specifies a memory address
PORT=*number*	Specifies an I/O port
SLOT=*number*	Specifies the slot in which the applicable board is installed

UPS STATUS

Use the UPS STATUS command to check the status of the UPS (Uninterruptible Power Supply) attached to the file server. This command displays the following types of information:

- ▸ The power being used (commercial or battery)

- ▸ The discharge time requested/remaining (which shows the estimate of how long the server can run safely on the UPS battery and the amount of time remaining if the server is currently running on battery power)

- ▸ The battery's status (recharged, low, or being recharged)

- ▸ The recharge time requested/remaining (which shows the estimate of the total time required to recharge the battery fully and the amount of time needed to recharge the battery in its current state)

- ▸ Current network power status (normal, server down, or server going down in the displayed number of minutes)

This command displays information only about the UPS. To make the file server recognize the UPS hardware, you must load the UPS.NLM loadable module. To change the amount of time you want the UPS to discharge and recharge, use the UPS TIME command.

UPS TIME

Use the UPS TIME command to change the amount of time the UPS should take to discharge and recharge. The discharge time is the length of time the file server will run on the UPS's battery if commercial power goes out. The recharge time is the time needed to recharge the battery after the file server has been running on the UPS's battery.

The manufacturer's documentation should have recommendations for these times.

To set the discharge and recharge times, use the command format

```
UPS TIME DISCHARGE=minutes RECHARGE=minutes
```

Alternatively, you can just type

```
UPS TIME
```

and answer the prompts for the discharge and recharge time.

VERSION

Use the VERSION command to display the version of NetWare running on the file server.

VOLUMES

Use the VOLUMES command to list the volumes that are currently mounted on the file server. This command also displays the name spaces supported by each volume.

CHAPTER 11

NetWare 3.12
Workstation Utilities

NetWare 3.12 provides many utilities you can use from a workstation to control, view, or change different aspects of a network. This chapter lists these workstation utilities.

Types of Workstation Utilities

Some workstation utilities are menu utilities, which means that when you execute the utility, a menu appears from which you can select options. Other workstation utilities are command-line utilities, which means you simply type a command, possibly with some parameters, at the DOS prompt, and the utility executes.

Some utilities allow you to do different tasks depending on whether or not you have Supervisor rights. For example, the SYSCON utility allows the Supervisor to create new users, modify the system login script, and set accounting features, but ordinary users can use SYSCON only to view and modify some of their own information, not that of other users.

All of the NetWare 3.12 workstation utilities are listed in the following sections.

ACONSOLE

Use the ACONSOLE utility to start a Remote Console session on a workstation that is connected to the file server across asynchronous telephone lines, via a modem. By running Remote Console you can turn your workstation into the file server's keyboard and monitor.

To start a Remote Console session on a workstation that is directly connected to the file server's cabling system, use RCONSOLE instead.

To use ACONSOLE, two NLMs must already be loaded on the file server: RS232.NLM and REMOTE.NLM.

To execute ACONSOLE, type

ACONSOLE

You are prompted for the modem's telephone number and baud rate, as well as for the server to which you want to connect.

After you've started a Remote Console session with ACONSOLE, you can work with the console as follows:

- To access Remote Console's Available Options menu, press the asterisk (*) key on the number pad of your keyboard.

- To move between active file server screens, such as between MONITOR and the console prompt, press the minus (−) and plus (+) keys. Note that these keys do not work in the Available Options menu.

- To run a server utility, go to the console prompt and type the server utility command.

- To exit Remote Console, select Available Options ➤ End Remote Session with Server.

ALLOW

Use the ALLOW utility to see or change a file or directory's Inherited Rights Mask. Use the command format

```
ALLOW path rights
```

Replace *path* with the directory path or file whose Inherited Rights Mask you want to see.

If you do not specify any *rights*, ALLOW displays the current trustee rights allowed by the Inherited Rights Mask. To change the rights allowed in the Mask, you list the rights you want to grant. (Use the abbreviation for the right, as shown in the following list.) To list several rights, separate each one with a space.

RIGHT	DESCRIPTION
ALL	Allows users to inherit all eight rights
N	(Nothing) Prevents any rights from being inherited, except the Supervisory right, which can't be overridden
S	(Supervisory) Allows users to inherit the Supervisory right
R	(Read) Allows users to inherit the Read right
W	(Write) Allows users to inherit the Write right
C	(Create) Allows users to inherit the Create right
E	(Erase) Allows users to inherit the Erase right
M	(Modify) Allows users to inherit the Modify right
FS	(File Scan) Allows users to inherit the File Scan right
A	(Access Control) Allows users to inherit the Access Control right

For more information about trustee rights, see Chapter 4.

ATOTAL

Use the ATOTAL utility to total the usage numbers for the accounting feature if it has been activated on your file server.

When you use this utility, you will probably find it easier to redirect the utility's output to a file than to just watch it scroll by on the screen. To do this, use the command

```
ATOTAL > filename
```

Replace *filename* with any file name you choose. The output is then saved as a text file, with the name you specified. You can print the file using any word processor or text editor.

ATTACH

Use the ATTACH utility to connect to additional file servers after you've already logged in to one. The ATTACH utility gives you a connection to the server and lets you access that server's resources, but it doesn't execute a login script to redefine your workstation's environment.

To attach to a server, use the command format

```
ATTACH server/username
```

Replace *server* with the name of the server to which you want to connect, and replace *username* with the user's login name.

There is a login script command, also called ATTACH, that allows users to automatically attach to other servers during the login process.

BINDFIX

Use the BINDFIX utility to repair structure problems in the NetWare bindery (the database of information about network objects, such as servers and users). As it repairs the bindery, BINDFIX creates new versions of the NET$OBJ.SYS, NET$PROP.SYS, and NET$VAL.SYS files and renames the originals with an .OLD extension.

The following types of problems usually indicate that you should run BINDFIX:

- ▸ A user's password can't be changed.

- ▸ A user's name can't be changed or deleted.

- A user's trustee rights can't be changed. (This may also indicate that you should run VREPAIR.)

- The file server displays error messages about the bindery.

- The error message "unknown server" appears when you are print-spooling to the default server.

If the repaired bindery does not fix the problem and you have a backup copy of the .OLD files, copy those .OLD files to SYS:SYSTEM. Then you can restore the original version of the bindery by running the BINDREST utility.

When BINDFIX is running, users who are logged in will not be affected, except that they will not be able to change trustee assignments or recalculate their effective rights. New users cannot log in until after BINDFIX is finished. For this reason you may want to run BINDFIX after work hours.

BINDREST

Use the BINDREST utility to restore a bindery to the state it was originally in before you ran the BINDFIX utility. BINDREST restores the original bindery by closing the current bindery, searching for bindery files with the .OLD extension, renaming those files with .SYS extensions, and then reopening the bindery.

CAPTURE

Use the CAPTURE utility to redirect a workstation's LPT printer port to a print queue instead of a locally attached printer. That way, print jobs will be sent to a network print queue. Use the following command format:

```
CAPTURE parameters
```

Replace *parameters* with any of the following:

PARAMETER	DESCRIPTION
A	(Auto Endcap) Sends the data, such as multiple screen shots, to the printer when you exit or enter an application. This parameter is enabled by default
B=*name*	(Banner) Specifies the text (12-character limit) that should appear on the lower part of a banner page. Default: Your login name and the print job's file name
C=*number*	(Copies) Specifies how many copies of the file to print (up to 999). Default: 1
CR=*path*	(Create) Specifies a directory path and file in which to store the data instead of sending it to a printer. Replace *path* with the full path to the directory and file name
F=*form*	(Form) Specifies which form type (paper) to print the job on. Replace *form* with the name or number of the form defined in the PRINTDEF utility. Default: 0
FF	(FormFeed) Forces a form feed at the end of your print job, allowing the next print job to start at the beginning of the next page. Use this option only if your application doesn't already force a form feed, or an extra blank page will be fed through the printer

PARAMETER	DESCRIPTION
J=*name*	(Job Configuration) Specifies which print job configuration to use. Replace *name* with the name of the print job configuration defined in the PRINTCON utility. If you run CAPTURE with no parameters, the default print job configuration is used. You define the default configuration in PRINTCON
K	(Keep) Specifies that the file server keep all data from your workstation in case your workstation loses its connection (hangs, loses power, and so on). The server will send the data to the printer if it detects that your workstation is gone. Use this parameter if you will be capturing data over a period of time and don't want to risk losing any captured data before you send the data to the printer
L=*number*	(Local) Specifies which logical LPT port to capture (1, 2, or 3). Default: 1
NA	(No Auto Endcap) Prevents data from being sent to a printer when you enter or exit a file
NAM=*name*	(Name) Specifies the text (12-character limit) that should appear on the upper part of a banner page. Default: Your login name
NB	(No Banner) Prevents a banner page from being printed
NFF	(No FormFeed) Disables form feed at the printer

PARAMETER	DESCRIPTION
NONOTI	(No Notify) Prevents a message from appearing that tells you your data has been printed. You need to use this parameter only if NOTI is turned on in the print job configuration and you want to override it. By default, NONOTI is enabled
NOTI	(Notify) Makes a message appear at the bottom of your screen when your data has been printed. By default, NOTI is disabled
NT	(No Tabs) Allows the application's print formatter to determine how many spaces are in a tab stop. Use this option only if your application has a print formatter and you have problems printing graphics or the format of your printout is not as you expected
Q=*name*	(Queue) Specifies which print queue to send the print job to. If you do not specify a queue or a default print job configuration but you have used the SPOOL console command to map Spooler 0 to a queue, the default will be Spooler 0's queue
S=*name*	(Server) Specifies which file server to send the print job to. Default: The default file server
SH	(Show) Displays the currently captured ports
T=*number*	(Tabs) Specifies the number of spaces that should be in each tab stop. Use this parameter only with applications that do not have a print formatter. Default: 8
TI=*number*	(Timeout) Specifies the number of seconds to wait before printing (instead of waiting for you to exit the application). Default: 0 (timeout disabled)

To place a CAPTURE command in a login script, precede the CAPTURE command with a # symbol, such as

```
#CAPTURE L=1 Q=Queue1 TI=5 NB
```

CASTOFF

Use the CASTOFF utility to prevent messages being sent from other workstations or the server from appearing on your workstation. To block messages from other workstations but allow messages from the file server, type

```
CASTOFF
```

To block messages from the file server and all workstations, type

```
CASTOFF ALL
```

To make it so you can receive messages again, use CASTON.

CASTON

Use the CASTON utility to allow your workstation to receive messages from other workstations and the file server. You need to use this command only if you've executed the CASTOFF command.

CHKDIR

Use the CHKDIR utility to display storage information for volumes and directories. Use the command format

```
CHKDIR path
```

Replace *path* with the path for the volume or directory whose information you want to display. This utility displays the following types of information for the volume and directories you specify:

▸ The maximum disk space

▸ The amount of disk space currently in use

▸ The amount of disk space still available

CHKVOL

Use the CHKVOL utility to display information about how the disk space on a volume is being used. Use the command format

```
CHKVOL path
```

Replace *path* with the path for the volume whose information you want to display. This utility displays the following types of information for the volume you specify:

▸ The total disk space on the volume

▸ The disk space currently being used by all files

▸ The disk space being used by deleted files (which are kept in a salvageable state until they are purged)

▸ The disk space available from those deleted files if you purge them

▸ The disk space that is still available on the volume

▸ The disk space available to you on this volume, assuming you have enough trustee rights to use this volume

COLORPAL

Use the COLORPAL utility to change the colors of the menus in menu utilities. You need to use this utility only if you have a computer that runs a monochrome monitor from a composite color adapter, such as a Compaq or an AT&T 6300 computer. Those computers may have trouble displaying the NetWare menu utilities in the default colors. (You can change the colors of menus for other computers, as well, but it isn't necessary, and it could create more problems than it's worth if you end up with colors that make the screens hard to read.)

To change the colors for all color monitors on the network, run COLORPAL from the SYS:PUBLIC directory. If you want to change the colors for your workstation only, copy COLORPAL to a different directory (such as your home directory) and run it from there instead.

Once you are running COLORPAL, you can select the colors in which you want aspects of the menus to be displayed. Each color scheme is called a palette.

DOSGEN

Use the DOSGEN utility to allow diskless workstations to boot DOS from the file server instead of from a local disk. To use DOSGEN, you create a DOS boot diskette that can be used to boot the workstation to DOS and load the NetWare client software, up to the point where the network drive appears (F:\LOGIN). DOSGEN then creates an image file from this diskette that can be used by a diskless workstation. The image file is called NET$DOS.SYS and is stored in SYS:LOGIN.

DSPACE

Use the DSPACE utility to limit the amount of disk space that can be used by a directory or a user.

To limit the amount of disk space that can be used for a given directory, select the Directory Restictions option from DSPACE's main menu. Enter the path to the desired directory, or press the Ins key to choose the path from a menu. Then specify the number of kilobytes the directory should use.

To limit the amount of disk space a user can use, select User Restrictions from the main menu, select the user from the list that appears, and then select the volume whose space you want to limit for the user. Then change the Limit Space option to Yes and enter the number of kilobytes the user can use.

ENDCAP

Use the ENDCAP utility to stop redirecting (capturing) the workstation's LPT printer ports to a print queue. Use the command format

```
ENDCAP parameters
```

Replace *parameters* with one of the following:

PARAMETER	DESCRIPTION
L=*number*	(Local) Specifies which LPT port to stop capturing (1, 2, or 3)
ALL	Ends the capture for all LPT ports on the workstation
C	(Cancel) Stops the capture and discards the data that was being stored without printing it. You can use this parameter in conjunction with the other two parameters, such as ENDCAP C ALL or ENDCAP C L=2

FCONSOLE

Use the FCONSOLE utility to display and change the status of the file server, display information about user connections, and broadcast messages to network users. Only users with Supervisor rights can use most of the features of this utility.

This menu utility lets you select from the following options:

- **Broadcast Console Message:** Lets you send messages to all other network users who are logged in or attached to the server.

- **Change Current File Server:** Lets you change to a different file server to see that server's information. To select a server that isn't in the current list of servers you're logged in to, press the Ins key and choose a server. Then enter your user name and password.

- **Connection Information:** Lets you select a user and view information about that user's current connection to the file server. It also lets you send a message to that user.

- **Down File Server:** Lets you cleanly shut down the file server from a workstation, closing all open files, flushing cache buffers to disk, and so on.

- **Status:** Displays the server's date and time, shows whether users can log in, and shows whether TTS is enabled. You can also change this information.

- **Version Information:** Displays the version of NetWare that is running on the file server.

FILER

Use the FILER utility to work with volume, directory, and file information and to display and change directory and file security. You can use the following options of this menu utility:

- **Current Directory Information:** Lets you see and change the following information about the current directory: its owner, its creation date and time, its attributes, its Inherited Rights Mask, the trustees who have rights to it, and your current effective rights in it.

- ▸ **Directory Contents:** Lets you work with many different types of information about network directories. For instance, you can copy files and whole directory structures, create or delete subdirectories, see who has rights to a directory, change the Inherited Rights Mask, specify whether Hidden and System files can be viewed, and so on.

- ▸ **Select Current Directory:** Lets you change your current directory path to see a different directory's information.

- ▸ **Set Filer Options:** Lets you specify how FILER operates on files and directories. For example, you can specify whether or not it asks you to confirm deletions, copies, and overwrites. In addition, you can tell it whether or not to preserve file attributes, and you can specify file name patterns (using wildcard characters) to search for or to exclude from searches.

- ▸ **Volume Information:** Lets you see information about the volume on which your current directory is located. You can see the server name, the volume name, the volume type (fixed or removable), the volume's maximum and available disk space, and the volume's maximum and available number of directory entries.

FLAG

Use the FLAG utility to display and change the file attributes assigned to files. Use the command format

```
FLAG path attributes
```

Replace *path* with the directory path and file name of the file whose attributes you want to see.

If you want to change the file's attributes, replace *attributes* with the attributes you want to assign to the file. The following attributes (and options) are available.

ATTRIBUTE	DESCRIPTION
ALL	Assigns all attributes to the file
N	(Normal) Flags the file Read Write, which is the default for most files
SUB	(Subdirectory) Displays or changes the attributes for files in subdirectories
Ro/Rw	Read Only/Read Write (These attributes toggle with each other.)
S	Shareable
A	Archive Needed
X	Execute Only (Because this attribute can never be removed, even by the Supervisor, it's a good idea to not use this. Use Read Only instead.)
H	Hidden
Sy	System
T	Transactional
P	Purge
Ra	Read Audit (not used)
Wa	Write Audit (not used)
CI	Copy Inhibit
DI	Delete Inhibit
RI	Rename Inhibit

To replace the file's existing attributes with the ones you specify, just list the abbreviations of the attributes you want, separated by spaces. For example, type

```
FLAG MYFILE A Ro S
```

To add attributes to the ones the file already has, use a plus sign. For example, to add the Purge attribute to the MYFILE file in the preceding example, type

```
FLAG MYFILE +P
```

To delete an attribute from the file but leave the rest of the attributes intact, use a minus sign. For example, to delete the Ro attribute from MYFILE, type

```
FLAG MYFILE -Ro
```

You can delete and add attributes in the same command. For example, the following command adds the Ro attribute and deletes the A and S attributes:

```
FLAG MYFILE +Ro -A S
```

For more information about file attributes, see Chapter 4. To change the attributes of a directory, see FLAGDIR.

FLAGDIR

Use the FLAGDIR utility to display and change the directory attributes assigned to a directory. Use the command format

```
FLAGDIR path attributes
```

Replace *path* with the directory path and name of the directory whose attributes you want to see.

If you want to change the directory's attributes, replace *attributes* with the attributes you want to assign. The following attributes are available:

ATTRIBUTE	DESCRIPTION
N	(Normal) Removes all attributes from the directory, which is the default for most directories
Sy	System
H	Hidden
DI	Delete Inhibit
P	Purge
RI	Rename Inhibit

To replace the directory's existing attributes with the ones you specify, just list the abbreviations of the attributes you want, separated by spaces. To add or delete attributes from the existing ones, use the plus and minus signs as explained in the description of the FLAG utility.

For more information about directory attributes, see Chapter 4. To change the attributes of a file, see FLAG.

GRANT

Use the GRANT utility to assign trustee rights to users. Use the command format

```
GRANT rights path TO name /parameters
```

Replace *rights* with the list of rights you want to explain. Use the abbreviation for the right, and separate each one with a space.

Replace *path* with the directory path and name of the file or directory for which you are assigning rights.

Replace *name* with the name of the user or group to whom you are granting rights. (If a user and a group have identical names, use the word USER or GROUP in front of the name, such as USER BOB and GROUP BOB.)

Replace */parameters* with either /S for subdirectories or /F for files (the slash is necessary).

The available rights are

RIGHT	DESCRIPTION
ALL	Grants all eight rights to the user or group
No Rights	Revokes all trustee rights for the user or group
S	Supervisory
R	Read
W	Write
C	Create
E	Erase
M	Modify
FS	File Scan
A	Access Control

For more information about trustee rights, see Chapter 4.

LISTDIR

Use the LISTDIR utility to see information about the subdirectories in a directory. Use the command format

```
LISTDIR path /parameters
```

Replace *path* with the directory path for the directory whose information you want to see. If you don't include any parameters, a list of the directory's subdirectories is displayed. To see specific information about the subdirectories, replace */parameters* with any of the following (the slash is necessary):

/Rights	Displays the Inherited Rights Mask of all subdirectories in the directory
/Effective Rights	Displays your effective rights in all subdirectories in the directory
/Date (or /Time)	Both of these parameters display the date and time each subdirectory in the directory was created
/Subdirectories	Displays this directory's subdirectories and all their subdirectories
/All	Displays all the information from the other four parameters

LOGIN

Use the LOGIN utility to log in to a file server. LOGIN executes both the system login script and a user login script, if one is available. If a user login script doesn't exist, LOGIN executes its own default login script, which contains a few basic drive mappings to NetWare login directories. Use the command format

```
LOGIN server/user
```

Replace *server* with the name of the file server to which you want to log in. Replace *user* with the login name you are using.

Every time you log in to a new file server using LOGIN, you are automatically logged out of the original server, and a login script for the new server is executed. To attach to additional file servers without logging out of the first file server and to avoid executing additional login scripts, use the ATTACH utility instead.

LOGOUT

Use the LOGOUT utility to log out of a network. To log out of all file servers you're attached to, type

```
LOGOUT
```

To log out of a single file server while retaining your connection to others, type

```
LOGOUT server
```

Replace *server* with the name of the server from which you want to log out.

MAKEUSER

The MAKEUSER utility is useful for creating and deleting numerous user accounts or objects on a frequent basis. There are two versions of this utility: a menu version and a command-line version. With the menu version, you create a USR file, which contains the information necessary to create users, assign them rights and restrictions, or delete existing users. After you create the USR file, you can process it using either the menu or the command-line version of MAKEUSER.

To process a USR file with the menu version of MAKEUSER, select Process USR File from the main menu. To process a USR file using the command-line version, type

```
MAKEUSER filename
```

Replace *filename* with the name of the USR file.

When you create the USR file, you use keywords to define information for the users. Each keyword must be on its own line in the file. All keywords except #CREATE and #DELETE are optional, and any keywords you want to apply to specific users must precede the #CREATE or #DELETE keyword. The keywords you can use in the USR file are

KEYWORD	DESCRIPTION
#ACCOUNT EXPIRATION *month day year*	Specifies when users' accounts expire
#ACCOUNTING *balance, lowlimit*	Assigns an account balance and low balance limit for the users you create (Accounting must be installed on the file server for this keyword to work.)
#CLEAR	Begins a new set of keywords in the same USR file. Previous keywords in the file do not apply to the rest of the file (same as #RESET)
#CONNECTIONS *number*	Specifies the maximum number of simultaneous connections each user can have to a server
#CREATE *username; fullname;password;group; directory rights*	Creates the user and specifies other options for the user. The *username* is mandatory; all other options in this keyword command are optional. If you specify some but not all options, indicate missing ones with a double semicolon(;;). Separate multiple group names with a comma, and separate multiple directory paths and their rights with a comma. If the keyword goes beyond a single line, use a plus sign after the last variable in a line to indicate that the next line is part of the same command

KEYWORD	DESCRIPTION
#DELETE *username*	Deletes the user specified in *username*
#GROUPS *groupname*	Assigns users to groups (which must have already been created using SYSCON)
#HOME_DIRECTORY *path*	Assigns or deletes a home directory when creating or deleting a user
#LOGIN_SCRIPT *path*	Specifies the location of a file that contains login script commands that should be copied into the login script for each user
#MAX_DISK_SPACE *volume, number*	Specifies the maximum number of 4K disk blocks each user can use on the volume. Default: unlimited
#NO_HOME_DIREC-TORY	Specifies that a home directory should not be created for the user
#PASSWORD_LENGTH *length*	Specifies the minimum length for users' passwords (Use #PASSWORD_RE-QUIRED before using this keyword.)
#PASSWORD_PERIOD *days*	Specifies how many days before passwords expire (Use #PASSWORD_RE-QUIRED before using this keyword.)
#PASSWORD_RE-QUIRED	Requires users to have a password
#PURGE_USER_DIREC-TORY	Deletes any subdirectories owned by the user when the user is deleted
#REM	Allows you to write comments that aren't processed in the USR file

KEYWORD	DESCRIPTION
#RESET	Begins a new set of keywords in the same USR file. Previous keywords in the file do not apply to the rest of the file (same as #CLEAR)
#RESTRICTED_TIME *day, start, end*	Specifies times in a day that new users cannot log in to the file server. To specify times for multiple days, place a semicolon (;) at the beginning of each new *day*
#STATIONS *network, station*	Specifies the physical workstations from which a user can log in to the file server. To specify multiple stations, separate them with a semicolon (;)
#UNIQUE_PASSWORD	Prevents users from reusing any of their last eight passwords (Use #PASSWORD_REQUIRED before using this keyword.)

MAP

Use the MAP utility to map drive letters to network directories. You can also put MAP commands in a login script to ensure that those drive mappings will automatically be set up for your users every time they log in.

To map drives to network directories, use the command format

```
MAP letter:=path
```

For example, to map drive F to the VOL1:USERS\MARY directory, type

```
MAP F:=VOL1:USERS\MARY
```

To map a search drive, use a number preceded by an "S" instead of a drive letter. The system will automatically assign the search drive a letter. Also, include the word "INS" to insert the mapping into the workstation's DOS path environment instead of overwriting whichever path was already established. For example, to map your first search drive to the PUBLIC directory, type

```
MAP INS S1:=SYS:PUBLIC
```

Some applications require that they be installed at the root of the volume. If you would rather install the application in a subdirectory, you can use MAP to map a fake root to the subdirectory that contains the application.

For example, to map a fake root (and a search drive) to a directory called JOBMAKER, you might type

```
MAP ROOT S16:=VOL1:APPS\JOBMAKER
```

For more information about mapping drives, search drives, fake roots, and using drive mappings in login scripts, see Chapter 5.

NCOPY

Use the NCOPY utility to copy files. It is more reliable than DOS's COPY command when copying files on a network, and it preserves file attributes and name space information. Use the command format

```
NCOPY sourcefile destinationfile /parameter
```

For example, to copy the file TRIP-RPT.TXT from drive F to drive G and rename it TRIP-RPT.OLD, type

```
NCOPY F:TRIP-RPT.TXT G:TRIP-RPT.OLD
```

If you want the file to retain the same name in the new directory as it had in the original directory, you can eliminate the destination file name and just specify the destination directory. For example, type

```
NCOPY F:TRIP-RPT.TXT G:
```

You can also use wildcard characters to copy multiple files. The parameters you can use with NCOPY are

PARAMETER	DESCRIPTION
/A	(Archive bit) Copies only files that have the Archive Needed attribute. It does not remove the Archive Needed attribute, however (To remove the Archive Needed attribute, use /M.)
/C	(Copy) Copies files without preserving file attributes and name space information
/E	(Empty Subdirectories) Copies empty subdirectories (valid only if used with /S)
/F	(Force sparse files) Forces the operating system to write to sparse files
/I	(Inform) Notifies you with a warning message that name space information or attributes couldn't be copied because they are not supported on the destination volume
/M	(Archive bit) Copies only files that have the Archive Needed attribute, and removes that attribute (To retain the Archive Needed attribute, use /A.)

PARAMETER	DESCRIPTION
/S	(Subdirectories) Copies subdirectories as well as files
/V	(Verify) Verifies that the original file and the newly created file are identical

NDIR

Use the NDIR utility to list the files and subdirectories in a directory and to see information about them. You can list the files and subdirectories in various orders; display only files or directories with specified attributes; or list only files and directories with specified dates, sizes, or owners. Use the command format

```
NDIR path /parameters
```

Replace *path* with the path to the directory whose contents you want to list. Replace *parameters* with any of the following options. To use more than one parameter, separate each one with a space. The slash is necessary only before the first parameter.

PARAMETER	DESCRIPTION
/HELP	Displays the command format and parameters for NDIR
/DATES	Displays the dates the file was created, last modified, last archived, and last accessed
/DO	(Directories Only) Displays directories only
/FO	(Files Only) Displays files only
/SUB	(Subdirectories) Displays subdirectories and all subsequent subdirectories

PARAMETER	DESCRIPTION
/LONG	(Long Names) Displays Macintosh, OS/2, and NFS file names, which can be longer than DOS file names
/MAC	Displays Macintosh files and subdirectories
/RIGHTS	Displays the inherited and effective rights and file attributes for files and subdirectories
/attribute	Displays files that have the specified attribute. Use file attribute abbreviations, and separate each with a space
/NOT /attribute	Displays files that do not have the specified attribute. Use file attribute abbreviations, and separate each with a space
/OW EQ username	(Owner Equal to username) Displays files that have the specified user as the owner. You can also use NOT (as in /OW NOT EQ username) to display files that are owned by anyone except the specified user
/SI GR number	(Size Greater than number) Displays files that are larger than the specified number of bytes. Can also use NOT (as in /SI NOT GR number) to display all files except those that are larger than the specified size
/SI EQ number	(Size Equal to number) Displays files that are exactly the specified number of bytes. You can also use NOT (as in /SI NOT EQ number) to display all files except those that match the specified size

PARAMETER	DESCRIPTION
/SI LE *number*	(Size Less than *number*) Displays files that are smaller than the specified number of bytes. You can also use NOT (as in /SI NOT LE *number*) to display all files except those that are smaller than the specified size
/UP BEF *date*	(Updated Before *date*) Displays files that were updated before the specified date (in mm-dd-yy format). You can also use NOT (as in /UP NOT BEF *date*) to display all files except those that were updated before the specified date
/UP EQ *date*	(Updated Equal to *date*) Displays files that were updated on the specified date (in mm-dd-yy format). You can also use NOT (as in /UP NOT EQ *date*) to display all files except those that were updated on the specified date
/UP AFT *date*	(Updated After *date*) Displays files that were updated after the specified date (in mm-dd-yy format). You can also use NOT (as in /UP NOT AFT *date*) to display all files except those that were updated after the specified date
/CR BEF *date*	(Created Before *date*) Displays files that were created before the specified date (in mm-dd-yy format). You can also use NOT (as in /CR NOT BEF *date*) to display all files except those that were created before the specified date

PARAMETER	DESCRIPTION
/CR EQ *date*	(Created Equal to *date*) Displays files that were created on the specified date (in mm-dd-yy format). You can also use NOT (as in /CR NOT EQ *date*) to display all files except those that were created on the specified date
/CR AFT *date*	(Created After *date*) Displays files that were created after the specified date (in mm-dd-yy format). You can also use NOT (as in /CR NOT AFT *date*) to display all files except those that were created after the specified date
/AC BEF *date*	(Accessed Before *date*) Displays files that were accessed before the specified date (in mm-dd-yy format). You can also use NOT (as in /AC NOT BEF *date*) to display all files except those that were accessed before the specified date
/AC EQ *date*	(Accessed Equal to *date*) Displays files that were accessed on the specified date (in mm-dd-yy format). You can also use NOT (as in /AC NOT EQ *date*) to display all files except those that were accessed on the specified date
/AC AFT *date*	(Accessed After *date*) Displays files that were accessed after the specified date (in mm-dd-yy format). You can also use NOT (as in /AC NOT AFT *date*) to display all files except those that were accessed after the specified date

PARAMETER	DESCRIPTION
/AR BEF *date*	(Archived Before *date*) Displays files that were archived before the specified date (in mm-dd-yy format). You can also use NOT (as in /AR NOT BEF *date*) to display all files except those that were archived before the specified date
/AR EQ *date*	(Archived Equal to *date*) Displays files that were archived on the specified date (in mm-dd-yy format). You can also use NOT (as in /AR NOT EQ *date*) to display all files except those that were archived on the specified date
/AR AFT *date*	(Archived After *date*) Displays files that were archived after the specified date (in mm-dd-yy format). You can also use NOT (as in /AR NOT AFT *date*) to display all files except those that were archived after the specified date
/SORT O	(Sort by Owner) Displays files and subdirectories by owner's name in alphabetical order. You can also use /REV to reverse the order of the display (as in /REV SORT O)
/SORT SI	(Sort by Size) Displays files and subdirectories from smallest to largest. You can also use /REV to reverse the order of the display (as in /REV SORT SI)
/SORT UP	(Sort by Update date) Displays files and subdirectories from the earliest "last modified" date to the latest. You can also use /REV to reverse the order of the display (as in /REV SORT UP)

PARAMETER	DESCRIPTION
/SORT CR	(Sort by Creation date) Displays files and subdirectories from the earliest creation date to the latest. You can also use /REV to reverse the order of the display (as in /REV SORT CR)
/SORT AC	(Sort by Accessed date) Displays files and subdirectories from the earliest "last accessed" date to the latest. You can also use /REV to reverse the order of the display (as in /REV SORT AC)
/SORT AR	(Sort by Archive date) Displays files and subdirectories from the earliest "last archived" date to the latest. You can also use /REV to reverse the order of the display (as in /REV SORT AR)
/UN	(Unsorted) Prevents NDIR from sorting files and subdirectories. You can also use /REV to reverse the order of the display (as in /REV UN)

NETBIOS

Use the NETBIOS utility to see information about NETBIOS. To see the version, whether NetBIOS is loaded, and which interrupts it is using, type

```
NETBIOS I
```

To unload NETBIOS to free up memory used by NETBIOS, type

```
NETBIOS U
```

NMENU

Use the NMENU utility to execute the menus you create for your users. Use the command format

```
NMENU filename
```

Replace *filename* with the path and name of the menu file you want to execute.

To force users to enter a menu immediately when they log in, add the following line to the end of the login script:

```
EXIT "NMENU filename"
```

See Chapter 5 for more information about creating and using menus.

NPRINT

Use the NPRINT utility to print ASCII files or files that have been formatted for your printer. Use this utility if you will not be printing from within an application. Use the following command format:

```
NPRINT parameters
```

Replace *parameters* with any of the following:

PARAMETER	DESCRIPTION
B=*name*	(Banner) Specifies the text (12-character limit) that should appear on the lower part of a banner page. Default: Your login name and the print job's file name
C=*number*	(Copies) Specifies how many copies of the file to print (up to 999). Default: 1
D	(Delete) Deletes the file after it is printed

PARAMETER	DESCRIPTION
F=*form*	(Form) Specifies which form type (paper) to print the job on. Replace *form* with the name or number of the form defined in the PRINTDEF utility. Default: 0
FF	(FormFeed) Forces a form feed at the end of your print job, allowing the next print job to start at the beginning of the next page. Use this option only if your application doesn't already force a form feed, or an extra blank page will be fed through the printer
J=*name*	(Job Configuration) Specifies which print job configuration to use. Replace *name* with the name of the print job configuration defined in the PRINTCON utility. Default: the first print job configuration defined in PRINTCON
NAM=*name*	(Name) Specifies the text (12-character limit) that should appear on the upper part of a banner page. Default: your login name
NB	(No Banner) Prevents a banner page from being printed
NFF	(No FormFeed) Disables form feed at the printer
NONOTI	(No Notify) Prevents a message from appearing that tells you your data has been printed. You need to use this only if NOTI is turned on in the print job configuration and you want to override it. By default, NONOTI is enabled

PARAMETER	DESCRIPTION
NOTI	(Notify) Makes a message appear at the bottom of your screen when your data has been printed. By default, NOTI is disabled
NT	(No Tabs) Allows the application's print formatter to determine how many spaces are in a tab stop. In most cases this parameter is unnecessary. Use this option only if your application has a print formatter and you have problems printing graphics
PS=*name*	(Print Server) Specifies which print server to send the print job to
Q=*name*	(Queue) Specifies which print queue to send the print job to. Default: the queue that Spooler 0 is assigned to
S=*name*	(Server) Specifies which file server to send the print job to. Default: the default file server
T=*number*	(Tabs) Specifies the number of spaces that should be in each tab stop. Use this parameter only with applications that do not have a print formatter. Default: 8

NVER

Use the NVER utility to see the version numbers of the following programs running on your file server and workstation:

- NetBIOS
- IPX and SPX
- LAN driver

- Shell or NetWare DOS Requester
- Workstation operating system (such as DOS) and version
- File server name
- Version of NetWare on the file server

NWXTRACT

Use the NWXTRACT utility to locate and copy individual files from the NetWare 3.12 CD-ROM or installation diskettes onto your network or a local disk. Use the following command format:

```
NWXTRACT path filename destination /parameters
```

Replace *path* with the source path to the CD-ROM or installation diskette (such as D: or A:). Replace *filename* with the name of the file you want to copy. If you want the file to be copied to the default location where it was originally copied during installation, omit the *destination*. To specify another location, replace *destination* with the path you desire.

Replace *parameters* with one of the following:

PARAMETER	DESCRIPTION
/S=*name*	(Server) Copies files to the default location on the specified server
/T=*type*	(Type) Copies files of the specified type (DOS, MAC, OS2, SER [server], UNX, WIN)
/?	(Help) Displays online help

You can also specify a group of files to copy. To see a list of valid file group names, read the online help by typing

```
NWXTRACT /?
```

PAUDIT

Use the PAUDIT utility to display the accounting records for your file server. The NetWare Accounting feature must have already been installed on your network. With this utility you can view information such as when users logged in or out, the times when an intruder was detected trying to log in, and how services (such as blocks read, blocks written, and connect time) are being used.

PCONSOLE

Use the PCONSOLE utility to set up printing services on your network. With PCONSOLE, you can

- ▶ Create and modify print servers

- ▶ Create and modify print queues

- ▶ Assign operators and users to print queues and print servers

- ▶ Assign print servers to print queues

- ▶ Assign print queues to printers

- ▶ Assign printers to print servers

- ▶ Work with the print jobs in a print queue

The PSC utility allows you to do similar tasks by typing commands at the command line instead of using PCONSOLE's menus.

See Chapter 6 for more information about setting up NetWare printing services.

PRINTCON

Use the PRINTCON utility to create and use print job configurations. Print job configurations specify how a print job should be printed. For example, they can specify how many copies to print, which tab spaces to use, which server and print queue to use, whether to use form feed, which form (paper style) to use, and so on.

Each user can have his or her own print job configuration, which is stored in a database in the user's own MAIL directory.

PRINTDEF

Use the PRINTDEF utility to define the printer you're using and to define the paper forms (such as invoices, paychecks, and so on) that will be used. The information you specify with PRINTDEF is stored in a database that is used by PRINTDEF to define print job configurations.

PSC

Use the PSC utility to control print servers and printers. This utility accomplishes most of the same tasks as PCONSOLE, but in a command-line format instead of a menu format. Use the command format

```
PSC PS=printserver parameters
```

or

```
PSC P=number parameters
```

Replace *printserver* with the name of the print server you want to control. Similarly, replace *number* with the number of the printer you want to control.

Replace *parameter* with any of the following:

PARAMETER	DESCRIPTION
AB	(Abort) Stops the current print job and deletes it from the print queue

PARAMETER	DESCRIPTION
CD	(Cancel Down) If you selected the Going Down after Current Jobs option in PCONSOLE, this parameter lets you cancel that command to prevent the print server from going down
FF	(Form Feed) Causes the printer to do a form feed. The printer must be stopped or paused to do a form feed
M *character*	(Mark) Prints a line of the character you specified so you can see which line the printer will print on. Default character: *
MO=*form*	(Mount From) Tells the print server you have mounted a new paper form on the printer. Replace *form* with the number of the form defined in PRINTDEF
PAU	(Pause) Temporarily stops the printer
PRI	(Private) Prevents other users from printing on this printer by removing it from the print server's list of network printers and changing it to a local printer. This printer must be remote, which means it is connected to a workstation rather than to the file server. To revert to a network printer, use SH (Shared)
SH	(Shared) Removes the PRI (Private) parameter so the printer can once again be used by other network users
STAR	(Start) Restarts a printer that has been stopped or paused

PARAMETER	DESCRIPTION
STAT	(Status) Displays the status of printers being serviced by the print server
STO	(Stop) Stops the printer and deletes the current print job from the queue
STO KEEP	(Stop and Keep) Stops the printer, but instead of deleting the current print job, it resubmits it to the top of the queue when the printer is restarted

PSERVER

PSERVER.EXE is exactly the same as PSERVER.NLM, except that it loads the print server on a dedicated workstation rather than on the file server. Use the command format

```
PSERVER fileserver printserver
```

Replace *fileserver* with the name of the file server that will control this print server (not necessary if you want to use the default file server). Replace *printserver* with the name of the print server you created in PCONSOLE.

PURGE

Use the PURGE utility to permanently erase files from the server. When files are deleted, they are actually retained in a salvageable state on the server and are truly erased only if the file server needs the disk space. PURGE removes them completely without waiting for the file server to run out of disk space.

Use the command format

```
PURGE path
```

Replace *path* with the directory path or file name you want to purge. To purge all recoverable files in your current directory and all its subdirectories, replace *path* with /ALL.

To salvage (restore) a deleted file, use the SALVAGE utility.

RCONSOLE

Use the RCONSOLE utility to start a Remote Console session on a workstation that is directly connected to the file server's cabling system. By running Remote Console, you can turn your workstation into the file server's keyboard and monitor.

To start a Remote Console session on a workstation that is connected to the file server across asynchronous telephone lines, via a modem, use ACONSOLE instead.

To use RCONSOLE, two NLMs must already be loaded on the file server: RSPX.NLM and REMOTE.NLM.

To execute RCONSOLE, type

```
RCONSOLE
```

You will be prompted for the server to which you want to connect.

After you've started a Remote Console session with RCONSOLE, you can work with the console as follows:

- ▶ To access Remote Console's Available Options menu, press the asterisk (*) key on the number pad of your keyboard.

- ▶ To move between active file server screens, such as between MONITOR and the console prompt, press the minus (−) and plus (+) keys. Note that these keys do not work in the Available Options menu.

- ▶ To run a server utility, go to the console prompt and type the server utility command.

▸ To exit Remote Console, select Available Options ➤ End Remote Session with Server.

REMOVE

Use the REMOVE utility to remove a user or group from the trustee list of a file or directory. Use the command format

```
REMOVE name path parameters
```

Replace *name* with the name of the user or group whom you want to remove as a trustee. Replace *path* with the directory path (and file name, if necessary) from which you want to remove the user as a trustee. Replace *parameters* with one of the following:

PARAMETER	DESCRIPTION
–SUB	(Subdirectories) Removes the trustee from all subdirectories in the path
–F	(Files) Removes the trustee from all files in the directory

To remove a user's rights to a file or directory but leave the user on the file's or directory's trustee list, use REVOKE instead.

RENDIR

Use the RENDIR utility to rename a directory. Use the command format

```
RENDIR oldname newname
```

Replace *oldname* with the path and name of the directory you want to rename. To rename your current directory, replace *oldname* with a period (.). Replace *newname* with the new name you want to give the directory.

REVOKE

Use the REVOKE utility to take away a user's rights to a file or directory while leaving the user listed as a trustee of that file or directory. Use the command format

```
REVOKE rights path FROM user parameters
```

Replace *rights* with the list of rights you want to revoke. Use the standard rights abbreviations or the word ALL, and separate each right with a space. Replace *path* with the directory path to the file or directory from which you are revoking this user's rights. (Wildcards are supported.)

Replace *user* with the name of the user or group whose rights you are revoking.

Replace *parameter* with one of the following:

PARAMETER	DESCRIPTION
–SUB	(Subdirectories) Revokes the user's rights to all subdirectories
–F	(Files) Revokes the user's rights to all files in the directory

RIGHTS

Use the RIGHTS utility to see your own effective rights in a directory. Use the command format

```
RIGHTS path
```

Replace *path* with the directory path leading to the directory or file for which you want to see your effective rights.

RPRINTER

Use the RPRINTER utility to attach a printer to a workstation instead of to a file server. Such printers are called remote printers. Use the command format

```
RPRINTER printserver printernumber parameters
```

Replace *printserver* with the name of the print server that will service this printer.

Replace *printernumber* with the number of the printer, defined in PCONSOLE.

Replace *parameter* with one of the following:

PARAMETER	DESCRIPTION
−R	Disconnects the remote printer from the print server
−S	Displays the status of the remote printer

To select a print server from a list of available print servers, type RPRINTER with no parameters. Choose the print server you want, and then select a printer from the list of defined remote printers that appears. A message indicating that the remote printer has been installed appears.

SALVAGE

Use the SALVAGE utility to restore a file that was previously deleted. When files are deleted, they are actually retained in a salvageable state on the server and are truly erased only if the file server needs the disk space. SALVAGE, a menu utility, lets you recover these deleted files.

SALVAGE also lets you purge deleted files, if you wish, or you can use the PURGE utility instead. Purging a file erases it completely from the disk so that it cannot be restored.

Deleted files are stored in the directory from which they were deleted. If the directory itself has also been deleted, that directory's deleted files are stored in a directory under volume SYS, called DELETED.SAV.

SECURITY

Use the SECURITY utility to see what security holes may exist on your network. This utility displays information about users who have insecure passwords, no passwords, supervisor equivalence, or trustee rights at the root of volumes. It also shows which users have more rights than they should in the standard NetWare directories and whether or not users have user login scripts.

SEND

Use the SEND utility to send a one-line message to another workstation. Use the command format

```
SEND "message" server/user
```

Replace *message* with any text you want to send, up to 44 characters. The message must be enclosed in quotation marks.

Replace *server* with the server name of the user to whom you're sending the message. If the user is on the same server as you, omit *server* and the slash.

Replace *user* with the name of the user or group you want to receive the message. To send a message to multiple users, separate each name with a comma.

You can also use the SESSION menu utility to send messages.

SESSION

Use the SESSION utility to work with information about your current drive mappings and to send messages to users and groups. SESSION has the following options on its main menu:

- ▶ **Change Current Server:** Lets you switch to another file server to see your drive mapping or user information on that server

- ▶ **Drive Mappings:** Displays your current drive mappings for this server and lets you add or delete drive mappings

- ▶ **Group List:** Lists the groups on this server and lets you send a message to a group

- ▶ **Search Mappings:** Displays your current search drive mappings for this server and lets you add or delete search drive mappings

- ▶ **Select Default Drive:** Lets you switch your current default drive

- ▶ **User List:** Lists the users on this server and lets you send a message to a user

SETPASS

Use the SETPASS utility to change your password. This utility can also synchronize your new password on any other servers to which you are currently attached. Use the command format

```
SETPASS fileserver/user
```

Replace *fileserver/user* with the name of the file server and the username you have on that server. To change your password on your current default file server, you can omit the *fileserver/user* portion of the command.

SETTTS

Use the SETTTS utility to establish the number of logical and physical record locks that TTS (NetWare's Transaction Tracking Service) ignores before beginning to track a transaction.

This allows TTS to work with your application if the application requires you to set new transaction beginning points. Most applications do not require this utility to be run.

If an application does not make explicit transaction tracking calls, the NetWare operating system performs implicit transaction tracking when record locks are sent to the server. The server creates transactions based on record locks and unlocks from your application.

If you need to use this utility, use the command format

```
SETTTS logical physical
```

Replace *logical* with the number of logical record locks you want TTS to ignore. Replace *physical* with the number of physical record locks you want TTS to ignore.

SLIST

Use the SLIST utility to display a list of all file servers on the network. Use the command format

```
SLIST fileserver
```

If you want to see all file servers on the network, omit the *fileserver* parameter. To see only a file server of a particular name, replace *fileserver* with that server's name. You can also use wildcard characters with this parameter. For example, to see all servers beginning with the letter "A," type

```
SLIST A*
```

SMODE

Use the SMODE utility to specify the order in which an application searches through search drives. Use the command format

```
SMODE path mode parameter
```

Replace *path* with the directory path for the executable file whose search mode you want to set.

Replace *mode* with the number of the search mode you want to assign to this application. The possible mode numbers are

NUMBER	DESCRIPTION
0	Default. Specifies no search instructions. The executable file looks for instructions in the NET.CFG file
1	The program searches any directory specified in the executable file itself, the default directory, and then all mapped search drives
2	The program searches any directory specified in the executable file itself and then the default directory
3	The program searches any directory specified in the executable file itself and then the default directory. Then, if the open request is read only, the program searches all mapped search drives
4	Not used
5	The program searches any directory specified in the executable file itself and then all mapped search drives. If no path is specified in the executable file, the program searches the default directory and then all mapped search drives
6	Not used

NUMBER	DESCRIPTION
7	If a directory is specified in the executable file itself, the program searches that path first. Then, if the open request is read only, the program searches the search drives. If no path is specified, the program searches the default directory first. If the open request is read only, the program searches all mapped search drives

SYSCON

Use the SYSCON utility to control most of the user, group, acounting, and server information. SYSCON is usually the network supervisor's primary utility for managing access control for the network.

SYSCON has the following items on its main menu:

- ▶ **Accounting:** Lets you install and remove the accounting feature and set charge rates for server usage

- ▶ **Change Current Server:** Lets you switch to a different file server

- ▶ **File Server Information:** Lets you see information about the file server, such as the version of NetWare running, the level of System Fault Tolerance being used, whether TTS is enabled, the number of connections supported and in use, and the network and node addresses

- ▶ **Group Information:** Lets you create, list, and delete groups; add users to groups; and grant the group trustee rights to directories

- ▶ **Supervisor Information:** Lets you work with account balances, set time restrictions for all users, edit the system login script, activate the intruder detection system, edit the server's AUTO-EXEC.NCF file, read the system error log file, and create workgroup managers

▶ **User Information:** Lets you create and delete users, set their environment and password restrictions, edit users' login scripts, assign rights to users, and so on

SYSTIME

Use the SYSTIME utility to see the file server's date and time. Use the command format

```
SYSTIME fileserver
```

Replace *fileserver* with the name of the file server whose time you want to see unless you want to see the default server's time. In that case, omit *fileserver.*

TLIST

Use the TLIST utility to see all the users and groups that are trustees of a file or directory. Use the command format

```
TLIST path
```

Replace *path* with the directory path or name of the file whose trustees you want to list.

USERDEF

Use the USERDEF utility to create multiple users with a template. USER-DEF lets you use a template to create users. Using the template as a basis, it creates a USR file that is processed automatically by MAKEUSER.

If you have a lot of users to create, you may find it more efficient to use MAKEUSER to edit the USR file.

USERLIST

Use the USERLIST utility to list all users who are currently logged in to the file server. This utility also displays each user's connection number and login time.

Use the command format

```
USERLIST fileserver/user /parameters
```

Replace *fileserver,* if necessary, with the name of a file server whose users you want to list.

To list all users on a server, omit the *user* parameter. To see a particular user, replace *user* with the user's login name. You can also use wildcard characters.

Replace *parameters* with one of the following, if necessary:

PARAMETER	DESCRIPTION
/A	(Address) Displays the network address and node address of each user
/O	(Object) Displays the type of bindery object that is attached at that connection (such as "user")
/C	(Continuous) Allows the list of users to scroll off the page without pausing

VERSION

Use the VERSION utility to display the version of a NetWare utility. Use the command format

```
VERSION filename
```

Replace *filename* with the directory path and name of the file whose version you want to see. (If the file has an .EXE extension, you do not need to type the extension in the command.)

VOLINFO

Use the VOLINFO utility to see information about the volumes on your server. This utility displays the total amount of disk space and directory entries available on each volume, as well as the amount of that space that is still available. By default, the information is updated every five seconds. You can adjust the interval if necessary.

WHOAMI

Use the WHOAMI utility to see the servers you're logged in to, your username on each of those servers, the times you logged in, and so on. Use the command format

```
WHOAMI fileserver parameters
```

To see a list of all servers you're connected to and your user name and information on each of those servers, omit all parameters and just type WHOAMI.

Replace *fileserver*, if necessary, with the name of a particular server if you want to see your information for only that server.

Replace *parameters* with one of the following:

PARAMETER	DESCRIPTION
/A	(All) Displays all the information available with the other parameters
/C	(Continuous) Scrolls the display off the screen without pausing
/G	(Groups) Displays the groups you belong to

PARAMETER	DESCRIPTION
/O	(Object) Displays object supervisor information and the users and groups being supervised
/R	(Rights) Displays your effective rights
/S	(Security Equivalences) Displays your security equivalences
/SY	(System) Displays general system info
/W	(Workgroup Manager) Displays workgroup manager information

WSUPDATE

Use the WSUPDATE utility to update files on your workstation. This utility compares the dates of the files on the workstation with its source files and copies the source files onto the workstation if the source files' dates are more recent. Use the command format

```
WSUPDATE source destination /parameter
```

Replace *source* with the directory path and name of the file you want to update the workstation with. Replace *destination* with the drive you want the utility to check to find the workstation's version of the file. You can also replace *destination* with either ALL (to search all the workstation's drives) or ALL_LOCAL (to search only the workstation's local drives).

Replace *parameter* with one of the following:

PARAMETER	DESCRIPTION
/C	(Copy) Copies the new file over the old one. Does not keep a backup copy of the older file

PARAMETER	DESCRIPTION
/F=*path\filename*	Directs WSUPDATE to a file that contains commands for updating workstation files
/I	(Interactive) Prompts the user as to whether or not to update the file when it finds one that is outdated. This is the default
/L=*path\filename*	Creates a log file to track the messages created during updates
/N	(New) Creates the file and path if they don't already exist
/R	(Rename) Renames the old file with the extension .OLD and then copies the new file to the workstation
/S	(Search) Searches for the outdated files in all subdirectories of the specified destination drive
/V=*drive*	Updates the CONFIG.SYS file, making changes necessary to update it from NetWare 3.11 to NetWare 3.12

Worksheets

This appendix contains example worksheets you can use to document your network. You can photocopy these worksheets or develop your own. Many people find it more convenient to use a database to track their inventories. Use whichever method you prefer.

Worksheet A: Record of Hardware and Software Purchases

Name of product: _____

Version number: _____ Serial number/part number: _____

Manufacturer name, address, phone: _____

_____

_____

_____

_____

Vendor name, address, phone: _____

_____

_____

_____

_____

Purchase price: _____

Purchase date: _____

Purchase order number: _____

Length of the warranty: _____

Current location of hardware or software: _____

_____

Warranty or Registration Card mailed in? Yes _____ No _____

Comments: _____

_____

_____

_____

_____

_____

_____

_____

Worksheet B: Record of Hardware Configuration Settings

File server or workstation?_____

Current location:_____

Make and model: _____

Serial number/part number: _____

Size of floppy disk drives: A: _____ B: _____

Size of hard disk drives: C: _____ D: _____

Memory: _____

Network boards:_____

   Name: _____   Settings: _____

   _____   Node address: _____

   _____   LAN driver: _____

   Name: _____   Settings: _____

   _____   Node address: _____

   _____   LAN driver: _____

   Name: _____   Settings: _____

   _____   Node address: _____

   _____   LAN driver: _____

   Name: _____   Settings: _____

   _____   Node address: _____

   _____   LAN driver: _____

Other boards (graphics, modem, etc.): _____

   Name: _____   Settings: _____

   Name: _____   Settings: _____

   Name: _____   Settings: _____

   Name: _____   Settings: _____

Comments: _____

_____

_____

_____

Worksheet C: Record of Printer Configuration Settings

Current location: _____

Make and model:_____

Serial number/part number: _____

Local (attached to print server) or remote? _____

Printer number: _____

Serial printer configuration: _____

      Port (COM1 or COM2?): _____

      Baud rate:_____

      Word size: _____

      Stop bits: _____

      Parity: _____

      XON/XOFF: _____

      Poll:_____

      Interrupt (COM1=4, COM2=3): _____

Parallel printer configuration:_____

      Port (LPT1, LPT2, or LPT3?): _____

      Poll:_____

      Interrupt (LPT1=7, LPT2=8): _____

Print queues:_____

_____

_____

Print queue operators: _____

Print server operators:_____

Comments: _____

_____

_____

_____

Worksheet D: Hardware Maintenance Record

Name of product: _____

Serial number/part number: _____

Repair date: _____

Purchase order number: _____

Repair cost: _____

    Repaired under warranty? Yes _____ No _____

    New warranty given?   Yes _____ No _____

    Warranty expiration date: _____

Repair vendor name, address, phone: _____

_____

_____

_____

_____

_____

Comments: _____

_____

_____

_____

_____

Worksheet E: Backup Schedule

Server name:_____

Server location:_____

Location of backup media: _____

_____

_____

_____

Backup system used (hardware and software): _____

_____

_____

_____

Backup schedule:_____

    Full backup: _____

    Bindery backup: _____

    Incremental backup:_____

Media rotation schedule: _____

_____

_____

_____

_____

Media labeling instructions: _____

_____

_____

_____

Comments: _____

_____

_____

_____

_____

Resources and
Phone Numbers

Because NetWare is the most popular and widely used networking operating system in the world, an extensive number of resources are available to help you learn more about NetWare products.

You can find numerous magazines, newsletters, and books from various publishers (such as Novell Press) dedicated to the networking industry.

There are NetWare user groups and other professional organizations you can join. In addition, you can take NetWare classes throughout the world.

These and other resources can be invaluable to you. This appendix explains where and how to find information about many of these resources.

Novell Product Information

For all types of information about Novell or its products, you can call one easy number: 800-NETWARE.

When you call this number, you can receive information about Novell products, the locations of your nearest resellers, pricing information, Technical Support (see the section "Novell Technical Support" later in this appendix), and so on.

To order the printed manuals or the electronic manuals on CD-ROM for NetWare 3.12, you can use the order form that came in your NetWare 3.12 box, or call 800-336-3892 (in the United States) or 512-834-6905.

Using NetWire on CompuServe

NetWire is a collection of Novell forums on CompuServe that offer users access to a wide variety of information and files, such as technical advice from sysops (system operators) and other users, updated files and drivers, and the latest patches and workarounds. NetWire also includes forums for user-contributed files, classified and help wanted ads, developer support, and vendor information.

To see the latest list of Novell forums, download the FRMORG.EXE file from the NOVLIB forum.

NetWire is managed by Novell employees and by sysops who have extensive knowledge about NetWare. Public forums can be quite active, with many knowledgeable users offering advice to those with problems.

To get technical help with a problem, post a message and address the message to the NetWire sysops. (But don't send the sysops a personal email asking for help—the public forums are the approved avenue for help.)

If you have a CompuServe account, you can access the NetWire forums. There is no additional monthly fee for using NetWire, although you are charged the connection fee (on an hourly rate) for accessing the service.

If you do not yet have a CompuServe account, you can subscribe to CompuServe and NetWire by calling 800-524-3388 (ask for Operator 200). Outside the United States and Canada, call 614-529-1349.

Novell Information on the Internet

If you have a connection to the Internet, you can access Novell information through one of the following communication options:

- ▶ **World Wide Web:** Novell URL:http://www.novell.com/

- ▶ **Gopher:** gopher.novell.com

- ▶ **File Transfer Protocol (FTP):** anonymous FTP to ftp.novell.com

(Users in Europe should replace the .com with .de.)

After you access the Novell site, you can choose from the information categories to find specific topics. The Novell information available on the Internet includes

- Novell Technical Information Documents

- 30-day archives of Usenet (Novell's Internet news areas)

- Novell Labs hardware and software test bulletins

- All available NetWare patches, fixes, and drivers

- The *Novell Buyer's Guide*

- A Technical Support database for known problems and solutions

NetWare Users International (NUI)

NetWare Users International (NUI) is an organization that sponsors NetWare user groups. Worldwide there are over 250 groups and a total membership of over 140,000 end users.

In North America there are 13 regions of NUI, and each region has numerous local user groups. Each local NUI group elects a president to represent the local group on the regional board. Then each regional group elects a president to represent the region on the national scale. Internationally, there is a similar structure in Europe, Australia and Asia, Latin America, and Japan.

NUI offers the following benefits:

- Local user groups that hold regularly scheduled meetings

- *NetWare Connection,* a bimonthly magazine that provides feature articles on new technologies, network management tips, product reviews, NUI news, and other helpful information

- NUInet, an independent BBS (online bulletin-board system) that provides NetWare help and an email facility, as well as a way to communicate directly with NUI (Nonmembers can also use NUInet.)

- Regional NUI conferences, held in different major cities throughout the year

The best news is, there's usually no fee or only a very low fee for joining an NUI user group.

For more information or to join an NUI user group, call 800-228-4NUI or 801-429-7177.

For a free subscription to *NetWare Connection*, fax or mail your name, address, and request for a subscription to

NetWare Connection
P.O. Box 1928
Orem, UT 84059-1928
USA
Fax: 801-429-3056

Novell Education Classes and CNE Certification

Novell offers a variety of classes on various aspects of running NetWare networks. The classes are taught at over a thousand Novell Authorized Education Centers (NAECs) throughout the world. They are also taught at more than a hundred NAEPs (Novell Authorized Education Partners), which are universities and colleges that teach these courses.

These classes are not required, but they often offer the best way to get some direct, hands-on training in just a few days. Some of the classes are also available in Computer-Based Training (CBT) form in case you'd rather work through the material at your own pace, on your own workstation, than attend a class.

These classes also help prepare you if you want to become a Certified NetWare Engineer (CNE).

The Novell CNE program provides a way to ensure that networking professionals meet the necessary criteria to adequately install and manage NetWare networks. To achieve CNE status, you take a series of exams on different aspects of NetWare. In most cases you will probably want to take the classes Novell offers through its NAECs to prepare for the exams.

The classes and exams you take depend somewhat on the level of certification you want to achieve. While there are certain core exams that are required for all levels, you can choose from additional "electives" to achieve the certification you want.

The following levels of certification are available:

- **CNA (Certified NetWare Administrator):** This certification is the most basic level. It prepares you to manage your own NetWare network. It does not delve into the more complex and technical aspects of NetWare. If you are relatively new to NetWare, the classes offered for this certification are highly recommended.

- **CNE (Certified NetWare Engineer):** This certification level ensures that you can adequately install and manage NetWare networks.

- **ECNE (Enterprise Certified NetWare Engineer):** This certification level's series of tests emphasizes aspects of networking encountered in larger, enterprise-wide networks, such as routing, gateways, NetWare Directory Services, and so on.

- **CNI (Certified NetWare Instructor):** CNIs are authorized to teach NetWare classes through NAECs. The tests and classes specific to this level ensure that the individual taking them will be able to adequately teach others how to install and manage NetWare.

CNEs and ECNEs qualify for membership in the NetWare Professional Association (NPA), which is explained in the following section.

For more information about Novell Education classes or to find the nearest NAEC near you, call 800-233-3382.

To purchase a CBT version of a class, contact your nearest NAEC.

NetWare Professional Association

The NetWare Professional Association (NPA), formerly called CNEPA, is an organization for network computing professionals. Its goal is to keep its members current with the latest technology and information in the industry.

To be a member, you must be certified as one of the following:

- Certified NetWare Engineer (CNE)
- Enterprise Certified NetWare Engineer (ECNE)
- Certified Banyan Engineer (CBE)
- Certified Banyan Specialist (CBS)
- Microsoft Certified Systems Engineer (MCSE)

Associate memberships are available for the following people:

- Those who have begun the CNE, CBS, or MCSE certification process but who have not yet completed it
- Certified NetWare Administrators (CNA)
- Lotus Certified Notes Specialists (LCNS)
- WordPerfect Certified Systems Engineers (CSE)
- Microsoft Certified Product Specialists (MCPS)

Benefits of belonging to NPA include

- ▶ Local NPA chapters (more than 80 worldwide) that hold regularly scheduled meetings that include presentations and hands-on demonstrations of the latest technology

- ▶ *Network News,* a monthly publication that offers technical tips for working with NetWare networks, NPA news, classified ads for positions, and articles aimed at helping CNEs make the most of their careers

- ▶ Discounts on NPA Satellite Labs (satellite broadcasts of presentations)

- ▶ Product discounts from vendors

- ▶ Hands-On Technology Labs (educational forums at major trade shows and other locations as sponsored by local NPA chapters)

- ▶ Discount or free admission to major trade shows and conferences

Membership in NPA costs $150 per year. For more information or to join NPA, call 801-429-7227.

Novell Technical Support

Whenever you encounter a problem with your network that you can't solve on your own, it's usually best to go to your reseller or consultant first. Novell Technical Support is available if your reseller can't help you.

Novell Technical Support charges a fee for each incident (an incident may involve more than one phone call, if necessary), and the fee depends on the product for which you're requesting support.

When you call Technical Support, make sure you have all the necessary information ready, such as the versions of NetWare and any utility or application you're using, the type of hardware you're using, network or node addresses and hardware settings for any workstations or other machines being affected, and so on. You'll also need a major credit card.

To get Technical Support, call 800-NETWARE.

NetWare Support Encyclopedia

The *Novell Support Encyclopedia Professional Volume* (*NSEPro*) is a CD-ROM of technical information that is available by subscription. The *NSEPro* is updated as many as 12 times a year to provide the most current technical information about NetWare. The *NSEPro* contains

- ▶ Novell Technical Information Documents

- ▶ Novell Labs hardware and software test bulletins

- ▶ Product documentation

- ▶ Novell Application Notes

- ▶ Professional Developer Bullets

- ▶ All available NetWare patches, fixes, and drivers

- ▶ The *Novell Buyer's Guide*

- ▶ Novell corporate information, such as event calendars and press releases

The *NSEPro* includes the Folio 3.0 information-retrieval software that allows you to access and search easily through the *NSEPro* information from your workstation using DOS, Macintosh, or Microsoft Windows.

You can obtain a subscription to the *NSEPro* from any Novell Authorized Reseller or directly from Novell at 1-800-377-4136 (in the United States and Canada) or 303-297-2725. Credit card orders can be faxed to 303-294-0930.

Novell Developer Support

If you are a developer creating applications to run on NetWare, you may qualify to join Novell's Professional Developers' Program. Joining the developers' program provides the following benefits:

- Ability to purchase Software Development Kits (SDKs), which include development tools you can use to create and test your application

- Special technical support geared specifically at developers

- *Developer Notes,* a bimonthly publication from the Novell Research department, that covers software development topics for NetWare products

- *Bullets,* a monthly technical journal

- Access to Novell's developer forums on CompuServe

- Opportunity to attend Skills Transfer Workshops, which offer training, and Novell Compass SIGs (Special Interest Groups)

Membership in the Professional Developers' Program is free.

For more information, to apply for membership, or to order an SDK, call 800-REDWORD or 801-429-5281, or contact the program administrator via email at devprog@novell.com.

Novell Application Notes

Application Notes is a monthly publication created by the Novell Research department. Each *Application Notes* issue contains research reports and articles on the following topics:

- ▶ Network design and optimization strategies

- ▶ Network management tactics

- ▶ NetWare internals and theory of operations

- ▶ Novell product implementation guidelines

- ▶ Integration solutions for third-party products

- ▶ NetWare programming techniques

A year's subscription costs $95 ($135 outside the United States), which includes access to the *Application Notes* in their electronic form on NetWire. An electronic-only subscription costs $35 (plus access charges).

To order a subscription, call 800-377-4136 or 303-297-2725. You can also fax an order to 303-294-0930.

Novell Press and Other Books

There are dozens of books about NetWare products available from many different publishers, including Novell Press. The following are just a few examples of books that you may find to be useful resources:

Chappell, Laura, and Dan Hakes. *Novell's Guide to NetWare LAN Analysis* (San Jose CA: Novell Press, 1993. ISBN 0-7821-1362-1)

Chappell, Laura A., and Roger L. Spicer. *Novell's Guide to Multiprotocol Internetworking* (San Jose CA: Novell Press, 1994. ISBN 0-7821-1291-9)

Clarke, David James IV. *Novell's CNA Study Guide* (San Jose CA: Novell Press, 1993. ISBN 0-7821-1139-4)

Clarke, David James IV. *Novell's CNE Study Guide* (San Jose CA: Novell Press, 1994. ISBN 0-7821-1502-0)

Currid, Cheryl and Co. *Novell's Guide to NetWare 3.12 Networks* (San Jose CA: Novell Press, 1993. ISBN 0-7821-1093-2)

Liebing, Edward. *NetWare User's Guide* (New York: M&T Books, 1993. ISBN 1-55851-318-3)

Lindberg, Kelley J. P. *Novell's Guide to Managing Small NetWare Networks* (San Jose CA: Novell Press, 1993. ISBN 0-7821-1238-2)

If you want to find more information about AppleTalk and Macintosh networking, you'll find several good books from Addison-Wesley, such as *Inside AppleTalk, Inside Macintosh: Networking, AppleTalk Network System Overview,* and *Planning and Managing AppleTalk Networks.*

Glossary

Account restrictions Settings that restrict how users can access the network. For example, you can limit the hours that users can log in, the workstations they can use, the disk space they can fill up, or how long they can use the same passwords. If a user exceeds one of these restrictions, that user's account is disabled, and the user is locked out of the network. You can specify system-wide restrictions, which apply to every user created from that point on, or user restrictions, which apply only to individual users. Individual user assignments override any system-wide restrictions you may have already set.

AppleTalk A protocol used by Macintosh workstations and other devices to communicate on a network.

AppleTalk network, extended An AppleTalk network that allows far more than 254 nodes to be connected to the network (theoretically, up to more than 16 million nodes). In addition, extended networks can have multiple zones (up to 255). Ethernet and Token-Ring networks are extended AppleTalk networks.

AppleTalk network, nonextended AppleTalk networks that can support only up to 254 nodes, which are all contained in a single zone. EtherTalk 1.0, Arcnet, and LocalTalk are all nonextended AppleTalk networks.

AppleTalk print server Print server software that takes print jobs from a NetWare queue and sends those jobs to a printer on the Apple-Talk network.

AppleTalk print spooler (Formerly called an AppleTalk Queue Server) Software that looks like a regular Apple printer to a Macintosh workstation, so the workstation will send a print job to it. The AppleTalk print spooler then sends the job to the NetWare print queue, where the Macintosh's print job joins any other print jobs from other Macintosh or DOS workstations and waits its turn to be printed. When a printer is available, the print server takes the job from the queue and sends it to the printer.

AppleTalk router Software (APPLETLK.NLM) that, when loaded on a NetWare file server, allows Macintoshes to communicate with the IPX network or with other AppleTalk networks on the other side of the file server. The AppleTalk router contains an internal network (contained within the router's software rather than encompassing any workstations) and communicates with an external network (to which the Macintosh workstations are attached). *See also* **External network, Internal network,** and **Seed router.**

AppleTalk zones. *See* **Zone.**

ASCII American Standard Code for Information Interchange; a standard way of encoding letters, numbers, and punctuation as bits in a file. ASCII is a standard used for moving text files from one computer to another, as well as for printing files without an application.

Attributes Attributes are assigned to NetWare files and directories. They control such things as whether the file or directory can be shared by several users, whether it can be deleted, and so on. Attributes override any trustee rights a user may have. Attributes are sometimes called flags. To set file attributes, use the FLAG utility. To set directory attributes, use the FLAGDIR utility. Note that FLAG and FLAGDIR do not affect files and directories stored on a local disk.

AUTOEXEC.BAT file A batch file, which is a file that executes commands automatically when a DOS workstation is turned on. The AUTOEXEC.BAT file, located on a workstation's boot disk, can take care of several networking startup steps, including loading the necessary NetWare shell files, changing to the network drive, and executing the LOGIN command with the user's name.

AUTOEXEC.NCF file   Executes on the file server automatically after STARTUP.NCF and continues the process of preparing the server to run the network by loading the LAN drivers, specifying the server name and internal network number, mounting volumes, automatically loading additional NLMs (such as MONITOR), specifying SET parameters, and so on.

Backup   A copy you make of an application or of files. If you lose files because of a system failure or an accident, you can restore the backup copy. Some backup products, such as the NetWare utility SBACKUP.NLM, back up trustee information and attributes for files in addition to the files themselves.

Banner page   A page that prints before a print job, usually containing the name of the user that sent the print job and the file that was printed.

Batch file   An ASCII file that contains a series of commands that execute when you run the file. A batch file's name has the extension .BAT. A common batch file on boot disks is AUTOEXEC.BAT, which can be used to execute NetWare workstation files and log the user in to the network.

Bindery   A server-based database of information about each object in the network, such as users, print servers, and print queues. Each object has properties that describe it, such as addresses, attributes, or passwords. These properties are also stored in the bindery, and they control how the objects can behave on the file server.

Boot disk   A floppy diskette or workstation hard disk that contains the files necessary for booting the workstation with DOS. Most boot disks for NetWare workstations also configure the workstation's environment, load the NetWare shell files, and log the user into the network.

Booting Turning on a computer so that its operating system and other necessary files load. *See also* **Remote reset**.

Capture Redirecting a workstation's LPT printer port to a print queue or file instead of a locally attached printer. That way, print jobs will be sent to a network print queue (or file).

CD-ROM Compact disk, read-only memory; a technology that allows for the retrieval of large amounts of data on a small compact disk.

Client A device, such as a workstation, that requests services from the network file server.

Code Page *See* **DOS code page**.

Command-line utilities NetWare utilities that let you perform a network task by typing a command at the system prompt rather than selecting an option from a menu

Compile: To convert a file into a program, or executable, file. The MENUMAKE utility compiles a text file containing menu-formatting commands into a data file with a .DAT file name extension, which the menu program can use to display the menu options.

CONFIG.SYS A DOS file that allows you to customize the DOS environment for a workstation. You also load device drivers from CONFIG.SYS. If you are using DR DOS 6.0 or MS DOS 5.0, this file was created when you installed DOS. Commands in CONFIG.SYS take effect when the workstation is booted. If you modify CONFIG.SYS, the changes will not take effect until you reboot the workstation.

Console A common name for the file server's keyboard and monitor. For example, you run server utilities by typing commands at the file server console. You can use Remote Console to turn your workstation's keyboard and monitor into the file server's console.

Controller board   A circuit board that controls the hard disks installed in a file server.

Data fork   The portion of a Macintosh file that contains the text of the file. DOS files are equivalent to the Macintosh file's data fork. Macintosh files also have a resource fork, for which there is no DOS equivalent. *See also* **Resource fork**.

Database   A collection of information that is accessible to computer programs. The database can be an integral part of a program, or it can be a separate file accessed by a database program. One example of a simple database is a collection of telephone numbers with names and addresses. The NetWare bindery is a database of network information.

Dedicated   A computer on the network that is reserved for one specific task. For example, you can use a dedicated workstation as a print server.

Dedicated IPX driver   A type of driver used by NetWare workstations. Dedicated IPX drivers understand only the IPX protocol. Dedicated IPX drivers have been largely replaced by ODI drivers. *See also* **ODI driver**.

Default   The choice a program makes if a user does not select another choice. Your default directory is the directory in which you are currently working.

Default login script   *See* **Login script**.

Directory entry   Provides information about a file or directory, such as the file or directory's name, creation date and time, size, and so on. A directory entry for a file is also used as a pointer to the first disk block used to store the file. Each directory, DOS file, and trustee list on the network uses up one directory entry. Each Macintosh file uses two directory entries. If you run out of directory entries on your disk, no one will be able to create a new file or directory.

Disk-controller board A circuit board that controls the hard disks installed in a file server.

Disk duplexing Duplicating network data on two identical hard disk channels so that if one goes bad, the other can continue to operate. When two disks are duplexed, the disk-controller boards, cables, power supplies, and disks are all duplicated. *See also* **Disk mirroring**.

Disk mirroring Duplicating network data on two identical hard disks so that if one goes bad, the other can continue to operate. When two disks are mirrored, they are both running on the same disk channel, meaning that both disks share the same disk-controller board, cable, and power supply. This is less protected than disk duplexing, which duplicates all of the disk channel hardware. *See also* **Disk duplexing**.

DOS code page A table DOS uses to determine which numerals, letters, and symbols are supported by the version of DOS running on the computer. Since computer hardware and DOS versions can vary from country to country, different countries may use different DOS code pages.

DOS partition *See* **Partition**.

DOS Requester *See* **NetWare DOS Requester**.

Drive mapping Assigning letters to local or network directory paths. Mapping drives to directories makes it easier for both users and applications to find files located in those directories.

Driver Software that allows hardware and software to communicate with each other. For example, LAN drivers allow network communication to travel across network boards and cables, printer drivers allow your printers and applications to communicate, and tape drivers allow tape backup systems to receive network data from the backup program.

Duplexing *See* **Disk duplexing**.

DynaText Novell's online documentation, included in the second release (the international version) of NetWare 3.12. It replaces Novell ElectroText, which shipped in the first (English-only) release.

Effective rights The sum of trustee rights a user can ultimately exercise in a directory or file, taking into consideration specific user and group trustee assignments, security equivalences, rights inherited from parent directories, and the Rights Masks assigned to the directory or file.

ElectroText *See* **DynaText; Novell ElectroText**.

Error log file Whenever an error occurs with the file server or the volume, NetWare records the error in an error log file. There are three error log files: SYS$LOG.ERR, for file server errors; VOL$LOG.ERR, for volume errors; and TTS$LOG.ERR, for NetWare's Transaction Tracking System (TTS).

Ethernet frame type The packet format Ethernet uses to send data across the network. In NetWare versions 2.2 and 3.11, Novell used an Ethernet frame type called 802.3 by default. In NetWare 3.12 Novell changed the default frame type to 802.2, which is an industry standard.

Executable file A program file that performs a task or set of tasks. For example, the executable file that runs WordPerfect is WP.EXE. Common executable file name extensions are .EXE, .COM, .BAT, and .NLM.

External network The network of Macintosh workstations that an AppleTalk router is aware of. The AppleTalk router also contains an internal network, which doesn't actually encompass any hardware; it is just a software feature of the router. The internal and external networks have to be configured with separate, unique network numbers (or ranges of numbers). *See also* **AppleTalk router** and **Internal network**.

External router *See* **Router**.

Fake root Some applications require that they be installed at the root of the volume. If you would rather install the application in a subdirectory, you can map a fake root to the subdirectory that contains the application, and the application will think it is located at the root of the volume instead of in a subdirectory.

File server The computer on the network that has the NetWare operating system running on it. The server provides common access to network files and directories, controls resource sharing on the network, and regulates network communications.

Flags *See* **Attributes**.

Form *See* **Print form**.

Frame type *See* **Ethernet frame type**.

Grace login When a user logs in after his or her password has expired, a grace login allows the user to finish logging in using the old password without changing it. You can set the number of grace logins a user is allowed.

Group A set of network users who have been assigned to a NetWare user group so that they all have the same level of security in the same directories. A group can contain other groups.

Home directory   A directory that the SYSCON and MAKEUSER utilities can create automatically for a network user. A home directory is named with the user's login name and is typically used by the user to store personal files.

Hot Fix   A fault-tolerant technique for ensuring that data does not get written to bad blocks on the file server's hard disk. When NetWare writes data to a disk block, the data is read again and compared to the data still in memory. If the data written to disk does not match the data still in memory, Hot Fix detects the problem, redirects the data to be written into another area reserved for the Hot Fix function (called the redirection area), and modifies the bad block table to make sure the bad block does not get used again. Hot Fix does not redirect data if the disk block goes bad after the data has already been stored there.

I/O address   Input/output address; used by the computer's microprocessor to communicate with peripheral boards. No two boards in the same computer can share the same address, so part of the board installation process is locating an open I/O address.

Identifier variable   A word or phrase used in login script commands that is replaced by a real value determined when the user logs in. For example, the identifier variable LOGIN_NAME is replaced by the user's name when the command that contains that variable is executed. Identifier variables can be used in generic login script commands that become customized for a user when that user logs in.

Inherited Rights Mask   A list of the trustee rights users are allowed to inherit from a trustee assignment to a parent directory. An Inherited Rights Mask is assigned to every directory and file. The Inherited Rights Mask affects only inherited rights, not explicit trustee assignments.

Internal network A logical network contained completely within the AppleTalk router software. Such an internal network doesn't actually encompass any hardware; it is just a software feature of the router. Besides the internal network, the AppleTalk router is aware of at least one external network—the "real" network that contains all the Macintosh workstations. The internal and the external networks have to be configured with separate, unique network numbers (or ranges of numbers). *See also* **AppleTalk router** and **External network**.

Internal router *See* **Router**.

IPX Internetwork Packet eXchange; a network-level protocol developed by Novell to move communications packets from one node (such as a computer) to another across a network.

IRM *See* **Inherited Rights Mask**.

IRQ Interrupt; used by peripheral devices to let the computer know they are waiting to be serviced. Generally, no two boards in the same computer can share the same IRQ, so part of the board installation process is locating an open IRQ.

Loadable module *See* **NetWare loadable module**.

Local area network (LAN) See **Network**.

Local drive A disk drive on the user's workstation, as opposed to a network drive, which is mapped to a directory located on the file server.

Local printer A printer that is attached to a file server or workstation that is running the print server.

LocalTalk Built-in networking capability for Macintoshes. If you use LocalTalk to connect your Macintoshes, you do not need to insert network boards in each workstation; simply connect the workstations with cables. LocalTalk is less expensive but generally slower than alternatives such as Ethernet and Token-Ring.

Log in The procedure by which a user accesses a network server. To log in to a NetWare network, type LOGIN. The LOGIN utility requests the user's name and password and then executes a login script, which sets up a user's working environment.

Log out The procedure by which a user exits the network. To log out of the network, type LOGOUT.

Login script A file that contains commands that set up a user's work environment. For example, a login script may set up drive mappings, display messages on the user's screen, and so on. The login script is executed by the LOGIN utility. The two types of login scripts are the system login script, which executes for all users who log in to the file server, and user login scripts, which belong to individual users. User login scripts execute after the system login script. If a user doesn't have a user login script, a default login script executes. The default login script is part of the LOGIN utility.

Maximum Rights Mask Used in NetWare 2.2 and earlier versions to list the rights users can exercise in a directory. A Maximum Rights Mask is assigned to every directory and can block both inherited rights and specific trustee assignments. The Maximum Rights Mask has been replaced in NetWare 3 and 4 by the Inherited Rights Mask. *See also* **Inherited Rights Mask**.

Menu program A program that allows users to select tasks from a list of options displayed on the computer screen. The menu program hides underlying commands that may not be user friendly to some network users. You can create your own menu programs and execute them using NetWare's NMENU utility.

Menu utilities NetWare utilities, such as SYSCON and FILER, that allow you to perform network tasks by selecting options from a list displayed on the computer screen.

Mirroring *See* **Disk mirroring.**

Modem MODulator/DEModulator; a device that lets computers communicate over telephone wires by converting digital computer signals to analog telephone signals and back again.

Name space module A software program you load on your file server if you are using NetWare for Macintosh, NFS, or OS/2 and its High Performance File System (HPFS) on your network. Macintosh, NFS, and OS/2 support longer file names than DOS does. The name space modules allow the NetWare file system to recognize other types of name spaces in addition to the default DOS name space.

NCP Packet Signature An optional NetWare security feature designed to prevent unauthorized intruders from forging packets and accessing network resources. Workstations and servers sign each NCP packet with a signature and change the signature for every packet.

NET.CFG A file that allows you to customize the NetWare environment on a workstation. You can use the NET.CFG file on workstations with either ODI drivers or dedicated IPX drivers. The SHELL.CFG file is a similar file that can be used only on workstations with dedicated IPX drivers.

NetBIOS A basic input/output system; an IBM protocol for network communications.

NetWare A network operating system from Novell, Inc., that lets you connect together a variety of computers so users on all these computers can share the same files, applications, printers, and so on.

NetWare DOS Requester The workstation software shipped in NetWare 3.12. The DOS Requester includes VLMs (Virtual Loadable Modules), which control how the workstation connects to and communicates with DOS and with the network. The DOS Requester replaces NETX, EMSNETX, and XMSNETX.

NetWare Loadable Module *See* NLM (NetWare Loadable Module).

NetWare Notify A module that lets Macintosh users send and receive short messages.

NetWare partition *See* Partition.

NetWare Tools An application for Macintosh workstations that allows the network supervisor to manage all NetWare users, groups, security, and printing from a Macintosh.

NetWare UAM (User Authentication Module) A module that encrypts Macintosh users' passwords before sending them across the network.

Network A group of computers that are connected so they can share files, applications, and other resources (such as disk space and printers). The NetWare operating system runs on the file server computer and controls communications across the network.

Network board A circuit board that allows a computer to communicate on the network. Each workstation and file server on the network must have a network board installed in it. Network cables connect the boards to the rest of the network. Network boards are sometimes called network interface cards (NICs) or network adapters.

Network drive A letter (such as F or Y) that is mapped to a directory located on the file server.

Network operating system The software that runs on the file server and controls network communications, including file sharing and print services. NetWare is a network operating system.

Network supervisor The user who has all rights to a given file server. The network supervisor can modify any file on the file server and can install or modify network resources. Typically, network administrators log in to the server as the user SUPERVISOR to perform management or maintenance tasks.

NLM (NetWare Loadable Module) A software program that runs on the file server and adds a particular feature to the network. For example, the SBACKUP.NLM loadable module allows you to back up network files from your file server.

Node address Physical workstation address; each workstation must have a unique node address.

Nondedicated Refers to a computer on the network that can fulfill two different functions at the same time. For example, a nondedicated file server can also be used as a workstation.

Novell ElectroText Novell's online documentation, included in the initial (English-only) CD-ROM version of NetWare 3.12. Replaced by DynaText in the International release of NetWare 3.12.

ODI driver Open DataLink Interface driver; a type of driver installed on a workstation. ODI drivers can handle more than one type of protocol. In addition, ODI drivers can handle different Ethernet frame types. *See also* **Dedicated IPX driver**.

Operating system A program that controls the way a computer handles communication between input and output devices. PCs can use either the DOS or OS/2 operating system. Macintosh computers use an operating system called System. NetWare is a network operating system that controls the entire network's communications.

Packet Signature *See* **NCP Packet Signature**.

Parent directory Any directory that contains other directories (called subdirectories).

Partition A logical segment of a hard disk. The DOS partition on a file server's hard disk contains DOS boot files and other files as necessary. The NetWare partitions on a server's hard disk contain all the network files and data, as well as the NetWare utilities and other software.

Password A word, phrase, or other combination of characters you type to prove that you are authorized to log in to the network. Each user should have a unique username and password to make sure the network cannot be accessed by unauthorized people.

Patch A small program designed to fix a bug in a product that has already been released.

Path (directory) The series of directories you follow to reach a particular file. For example, if you've stored a file called ARTICLE in a subdirectory called LENSES in another directory called PHOTO on the volume VOL1, the directory path to that file is VOL1:PHOTO\LENSES\ARTICLE.

Path (DOS) DOS allows you to set paths to directories. These paths tell DOS which directories to search through when looking for executable files that are not found in your current directory. NetWare search drives are added to the workstation's path environment variables.

Peripheral A device, such as a printer, modem, or tape drive, that is attached to the network or workstation.

Port An outlet on a computer that allows the computer to communicate with printers, modems, or other peripheral devices.

Print form   A style of paper you define for your printer. For example, you may define a paycheck form, an invoice form, or a statement form.

Print job   A file that has been sent to be printed.

Print queue   A directory on the file server that holds a print job temporarily until the print server is ready to take the print job and send it to the printer. Print jobs are held in the print queue in first-come/first-served order.

Print server   NetWare software that controls how print jobs are taken from print queues and directed to printers. The print server software can be installed on either a file server or a dedicated workstation.

Prompt   The mark the operating system or application puts on the screen to indicate that it's ready to accept another command. In DOS, the DOS prompt usually shows the drive you are currently working in, followed by an angle bracket (>). On a NetWare file server, the console prompt is a colon (:).

Protocol   The method of exchanging data between two systems. The protocol dictates how data is formatted, packaged, sent, and acknowledged between two systems. IPX, SPX, AppleTalk, and TCP/IP are all examples of communication protocols.

Purge   To remove deleted files from the disk. In NetWare 3.12, deleted files are stored in a salvageable state in their original directory, where they are hidden but still available should you need to retrieve them. If the original directory is also deleted, the files' entries are moved to a directory called DELETED.SAV in the root of the volume where the original directory was stored. Purging completely removes deleted files.

RAM   Random-access memory; the memory used by the computer to manipulate and temporarily store information. This memory is dynamic, which means that any information stored in it will be erased when the computer's power is turned off. Some applications require a large amount of RAM to run successfully.

Redirection area   A portion of the file server's hard disk set aside at installation. If NetWare attempts to write data to a bad block on the disk, a NetWare feature called Hot Fix detects the error and re-directs the data to be written in the redirection area instead. This helps protect network data from bad blocks on the hard disk. *See also* **Hot Fix**.

Remote Console   NetWare software that lets you manage a file server from a workstation. Your workstation screen and keyboard appear to be the file server's screen and keyboard. You can type commands from the workstation, and those commands will execute on the file server. Although you control the keyboard input from the workstation, the execution actually occurs on the file server. You cannot execute utilities or programs from the workstation itself.

Remote printer   A printer attached to a workstation that is not running a print server. The workstation must be running RPRINT-ER.EXE to allow other network users to send print jobs to that printer.

Remote reset   The installation of boot files on the file server so diskless workstations can boot and access the network. Also called remote boot.

Resource fork   The portion of a Macintosh file that contains information about the file, such as how the file's icon should display, which application was used to create the file, and so on. The data fork contains the actual text of a Macintosh file. The content of a

DOS file is equivalent to the Macintosh file's data fork, but there is no DOS equivalent to a resource fork. *See also* **Data fork.**

Restore   To retrieve files from a backup disk or tape and place them back on the network.

Rights   *See* **Trustee rights.**

Rights Mask   *See* **Inherited Rights Mask.**

Router   A software connection between two networks that allows them to communicate with each other. A router passes data packets to a network only when the packet is destined for that network. (A bridge forwards all packets regardless of their destinations.) When a file server contains two or more network boards, each connecting to a different network, the router that connects those networks is called an internal router. When networks are connected through a workstation that contains two or more network boards, it is called an external router. *See also* **AppleTalk router.**

Salvage   To retrieve a file that had been deleted. In NetWare 3.12 deleted files are stored in a salvageable state, hidden but still available should you need to salvage them. Purging completely removes those deleted files. See *also* **Purge.**

Search drive   A special type of drive mapping to a directory. If a search drive is mapped to a directory, the system will look in that directory for executable files if it can't find them in a user's current directory. For example, the NetWare utilities are located in the SYS:PUBLIC directory. A search drive to that directory is placed in the system login script so the utilities can be executed by users no matter which directory those users are currently using. Search drive mappings are added to the workstation's path commands.

Seed router   An AppleTalk router whose configuration has been explicitly set. Any additional AppleTalk routers can be set to learn their external network configuration from the seed router. By using a seed router, you do not have to explicitly assign network numbers and zones to additional AppleTalk routers' external networks.

Security The NetWare features that protect your network data. NetWare security includes user passwords, user account restrictions (which limit when users can log in), trustee rights (which are assigned to users to control the tasks they can perform with directories and files), file and directory attributes (which are assigned to directories and files and limit all users' access to them), and NCP Packet Signature (which prevents intruders from forging packets).

Security equivalence An assignment that grants one user identical trustee rights to another user. For example, if user Ed is given a security equivalence to user Jane, Ed can exercise the same trustee rights Jane can. However, the security equivalence lets Ed exercise only the trustee rights that are specifically assigned to Jane. Ed cannot exercise any rights Jane received through her security equivalences to other users.

Session In NetWare for Macintosh 3.12, a session is an instance of using a NetWare Tools utility to work with an entity, such as a user or a print queue.

Shell NetWare software that runs on the workstation and allows the workstation to communicate with the network. The NetWare shell (NETX) intercepts DOS commands and redirects them to the network. The NetWare DOS Requester (VLM) accepts commands from DOS only when the commands are requesting network services.

SHELL.CFG A file that allows you to customize the NetWare environment on a dedicated IPX workstation. (For an ODI workstation, use a NET.CFG file instead.)

Spooler assignments Spooler assignments give a corresponding printer number (0 through 4) to a print queue name so applications that require printer numbers can communicate with NetWare.

Stand-alone Any device, such as a computer or a printer, that is not connected to a network.

STARTNET.BAT A batch file that is automatically created during the DOS Requester installation. This batch file loads the LSL, LAN driver, and IPXODI files and then executes the VLM.EXE command, which loads all the necessary VLM files. (Most of these commands are put into the AUTOEXEC.BAT file in previous versions of NetWare. If this workstation was previously using NETX, you will need to edit the AUTOEXEC.BAT file and remove any lines that loaded the LSL, LAN driver, IPXODI, IPX, or NETX files.)

STARTUP.NCF file Used by SERVER.EXE to customize and auto-mate the initialization of the NetWare operating system. STARTUP.NCF executes on the file server automatically after SER-VER.EXE and loads disk drivers to support the file server's hard disks. It can load name space modules to support differing file for-mats (such as Macintosh or OS/2). It can also contain SET parame-ters, which modify default initialization values.

Subdirectory Any directory that is contained within another directory.

Surge suppressor A device that provides some protection for hardware against power peaks that occasionally come through the power-supply line.

System login script *See* **Login script**.

Trustee A user or group who has been granted rights to work in a network directory or file.

Trustee rights The means by which you control what a user can do to a particular directory or file. For example, trustee rights regulate whether a user can read a file, change it, change its name, delete it, or control other users' trustee rights to it. Trustee rights are assigned to individual users, and one user's rights can be different from another user's rights to the same directory.

TTS Transactional Tracking System; protects files such as databases, including the NetWare bindery, from being corrupted.

Unicode files Files necessary for the VLMs to work with the versions of DOS and Windows used in different countries and in different languages. Unicode files are automatically copied into the NWCLIET\NLS subdirectory on each workstation. Each Unicode file has a file name extension that indicates the country code and code page it supports. You need to keep only the files with the extension that matches your country and code page. Files for United States English have the .001 extension.

UPS Uninterruptible power supply; a device that provides alternative power to your file server if the main power supply is interrupted.

User account The definition of a network user. Every person who wants to log in to the server must have a user account.

User account restrictions A means by which you can restrict users' work with the network in various ways. For example, you can limit the hours users can log in to the network, the workstations they can use, the amount of disk space a user can fill up, or the length of time users can use the same password. You can assign account restrictions on a system-wide basis or to individual users.

User login script *See* **Login script**.

Utilities NetWare programs that allow you to perform tasks on the network. There are workstation utilities and server utilities. Generally, you use workstation utilities to work with users, files, directories, and so on. You use server utilities to change the way the file server operates. Some utilities are command-line utilities, which you execute by typing a command. Other utilities are menu utilities, which you execute by selecting an option from a menu displayed on the screen. NetWare 3.12 contains a feature called Remote Console, which lets you run server utilities from a workstation by accessing the file server from your workstation.

VAP Value-Added Process; a NetWare version 2.x software program that runs on the file server and adds a particular feature to the network. For example, NetWare for Macintosh VAPs allow you to connect Macintosh workstations to your NetWare 2.x network. VAPs have been replaced in NetWare 3 and NetWare 4 by NetWare Loadable Modules (NLMs). *See also* **NLM (NetWare Loadable Module)**.

VLMs (Virtual Loadable Modules) Programs that run on a DOS workstation as part of the DOS Requester workstation software. VLMs accept network requests from DOS and redirect those requests to the file server. VLMs replace NETX, EMSNETX, and XMSNETX.

Volume The top level of NetWare's directory structure. A volume is a portion of the file server's hard disk. The volume contains directories and files. A NetWare file server must have at least one volume, called SYS (for system), which contains all the files required to run NetWare. You may want to create additional volumes on your file server to contain applications and work files, as well as a separate volume to contain Macintosh files.

Wildcard character A character that can match any other character; used in specifying file names. The asterisk (*) stands for any series of characters. The question mark (?) represents any single character.

Workstation A personal computer on which users accomplish their daily work. Workstations on a NetWare network can be PCs (running DOS or OS/2) or Macintoshes. A NetWare workstation contains a network board, which connects it to the network cabling, and workstation software, which communicates with the file server.

Zone A collection of devices on an AppleTalk network that Macintosh users can access through the Chooser. For example, you might group related printers and file servers in the same zone so everyone in that area can easily find them.

I*ndex*

Symbols

login script command, explained, 113
* login script command, explained, 128
; login script command, explained, 128
%n variables, in login scripts, 129-131, 139

A

ABORT REMIRROR utility, explained, 228
Access Control right, explained, 95
access rights. *See* rights, trustee
ACCESS_SERVER identifier variable, explained, 138
account. *See* users
account restrictions. *See also* disk space
    assigning using SYSCON, 297-298
    explained, 89-92, 324, 344
accounting
    records, displaying, 285
    setting up, 297
    usage, totaling, 252-253
ACONSOLE.EXE, explained, 29, 250
ADD NAME SPACE utility, explained, 26-27, 228-229
addresses
    I/O, explained, 332
    IPX internal network number
        specifying, 16
        viewing, 233
    network,
        displaying in login script, 137
        specifying, 24
        viewing, 297
    network number, specifying for AppleTalk router, 184-190
    node,
        configuring in NET.CFG, 68
        displaying in login script, 136
        explained, 337
        viewing, 233, 297

administrator, primary tasks, 2-4
AFP.NLM, explained, 179, 211
alerts. *See* troubleshooting
Alloc Short Term memory pool, setting size of, 35
ALLOW utility, explained, 251-252
AM_PM identifier variable, explained, 135
API calls
    NetWare 3.0, displaying message when used, 45
    NETX, supported by VLMs, 61
AppleShare, version required, xxv
AppleTalk. *See also* NetWare for Macintosh
    explained, 324
    networks, extended and nonextended, explained, 184-185, 324
    print server, explained, 195, 324
    print spooler, explained, 195, 324-325
    protocol,
        loading and binding to driver, 185-190
        requires SNAP frame type, 202
        unbinding, 244-245
    Queue Server, explained, 195
AppleTalk router. *See also* NetWare for Macintosh
    configuring, 185-190
    explained, 178-179, 325
    internal and external network numbers, viewing, 201
    internal and external networks, explained, 182-183, 331, 333
    seed routers,
        explained, 341-342
        using, 189-190
    troubleshooting, 200-203
    viewing router table, 201
    zone list, viewing, 201
APPLETLK.NLM utility
    configuring, 185-190
    explained, 179, 211

D

data forks, explained, 193, 328
databases, explained, 328. *See also* TTS
date
   identifier variables, in login scripts,
      134-135
   server,
      changing, 242
      displaying, 244, 298
   server time zone, setting, 243
   sychronizing workstation's to server's, 77
DAY identifier variable, explained, 134
DAY_OF_WEEK identifier variable,
   explained, 134
DCB
   disk driver, using, 19
   using with a UPS, 226
dedicated IPX drivers, explained, 328
dedicated print servers, explained, 156. *See
   also* print servers
default login script. *See* login scripts
Delete Inhibit directory attribute, explained,
   99
Delete Inhibit file attribute, explained, 98
deleting files, preventing, 98, 99. *See also*
   purging files
developer support, 320
directories. *See also* drive mappings; home
   directories
   copying, 273-275
   for DOS, creating, 66
   hiding, 99
   information,
      viewing using FILER, 262-263
      viewing using NDIR, 275-280
   parent, explained, 338
   renaming, 290
   space on a volume,
      displaying, 31, 258-259, 263
      limiting, 40, 260-261
   subdirectories, setting maximum number,
      39
   subdirectory information,
      viewing with LISTDIR, 268
      viewing with NDIR, 275-280
directory attributes. *See* attributes

directory caching SET parameters, listed,
   37-38
directory entries
   explained, 328-329
   number in use, monitoring, 31, 263
   repairing problems with VREPAIR, 226
directory security. *See* attributes; rights, trustee
Directory Services VLM, explained, 59-60
DISABLE LOGIN utility, explained, 233
DISABLE TTS utility, explained, 233
disk-controller boards. *See also* disk drivers
   for disk duplexing and mirroring, 14
   explained, 329
   using memory below 16MB, 17-18, 19-20,
      37
disk drivers
   DCB, using, 19
   explained, 206
   listed, 18
   loading, 207-208
   loading during installation, 18-19
   using memory below 16MB, 17-18, 19-20,
      37
disk duplexing and mirroring
   explained, 329
   Hot Fix area, specifying size of, 21
   remirroring, 240
      aborting 228
   remirroring requests, setting number of, 43
   setting up, 21
   size of disks needed, 12-14
   status, monitoring, 31, 237
disk space
   in use, displaying, 31, 258-259, 263
   limiting, 40, 260-261
diskless workstations. *See* remote booting;
   workstations, diskless
disks, file server. *See also* disk duplexing and
   mirroring; volumes
   activating and deactivating, 216
   adding, 214
   blocks,
      number of, specifying, 21
      used for Hot Fix, monitoring, 31
   caching, SET parameters for, 36
   listing, 235

partition,
    DOS, creating for a server, 15
    explained, 338
    NetWare, creating for a server, 20-21
    NetWare, repairing, 47-48, 226
    scanning for newly installed, 240
    SET parameters, listed, 43
DISKSET utility
    explained, 234
    using with DCB disk driver, 19
DISMOUNT utility, explained, 234
dismounting volumes, 216, 234
DISPLAY login script command, explained,
    115. See also FDISPLAY login script
    command
DISPLAY NETWORKS utility, explained, 234
DISPLAY SERVERS utility, explained, 234
DMA channel, configuring in NET.CFG, 68
documentation,
    online. See DynaText; Novell ElectroText
    printed, ordering, 312
documenting the network
    backup information, 7
    explained, 4-5
    hardware configurations, 6
    hardware maintenance histories, 6
    inventory, 5
    login scripts, menus, boot files, 7
    network layout, 6-7
    worksheets, 305-309
DOS
    code page, specifying for server, 16-17
    COMMAND.COM, indicating location of,
    84, 114
    environment space, increasing, 84
    environment variables, in login scripts,
    129, 138
    file name format, specifying for server, 17
    identifier variable for version, 136
    languages, Unicode files for, 61-62, 85
    loading on network for diskless
    workstations, 66
    name, specifying for workstation, 74
    on server,
        accessing, 235
        removing, 103, 240, 241-242

System directory attribute, 99
System file attribute, 97
system files,
    on boot disk for NETX, 63
    on boot disk for VLMs, 56
DOS BREAK login script command,
    explained, 115-116. See also BREAK
    login script command
DOS partition
    creating on a server, 15
    explained, 338
DOS paths
    and search drive mappings, 125
    using SET PATH in login scripts, 129
DOS Requester. See NetWare DOS Requester
DOS VERIFY login script command,
    explained, 116
DOS workstation. See NetWare DOS
    Requester; workstations
DOS_REQUESTER identifier variable,
    explained, 136
DOSGEN utility, explained, 66, 260
DOWN utility, explained, 234-235
DRIVE login script command, explained, 116
drive mappings
    creating
        in login scripts, 123-127
        using MAP utility, 272-273
        using SESSION, 293-294
    explained, 123-127, 329
    fake root, explained, 126-127, 273, 331
    planning for login scripts, 111-112
    search drives,
        and effect on DOS paths, 125
        explained, 124-126, 273, 341
    troubleshooting, 152-153
drivers, explained, 329-330. See also disk
    drivers; LAN drivers
drives. See disks, file server; network drives
DSPACE utility, explained, 260-261
duplexing. See disk duplexing and mirroring
DynaText. See also Novell ElectroText
    explained, 168, 172-174, 330
    installing, 168-170
    printed manuals, ordering, 312
    setting up a workstation for, 172-174

R

GET A FREE CATALOG JUST FOR EXPRESSING YOUR OPINION.

us improve our books and get a *FREE* full-color catalog in the bargain. Please complete this form, pull out this page and send it in today. The address is on the reverse side.

Company _____

_____   City _____ State ____ Zip _____

_____

◄___)_____

would you rate the overall quality is book?

xcellent
ery Good
ood
air
elow Average
oor

t were the things you liked most ut the book? (Check all that apply)

ace
ormat
riting Style
xamples
ble of Contents
dex
rice
ustrations
ype Style
over
epth of Coverage
ast Track Notes

t were the things you liked *least* ut the book? (Check all that apply)

ace
ormat
riting Style
xamples
ble of Contents
dex
rice
ustrations
pe Style
over
epth of Coverage
st Track Notes

4. Where did you buy this book?

❏ Bookstore chain
❏ Small independent bookstore
❏ Computer store
❏ Wholesale club
❏ College bookstore
❏ Technical bookstore
❏ Other _____

5. How did you decide to buy this particular book?

❏ Recommended by friend
❏ Recommended by store personnel
❏ Author's reputation
❏ Sybex's reputation
❏ Read book review in _____
❏ Other _____

6. How did you pay for this book?

❏ Used own funds
❏ Reimbursed by company
❏ Received book as a gift

7. What is your level of experience with the subject covered in this book?

❏ Beginner
❏ Intermediate
❏ Advanced

8. How long have you been using a computer?

years _____
months _____

9. Where do you most often use your computer?

❏ Home
❏ Work

❏ Both
❏ Other _____

10. What kind of computer equipment do you have? (Check all that apply)

❏ PC Compatible Desktop Computer
❏ PC Compatible Laptop Computer
❏ Apple/Mac Computer
❏ Apple/Mac Laptop Computer
❏ CD ROM
❏ Fax Modem
❏ Data Modem
❏ Scanner
❏ Sound Card
❏ Other _____

11. What other kinds of software packages do you ordinarily use?

❏ Accounting
❏ Databases
❏ Networks
❏ Apple/Mac
❏ Desktop Publishing
❏ Spreadsheets
❏ CAD
❏ Games
❏ Word Processing
❏ Communications
❏ Money Management
❏ Other _____

12. What operating systems do you ordinarily use?

❏ DOS
❏ OS/2
❏ Windows
❏ Apple/Mac
❏ Windows NT
❏ Other _____

13. On what computer-related subject(s) would you like to see more books?

_____

_____

_____

14. Do you have any other comments about this book? (Please feel free to use a separate piece of paper if you need more room)

_____

_____

_____

_____

- - - - - - - - - PLEASE FOLD, SEAL, AND MAIL TO SYBEX - - - - - - - -

SYBEX INC.
Department M
2021 Challenger Drive
Alameda, CA
94501

1. Configure and install a network board, and connect the board to the network cabling.

2. Boot **DOS** on the workstation. (Do not run Windows.)

3. From the **WSDOS_1** diskette, type **INSTALL**.

4. Specify the directory to use (default is **C:\NWCLIENT**).

5. Specify whether or not to modify the **CONFIG.SYS** and **AUTOEXEC.BAT** files.

6. (Optional) Specify whether to install support for Microsoft Windows.

7. Select the LAN driver for the workstation network board:

   - Press Enter.

   - To select a driver supplied with NetWare 3.12, insert the WSDRV_2 diskette in drive A and press Enter.

   - To select a different driver, press Esc, insert the manufacturer's diskette, and press Enter.

8. When all selections are correct, press Enter.

9. When the installation is finished, press Enter to exit the program.

10. When prompted to "Insert disk with batch file, Press any key to continue...," insert the **WSDOS_1** diskette. It's looking for the **INSTALL.BAT** file.

11. If this workstation previously had **NETX** installed on it, edit the **AUTOEXEC.BAT** file to remove commands that loaded the **IPX** or **IPXODI** driver, the **LSL** driver, and the **NETX** file. These commands are now included in the **STARTNET.BAT** file instead.